Costing of Health Care Services in Developing Countries

Challenges in Public Health

Editor: Prof. Dr. Oliver Razum, Bielefeld

Formerly/früher: Medizin in Entwicklungsländern
Herausgegeben von
Prof. Dr. Hans Jochen Diesfeld, Heidelberg

Band 57

PETER LANG
Frankfurt am Main · Berlin · Bern · Bruxelles · New York · Oxford · Wien

Steffen Fleßa

Costing of Health Care Services in Developing Countries

A Prerequisite for Affordability, Sustainability and Efficiency

PETER LANG
Internationaler Verlag der Wissenschaften

Bibliographic Information published by the Deutsche Nationalbibliothek
The Deutsche Nationalbibliothek lists this publication in the Deutsche Nationalbibliografie; detailed bibliographic data is available in the internet at <http://www.d-nb.de>.

Cover design:
Atelier Platen, Friedberg

ISSN 1863-768X
ISBN 978-3-631-58408-8
© Peter Lang GmbH
Internationaler Verlag der Wissenschaften
Frankfurt am Main 2009
All rights reserved.

All parts of this publication are protected by copyright. Any utilisation outside the strict limits of the copyright law, without the permission of the publisher, is forbidden and liable to prosecution. This applies in particular to reproductions, translations, microfilming, and storage and processing in electronic retrieval systems.

www.peterlang.de

Acknowledgment

I would like to express my greatest gratitude to all colleagues who supported me during these studies. My sincere thanks go to Martin Blöcher, Dr. Mark Bura, Reinhard Hansen and the honorable Bishop Dr. Erasto Kweka for their support during the ELCT-study. Without their financial and personal encouragement I would have never started costing health services in developing countries. I also owe thanks to Dr. Nghiem Tran Dung for collecting the data of the Vietnam study. Dr. Bocar Kouyaté, Dr. Ali Sie and Dr. Paul Marschall thoroughly contributed to the research in Burkina Faso. Without their support the cost information system could not have been installed. Furthermore, I would like to express my gratitude to Dr. Cara Cocking and Prof. Dr. Gerhard Reinelt who took the lead in the mathematical modelling of the location analysis done in this health district. In addition, I strongly appreciate the support of the German Research Foundation (DFG) for the study in Nouna.

It is my severe hope that this research has not only resulted in a number of well-published papers, but that our work has an impact on the population in developing countries by encouraging others to cost their health services – for a more equitable, sustainable and efficient health care in developing countries.

Greifswald, January 2009

Steffen Fleßa

Preface: Creating evidence to improve the health of the world's poor

"Primary Health Care – Now More Than Ever" is the title of the World Health Report 2008. Dr Margaret Chan, Director-General of WHO, stresses in her opening message that policy-makers need more evidence to make health systems more equitable, inclusive and fair. At the same time, they need to think more comprehensively about the performance of the health system as a whole [1]. Only then will they be able to implement the necessary reforms to improve population health, and in particular the health of the most disadvantaged members of society.

One of the four sets of reforms delineated in the World Health Report 2008 concerns service delivery. Health services need to be reorganised so that they meet people's needs and expectations. In the context of this reform process, health care institutions may have to dynamically change their structure or function while remaining sustainable. For example, in the process of adapting hospitals to the needs of Primary Health Care, changes in function will often also require changes in structure. At this point, the health economists enter the scene: Among other things, they assess structural sustainability, using costing as a tool. The main purpose of costing is to increase efficiency.

The thinking of health economists in terms of efficiency has often been criticised, but has become literally indispensible. In all health care systems, resources are limited or scarce, so priorities have to be set. This will inevitably create moral dilemmas. Many health economists propose a utilitarian approach to find a way out of the specific dilemma of providing – or not providing – particular interventions in resource-poor developing countries with many competing health problems. A utilitarian approach in this context means that efficiency criteria are used to allocate the limited resources in such a way that as many lives as possible will be saved, or a quality of life as high as possible will be achieved.

Such an approach has practical problems that should not be underestimated. In no real-life situation will we have all the information we would like to have to make far-reaching decisions. Costing is no exception, and any estimates will have rather wide confidence ranges. This is a problem that will only be slightly mollified by more research. The tools that health economists use deliver necessary and valuable information on which decisions can be based. However, not all decisions can be determined by such tools alone, even if the underlying philosophy has been accepted.

There is a tendency in applied economics to reduce the utility-seeking behaviour of human beings to pure cost-effectiveness. Some economists even use the word "rational" as a synonym for efficiency. However, it is well accepted by public health specialists and by many professional economists that other factors need to be taken into consideration for decision-making in health care. For example, most people would behave "irrational" in the sense that they will rather dedicate money to finance an effective treatment for an individual who would otherwise die than to spend the same amount for preventive measures – even if the latter show a better cost-efficiency ratio. This is because most people do not feel the same empathy for the yet unknown person at risk as for the severely ill individual patient in front of them. Whether this is labelled culture, tradition or empathy – it has its own "rationality" that should not be ignored.

Real-life situations are often even more complex: Interventions can be efficient and at the same time increase inequity. Minor improvements in the health status of people who already enjoy good health and good access to health care can often be achieved more efficiently than major improvements for people who are disadvantaged and difficult to reach.

And yet, as Steffen Flessa convincingly shows in this book, we need more, rather than less, health economics. An equitable approach to health care is a fundamental prerequisite to improving the health of the world's poor. The Primary Health Care concept can contribute to this goal. For Primary Health Care to work, evidence-based interventions are needed – amongst other elements. To create an evidence base, the tools of health economics are indispensible. But employing these tools alone will not do the job: Their use needs to be embedded in an evidence-based public health approach that takes into consideration other crucial aspects, including socio-cultural aspects and values [2]. Flessa combines an ethical perspective with the methodological one of a health economist. He here presents approaches and instruments that contribute to decision-making in Primary Health Care that is at the same time rational *and* human. This is why his book is so important today.

Oliver Razum

Series editor

Table of Contents

1 Introduction 1
2 Essentials of Health Economics 3
   2.1 Ethics in Health Care 3
   2.2 Health Economic Framework 17
   2.3 Economic Evaluation 28
3 Methodology 33
   3.1 Concept of Cost-of-Illness 33
   3.2 Provider Cost 36
      3.2.1 Knowledge of Provider Cost 36
      3.2.2 Basic Terms 38
      3.2.3 Allocation of Costs 41
   3.3 Incomplete Data 46
      3.3.1 Donations and Grants 46
      3.3.2 Depreciation 47
      3.3.3 Charity Fund 50
   3.4 Concepts of Costs 50
4 Case Studies 55
   4.1 Costing Lutheran Hospitals in Tanzania 55
      4.1.1 Setting 55
      4.1.2 Findings 57
         4.1.2.1 Costs of Services 57
         4.1.2.2 Income Analysis 60
   4.2 Costing a Health District: Dodoma Rural in Tanzania 62
      4.2.1 Setting 62
      4.2.2 Findings 63
         4.2.2.1 Costs of Mvumi Hospital 63
         4.2.2.2 Costs of Primary Care 65
   4.3 Costing Governmental Hospitals in Vietnam 67
      4.3.1 Setting 67
      4.3.2 Findings 71

4.4	Costing a Health District in Burkina Faso		75
	4.4.1 Setting		75
	4.4.2 Findings		78
		4.4.2.1 Primary Care	78
		4.4.2.2 Secondary Care	82
		4.4.2.3 Total District Cost	87
		4.4.2.4 Capacity	88
5	Utilizing Costing Studies		93
	5.1 Estimating Standard Costs		93
		5.1.1 Costing a Pattern Health District in Tanzania	95
		5.1.2 Costing a Pattern Health District in Burkina Faso	108
	5.2 Resource Allocation		116
		5.2.1 Modelling Resource Allocation	116
		5.2.2 Model	117
		5.2.3 Results	121
		5.2.4 Policy Implications	129
	5.3 Setting a Premium for an Insurance Scheme		131
		5.3.1 Basic Model	132
		5.3.2 Results	135
		5.3.2.1 Fixed Income	136
		5.3.2.2 Non-linear Demand Increase	137
		5.3.2.3 Different Values for d_max and p_max	139
		5.3.2.4 Different Estimates of Willingness to Pay	140
		5.3.2.5 Effect of Pool Size	142
	5.4 Sustainability		143
		5.4.1 Assessing Static Sustainability	144
		5.4.2 Assessing Dynamic Sustainability	146
		5.4.3 Sustainability and Time Preference	152
		5.4.3.1 Model	152
		5.4.3.2 Results	157
6	Conclusions		161
Literature			165

1 Introduction

Equity and sustainability are of highest importance for policy makers in developed and developing countries [3-8]. In particular, equitable and sustainable health care is seen as a first-rank objective for most decision makers irrespective of their nationality and political orientation. Researchers and policy makers might disagree on definitions and implications, but most of them will strive for equitable and sustainable health services for their population. However, measuring equity and sustainability is difficult and sometimes seen as impossible. Decision makers in the health care sector are in urgent need of instruments to measure equity and sustainability of health care services.

Many authors have discussed the importance of equity and sustainability in developing countries under the public health perspective [9-12]. These contributions are of high importance for decision makers, but from a health economic point of view they frequently do not give sufficient attention to the macro economic environment in these countries. Developing countries are characterised as resource-poor, and their health care budgets are extremely low. Consequently, all explanations of inequality and low sustainability in health and health care provision that do not reflect on the chronic scarcity of resources are not sufficient to guide realistic decisions. On the contrary, we need wise decisions based on epidemiological *and* economic data.

The last few years have seen a strong increase in the knowledge of demographic and epidemiological data in developing countries [13, 14]. For instance, demographic surveillance systems have been installed in many health districts, and the number of papers published on the epidemiology of Aids, malaria and other major diseases is splendid. However, there hardly exist any data on the resource consumption of health care services. Without the knowledge of the resources which have to be invested in health care we will not be able to develop wise health policies. Our programmes will remain utopian wishes. *Only studies on resource consumption in combination with epidemiological research can guide our way towards a better health for all.*

In this booklet we would like to contribute to the knowledge of costs of health care services in developing countries. Furthermore, we would like to demonstrate how this knowledge can be used to guide policy decisions. The discussion is based on ten years of research and consultancies in different developing countries, including costing studies in Tanzania, Vietnam and Burkina Faso. As *Figure* 1.1 shows, health economic analysis can always be only one element of an entire system of evidence-based decision making. Health economics cannot contribute more than one component of policy making – but an essential one. Demographic and epidemiological research must be combined with health economic approaches in order to make wise decisions. Thus, if we focus on health economics and define basic terms from an economic perspective, it is not a shortcoming of our text, but a humble confession that health economics is an important dimension of real life that must be complemented by epidemiological and demographic research.

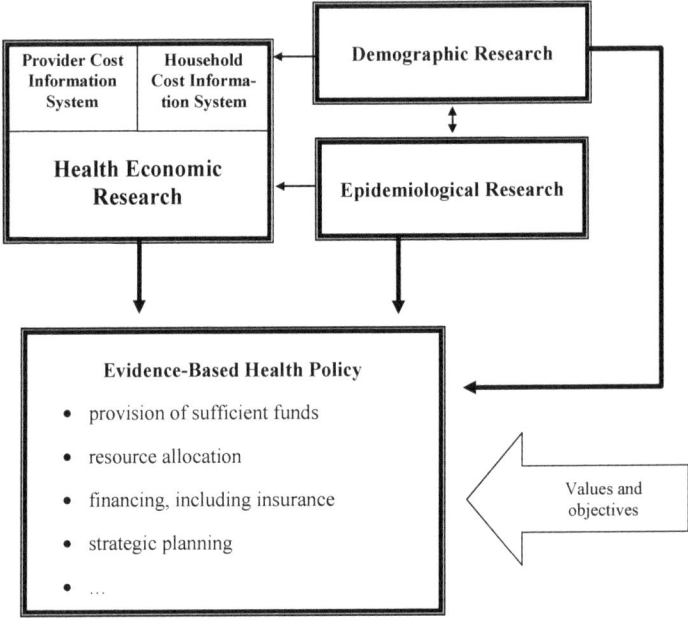

Figure 1.1   Health Economics as a component of evidence-based decision making

In addition, *Figure* 1.1 demonstrates that an evidence-based health policy also depends on the values and objectives of the society and the policy makers. *Therefore, any health economic analysis must start with some ethical consideration.* Only if we know what we want to achieve, health economists can gather appropriate data, analyse it for a specific question and provide an appropriate policy suggestion. Equity and sustainability are such values and objectives. We will demonstrate that affordability is a proxy for equity that can be assessed with an economic methodology, and sustainability can also be partly expressed in economic terms. However, we have to admit that not all aspects of equity and sustainability are quantifiable, so that *costing will provide an essential, but not a fully comprehensive view of equity and sustainability.*

In order to prove the importance of costing for equitable and sustainable health care in developing countries, we will first demonstrate the methodology of costing health care services in countries with poor accounting systems. Afterwards we will present some case studies from different countries. Finally we will show how this data can be translated into a health policy that follows these two basic values of health care.

2 Essentials of Health Economics

Economics is the science of describing, explaining and over-coming scarcity [15, 16]. Consequently, the health economist analyses all processes and institutions which determine the demand and supply of health care services. He assumes that these services will contribute positively to the health of people [17] and provides suggestions how to improve the public and individual health within the constraints of limited health care resources [18].

In a world of scarce resources, the health economist has to allot scarce resources to different programmes (e.g. Aids control programme) or service providers (e.g. hospitals) [19-22]. This allocation decision requires a clear and transparent goal system. For instance, he has to allocate resources to different spatial units (e.g. capital versus rural health districts), to different diseases (e.g. malaria versus diabetes), age sets (e.g. children versus adults) and social groups (e.g. wage-earners versus unemployed). *Whatever is transferred to one group, will not be available anymore for other groups* [23]. Therefore, any health economic discourse has to start with a brief analysis of the value and goal system. If we do not agree on values and objectives, we cannot agree on policies and decisions.

2.1 Ethics in Health Care

The discipline of ethics is an as essential dimension of practical philosophy, and it reflects on the appropriate and good life or behaviour [24]. Since Aristotle, philosophers have developed systems of societal values that should guide individual behaviour and policy decisions [25]. A generally accepted foundation of practical ethics is the Universal Declaration of Human Rights that was adopted and proclaimed by the General Assembly of the United Nations in 1948. This declaration is based on a long tradition of philosophy, Christianity and humanity as well as the declarations of civil rights of the French revolution and of the constitutions of free countries. It proclaims *the inherent dignity of all members of the human family as the highest value*. This dignity is protected by the right to medical care and necessary social services for every human being irrespective of its race, sex, income or property (Art. 25). It is the underlying obligation of all decision makers to defend this dignity and fight against all processes and conditions threatening it. Thus, *striving for better health in developing countries is a basic human responsibility for politicians, economists and other policy makers*.

Table 2.1 Millennium development goals (MDG)

MDG	Subgoal
Eradicate extreme poverty and hunger	Reduce by half the proportion of people living on less than one U.S. dollar a day.
	Reduce by half the proportion of people who suffer from hunger.
	Increase the amount of food for those who suffer from hunger.
Achieve universal primary education	Ensure that all boys and girls complete a full course of primary schooling.
	Increased enrolment must be accompanied by efforts to ensure that all children remain in school and receive a high-quality education.
Promote gender equality and empower women	Eliminate gender disparity in primary and secondary education preferably by 2005, and at all levels by 2015.
Reduce child mortality	Reduce the mortality rate among children under five by two thirds.
Improve maternal health	Reduce by three quarters the maternal mortality ratio.
Combat HIV/AIDS, malaria, and other diseases	Halt and begin to reverse the spread of HIV/AIDS.
	Halt and begin to reverse the incidence of malaria and other major diseases.
Ensure environmental sustainability	Integrate the principles of sustainable development into country policies and programmes; reverse loss of environmental resources.
	Reduce by half the proportion of people without sustainable access to safe drinking water.
	Achieve significant improvement in lives of at least 100 million slum dwellers, by 2020.
Develop a global partnership for development	Develop further an open trading and financial system that is rule-based, predictable and non-discriminatory. Includes a commitment to good governance, development and poverty reduction – nationally and internationally.
	Address the least developed countries' special needs. This includes tariff- and quota-free access for their exports; enhanced debt relief for heavily indebted poor countries; cancellation of official bilateral debt; and more generous official development assistance for countries committed to poverty reduction.
	Address the special needs of landlocked and small island developing States.
	Deal comprehensively with developing countries' debt problems through national and international measures to make debt sustainable in the long term.
	In cooperation with the developing countries, develop decent and productive work for youth.
	In cooperation with pharmaceutical companies, provide access to affordable essential drugs in developing countries.
	In cooperation with the private sector, make available the benefits of new technologies – especially information and communications technologies.

Source: [26]

2.1 Ethics in Health Care

Unhealth – as the opposite of health – is a major violation of dignity. It reduces the life expectancy, quality of life and the economic prospects of individuals and social groups. Therefore, fighting unhealth is a major mean of protecting the dignity of human beings and achieving the *Millennium Development Goals (MDG)*, in particular goals 4, 5, and 6 [27, 28]. *Thus, protecting the dignity of human beings is the most important objective of all development and of health economics.*

However, the achievement of dignity is difficult to measure, so that this basic value must be translated into *specific, measurable and realistic objectives*. The German constitution, for instance, regards freedom, equity and solidarity as basic values exemplifying the abstract term dignity. *Freedom* implies the autonomy of free development of one's personality, but also the right to live a healthy life and to participate in the processes influential on one's own existence. Therefore, unhealth is a major obstacle to freedom.

Equity is a complex and eclectic term. As we will see in the next chapter, different concepts of equity are irreconcilable and practical decisions based on equity are often considered as unfair by some stakeholders. However, it seems to the author that equity of health care provision in developing countries is easier to define. A policy that guarantees equal starting chances for each human being irrespective of the income, property and location is equitable. And a policy that safeguards access to basic health care services for all social groups irrespective of their poverty and place of living is protecting human dignity. Consequently, equity calls for a 'pro poor' policy in developing countries – a plea that is far from reality for poverty groups in many countries.

The third underlying value is *solidarity*. Solidarity in its narrow sense is a rational act. For instance, a contribution to a social health insurance is not induced by compassion or love, but it is a rational decision to subscribe to the insurance in order to receive coverage of health care costs in case of illness. However, in most of our cultures and religions we go beyond that rational decision and call for love and compassion for our neighbours. Solidarity in its broader sense demands more than giving to others just because we want to have some future gains. The majority of people will agree that the poor and suffering have a value of their own and humans have to take care of them – for the sake of dignity.

Dignity, freedom, equity and solidarity are abstract terms. They are underlying principles, but daily decisions must be based on specific, measurable and attainable *objectives*. These objectives must be inferable form the basic values, but they must be much more precise. Effectiveness and quality, affordability, sustainability as well as participation are such objectives that can be measured and that can serve as a foundation for policy decisions [29]. Figure 2.1 demonstrates the system of principle value, basic values and objectives.

Deriving a consistent goal system where the achievement of a specific, measurable and realistic objective highly correlates with the underlying basic value is difficult and frequently requires interdisciplinary cooperation. Health economists call for objectives the performance of which can be quantified, but politicians and ethicists frequently provide abstract and immeasurable values. However, for an equitable and sustainable health care, values and objectives must be consistent. *We must safeguard that daily life objectives reflect basic values. We cannot accept guidelines, regulations and daily life objectives that are not derived from principle values.*

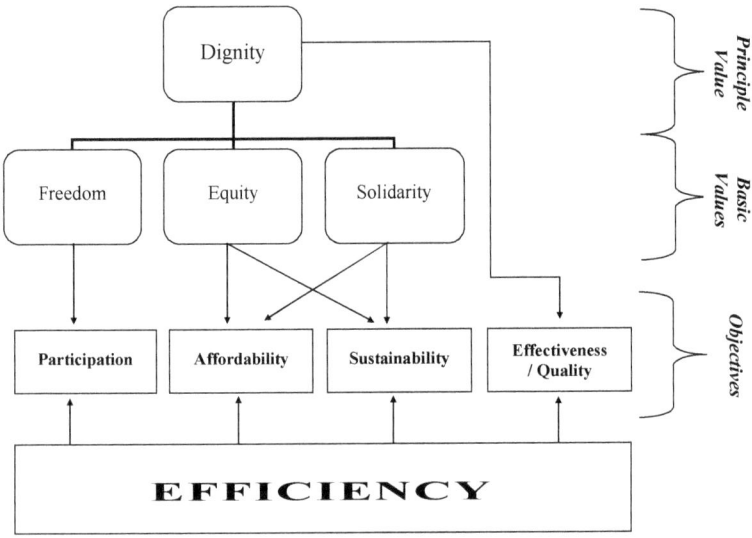

Figure 2.1 Values and objectives of health care[1]

Effectiveness and Quality

Health care services and programmes must be effective, i.e., they must achieve their goals. An ineffective anti-malaria drug is very unlikely to help the patient and is not protecting his dignity. A hospital where patients do not receive effective health care does not protect the basic rights of the patient. We can usually expect that services and programmes will be effective, if their quality is sufficient. Consequently, effectiveness is usually combined with quality.

Quality is difficult to define and to measure [30-33]. Corsten distinguishes objective and subjective quality [34]. Objective quality can be measured by scientific facts (e.g. germs per cm^2), whereas subjective quality reflects the perception of quality by customers. Health economists tend to use a subjective definition of quality [35]. This is partly due to the fact that the customer is part of the production process, so that he influences the production result. His subjective perception of quality will be of great influence on his ability and willingness to take a positive part in his healing process. Secondly, the basic value of freedom includes that every man should have autonomy

---

[1] Figure 2.1 does not reflect possible goal conflicts.

over his health. The patient should decide how he defines health and what he experiences as quality. An authoritarian determination of quality of health care services, as it was commonly done by colonial doctors [36], is not reflecting that health is more than physical well-being. It includes autonomy over processes that impact one's life [37, 38].

Subjective quality is the final point of a process of quality production [39, 40]. Input factors are transformed into outputs, and the individual perceives these outputs as input factors of its own production process of health. On a macro level this will again have consequences on other factors, such as the national product. Consequently, we can distinguish between structural, process and result quality as well as between outputs, outcomes and impacts [41].

Structural quality comprises the quality of input factors, such as quantity and quality of personnel, materials, equipment and buildings. Process quality expresses the goodness of the recombination processes, including documentation, waiting times, standardisation etc. Result quality expresses the (objective) quality of the outputs, e.g. hospital mortality, infection rates etc. [42-44].

It is a platitude that a perfect health service does not necessarily lead to a successful healing, i.e., even *a perfect output of the health service production process does not guarantee a satisfactory outcome* so that the result for the patient strongly differs from the output. Finally, the impact of the outcome can be economic growth, increase of herd immunity, eradication of a disease etc. Figure 2.2 demonstrates these steps.

Typical *indicators* of the structural quality are the cost per bedday, the occupied beds per member of a certain staff category (e.g. per physician) or the expenditure for personnel training. Typical indicators of the process quality are the existence of a standard treatment protocol, of a clinical pathway or of an essential drug list, as well as the quality of documentation. Furthermore, the percentage of patients seen by a physician on day of admittance and the percentage of patients seen by a physician on day of discharge are indicators of the process quality. Indicators of result quality are difficult to retrieve in developing countries, but the hospital mortality rate and the Caesarean section rate could serve as statistics, although they should be interpreted with caution.

Participation

Participation is the process of taking a stake in all conditions and processes that directly or indirectly affect oneself or those for whom we are responsible. Participation is a direct consequence of the basic value of freedom, as it means that all stakeholders [45] must be given a voice and a vote in a decision making process. It is generally accepted that participation of stakeholders is an important prerequisite of successful implementation, i.e., reforms which are not socially accepted cannot do well [46]. The more different stakeholders are integrated, the more likely an innovation will be accepted [47, 48]. However, we argue here that participation is more than a means to achieve a target. It is an objective of its own with the same importance as high quality, affordability and sustainability. Stakeholders have to be included in the decision making process, even if they cannot influence the implementation, because participation is consistent with the principal value of dignity. Withholding the right to decide on processes influential on their lives will harm the dignity of those for whom we plan and implement health services.

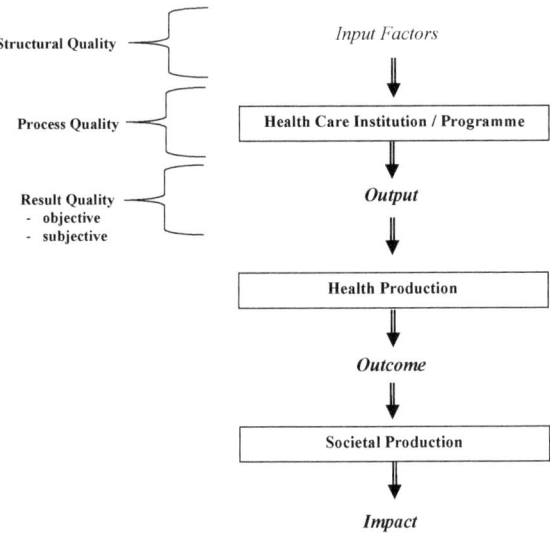

Source: [49]

Figure 2.2   Results: output, outcome, impact

Participation has been neglected a long time. A paternalistic approach dominated the management of health services in developing countries [50, 51] where doctors knew what their patients needed, whereas the patients were begging for help, in particular during the colonial period. The "big brothers" knew what their "little brothers" needed and how they could help them best [52-58]. This approach led to the establishment of big hospitals in the "mission field", in which white doctors, nurses and (later) administrators held all decision making power. These expatriates were usually quite committed and they received grants from their home churches to do their work. In this way they could offer their services at very low prices, sometimes free of charge. Their „white elephants" or „disease palaces" [59] were very well kept and fulfilled the objectives of affordability, quality and sustainability. However, participation of stakeholders was almost neglected.

Towards the end of the colonial period this concept of health care services was frequently criticized. In 1964 (Tübingen I, 19.-24. May 1964) directors of major protestant mission societies gathered in Tübingen, Germany, to analyse and discuss their work. They realised that their services could not reach the majority of people so that their system was very unjust. McGilvray, the former director of the Christian Medical Commission (CMC), describes the situation with the words: "... these church-related

2.1 Ethics in Health Care

institutions, together with all the other available facilities of Western medicine, were reaching only 20% of the population in these countries and were thus sustaining a grave injustice to the 80% who remained deprived of any services at all" [60]. In addition, they realised that due to technical progress the costs of medical treatment increased tremendously in the existing institutions, so that even the little that was done could not be sustained [61]. Most important in this consultation was, however, the insight that mission hospitals practised a type of medicine that was not in line with the biblical understanding of salvation and healing [62-64].

These statements were well received in the Christian churches world-wide. Several local consultations followed [65-67], and in 1967 (Tübingen II, 1.-8. September 1967) a new, community based approach was declared obligatory for church-related health care services [68]. The innovative work was co-ordinated by the newly founded Christian Medical Commission (CMC). From 1973 to the early 1980s this institution was in close contact with the World Health Organisation, highly influencing the development of the Alma Ata Declaration [69].

The World Health Organisation had to recognize that the most important health problems had not declined 25 years after its inauguration (07.04.48). On the contrary, financing the existing health services had become more and more difficult [70]. In search for new solutions, the Director General of the WHO, Halfdan Mahler, recognized that the decisions of Tübingen were relevant for all health care systems in developing countries, not only for church-related services. The concept of Primary Health Care (PHC) that was discussed and approved during the World Health Assembly in 1978 [71] can be interpreted as a secular advancement of the Declarations of Tübingen.

Primary Health Care is based on the traditional concept of hygiene, but enriched by a health political dimension and a strong element of participation [72-75]. Primary Health Care is a conception of health policy, i.e., it is not a level of health care, but a comprehensive philosophy of health care underlying all decisions in the health field. It is fundamentally oriented on the needs of the community, and intends to include the community in all processes of determining objectives and means of health care. The stakeholders of the community are to accept responsibility for their own health, so that institution or programme based health care becomes a *community based health care* (CBHC). Thus, PHC and CBHC are inducing the concept of participation as essential dimension of the health care objective system.

The strong community approach was rejected by many institutions and policy makers. Some saw it as expression of a left-wing political movement, as Art. III of the declaration refers to a „New International Economic Order", and Art. X states that high military expenditure are a major reason for poor health. Werner & Sanders write: „Many of the principles of Primary Health Care were garnered from China and from the diverse experiences of small, struggling non-governmental Community-Based Health Programmes (CBHP) in the Philippines, Latin America, and elsewhere. The intimate connection of many of these initiatives to political reform movements explains to some extent why the concepts underlying PHC have received both criticism and praise for being revolutionary" [76].

More important was the critic uttered by health specialists stating that PHC was utopic [52-55, 77-81]. They called for strict priorities, in particular the concentration on vertical programmes to fight childhood diseases. Contrary to the original "Comprehensive Primary Health Care" (CPHC) concept of the WHO, the "Selective Primary Health Care" (SPHC) and the „Expanded Programme on Immunisation" (EPI) [82, 83] in particular could work without strong community participation.

The failure of the implementation of the comprehensive primary health care concept in most developing countries has been frequently discussed and has many reasons. Flessa [84] developed an innovation model with several barriers of implementation, including meta-stability of the curative health care systems, high costs of building-up a CBHC-system, high time preference and low risk affinity of decision makers and an authoritarian leadership style. *In this booklet we merely have to state, that the objective of participation has almost disappeared from the agenda of health care policy makers.* Freedom as the fundamental right to participate in all processes with impact on one's life is reduced to the freedom to choose between different providers. Participation of the local population by setting priorities in health care, designing health care services and controlling institutions and programmes has almost disappeared from the political as well as from the research arena.

Affordability

Equity and solidarity call for accessibility to health care services for all groups of the society. However, in many developing countries, poverty groups have no access to modern health care services due to financial constraints and/or insurmountable distances from their place of living to the provider [81, 85, 86]. Consequently, morbidity and mortality of this subpopulation are above average [87-91]. The insufficient medical care for social groups might have two reasons [92-94]: low willingness to pay (WTP) or low ability to pay (ATP).

Many diseases in developing countries are life threatening so that we can in principle base further discussions on a high willingness to pay. Economists usually assume that people act rational, i.e., life threatening diseases call for strongest investments into health care [95], as long as these services are likely to produce health [96-99]. Consequently, the willingness to pay can be increased by quality improvements.

However, the income of most poor people in developing countries is so low, that they cannot even afford basic health care services necessary to fight even life threatening diseases and restore their ability to work as basis of the household wealth [100], even if they would like to do so. Higher mortality and morbidity of low income groups in developing countries are – opposite to the situation in developed countries – not primarily the consequence of poor health education or irrational behaviour, but of disability to pay. Consequently, people die from healable diseases as they cannot afford the costs of the health services. Theses costs can be user fees, transport charges and loss of labour of relatives who accompany the patient.

2.1 Ethics in Health Care

The ability to pay is a function of wealth and income. As in particular hospital fees are usually higher than the income, most households have to take from their savings or sell animals, houses or fields if one household member is sick. Thus, disability to pay from the normal income will frequently lead to the household's decline of economic production and constitutes a major risk of poverty. Chronic or frequent episodes of illness will reduce the future ability to pay, until the household is completely impoverished [92, 101].

Consequently, the analysis of the affordability of health care services is of highest importance for all health policy makers, and they must define criteria to measure affordability [102]. Su et al. [103, 104] calculate the household expenditure for health care based on a demographic surveillance system in a health district in Burkina Faso. They compare the expenditure for health care with the total income of the household. They conclude that poor families spend absolutely less on health care, but the household's health care expenditure forms a higher percentage of the total household income. In particular, the risk of so-called 'catastrophic' expenditure is much higher for poor households than for rich [101].

Studies like those presented by Su et al. require an existing surveillance system and a high precision of household data. An alternative would be to determine the catchment areas of existing health care institutions and mark the zones from which patients come. These maps can demonstrate that patients from urban slum areas are less likely to seek services at the hospital. Similarly, patients from rural villages will demand the less health care services the further away they are. Figure 2.3 gives an example from Masasi district hospital (Tanzania). The sample of 100 patient files was taken by the author in August 2001. It shows that about 75% of the inpatients came from the town, although according to official statistics 69% of the catchment populations live outside the town.

As stated before, the low demand for health services from outside the town has two reasons. Firstly, direct and indirect transport costs increase with distance so that the people coming from further away will not be able to afford the hospital services. Secondly, there is a tendency that rural people are poorer than urban people. Thus, user-fees are less likely a barrier for the urban than for the rural population to seek health care services.

In the last 15 years a number of health care institutions and health districts have introduced community health funds [105-109] in order to increase the affordability for the poor. These funds pool the risk of a catastrophic health expenditure so that in case of illness no or only little expenditure has to be shouldered by the household. Consequently, community health funds are frequently seen as an element of a *pro-poor policy*. However, these funds have to break-even, i.e., the expenditure must not exceed the income. In the absence of donations or government grants, the community health fund is only sustainable if the sum of premiums is not less than the sum of bills from the health care institutions and the administration costs of the fund. A community health fund must have a professional cost accounting system so that it can serve the poor with low premiums and remain viable.

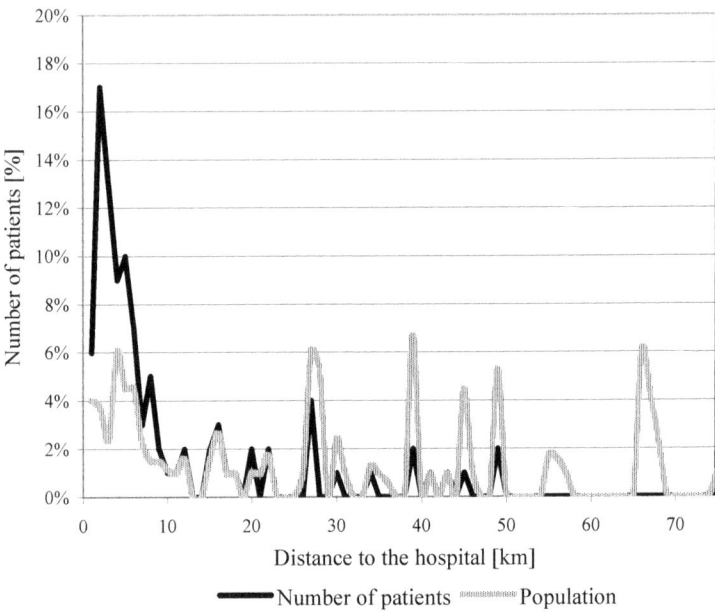

Figure 2.3   Catchment Analysis of Masasi hospital, Tanzania

Sustainability

Although the term sustainability has no generally accepted definition, it has become a high-rank objective of health care in developing countries. One could even talk about a new paradigm of development economics [100]. The word was originally used in forestry. During the Medieval Period the central European forests had been degraded to a degree that the rulers of that time had to make laws against the over-use of woodlands. It became a rule that the annual cut must not exceed the annual growth of wood in a forest. This was called sustainable as future generations will find the same quantity and quality of forests as the present generation.

Sustainability has been a key-word of development economics since the UN Conference on environment and development (Stockholm 1972) ended in a severe conflict between the interest of developed and developing countries. The latter insisted on their right to development, whereas the western world demanded more environmental protection. The solution for this conflict of goals was 'sustainable development'. Later conferences and reports, such as the Brundtlandt-Report (1987) [110] or the UN Conference on environment and development in Rio de Janeiro (1992) [111], developed the concept further. As a minimum it includes:

- *Development vs. growth:* the majority of economic theories analyze the economic growth by an increase in real national product per-capita. This incorporates that a nation can increase its economic growth by selling natural resources beyond their ability to regenerate them. The concept of development places particular emphasis on the complexity of a system, i.e. the number of elements and their relation to each other. This would mean that a nation which destroys its natural resources reduces its own complexity and thus induces negative development. The concept of sustainability calls for development instead of purely quantitative growth.
- *Intra-generational justice:* sustainable development includes that rich nations have a responsibility for the poorer nations. Resources should be distributed equally between the north and the south, but also regional disparities within a country should be reduced.
- *Inter-generational justice:* future generations should have the same access to resources as the present generation. This is the traditional meaning of the word as it was derived from agriculture and forestry.

The concept of sustainability has meanwhile entered other fields of development economics. We talk about 'sustainable programs' or 'sustainable institutions' and most development agencies demand sustainability for the programmes and institutions they support. However, if the concept of sustainability is not limited to natural resources but applied to many aspects of development, it should be clearly defined. This has hardly been attempted.

In this booklet sustainability is defined as the *ability of a system to provide services in the present without sacrificing the provision of services in the future*. Viability is a prerequisite of sustainability, but the persistent existence at a complete loss of any functionality might be called viability, but never sustainability. Assuming that the function of an open system in its environment is the transformation of inputs into outputs, sustainability includes the maintenance of a minimum structure (elements and relations) suited to combine the inputs in such a way that results are produced which are worthwhile for the environment. Thus, the concept of sustainability must distinguish:

- *Static vs. dynamic sustainability*: the term static sustainable should be used if a system can survive perpetually in its constant environment. On the contrary, the term dynamic sustainable should be applied if a system is able to react on changes of the environment so that it can survive under changed conditions. A system can exist forever under unchanging conditions, but it might be rapidly destroyed as soon as these conditions are modified.
- *Functional vs. structural sustainability*: a system is called functional sustainable if it is maintaining the original function. If the system is able to support its original structure (elements and relations) it is called structural sustainable.

Table 2.2 exhibits the combination of these dimensions. Many programmes and institutions in developing countries lack *static structural sustainability*. They were originally equipped with an expensive structure consisting of many elements and relations, but they cannot maintain them. The environment has not changed and the function of the system is constant. However, the input is inadequate to provide the system with sufficient agents of production so that it is able to fulfil its function and maintain its structure. Therefore, the system consumes its own elements. In that way the system is finally reduced to an energy level which can be maintained by the input. There are several examples of hospitals in developing countries for a low static structural sustainability.

Table 2.2 Concept of sustainability

	Functional Sustainability	Structural Sustainability
Static Sustainability	static functional sustainable	static structural sustainable
Dynamic Sustainability	dynamic functional sustainable	dynamic structural sustainable

Other hospitals in Africa have tried to maintain their structure but altered their functions. The original function of public and church-related hospitals was the provision of basic health services for the poor and needy within their catchment area. However, as this would usually mean that hospitals cannot be structurally sustainable, some decision makers made up their mind to increase the fees to an extent that these hospitals have become health institutions for a rich minority. They can break-even and re-invest money in order to keep the hospital at the same standard, but their fee policy excludes those patients for whom the hospital was originally built, i.e., they could not *sustain their function*. The environment has not changed dramatically and there would still be thousands of poor patients waiting to be treated, but these hospitals have reduced their functions in order to keep their structure.

There is a conflict between the desire to keep the function of a hospital and the necessity to keep the structure. In a long run systems which are structurally not sustainable will lose their functional sustainability as well. When all elements are consumed the system will cease away. In the case of church hospitals in low income countries this conflict has been solved for many years by donations. The function was kept up by consuming the structure. When the structure was in such poor a condition that the function could not be maintained anymore, donors gave a new structural input. Figure 2.4 demonstrates this development of donations and service level.

If the environment changes the system must react. Minor changes of the political or economic environment will usually not change the function. A flexible system can react by *changing its structure*. In Tanzania, for instance, nursing care had been to a large extent on the shoulders of untrained nursing attendants. This was due to the fact that only few professionally trained nurses were available. Today the situation has changed. Many training institutions were established and a sufficient number of qualified nurses is available on the labour market. Therefore, the structure of health care institutions has changed. More and more untrained nurses are substituted by professionally trained nurses.

2.1 Ethics in Health Care

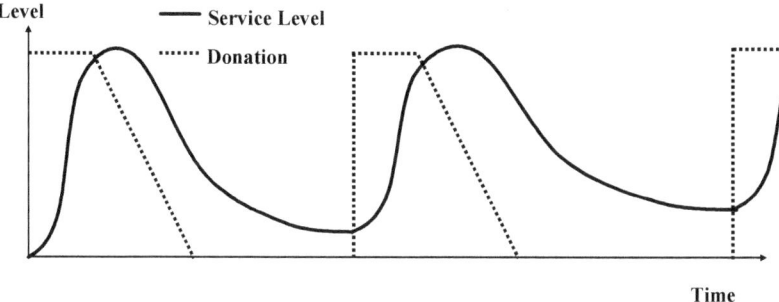

Figure 2.4   Development of donations and service level

More severe are usually changes of the environment that affect the function of a hospital. The analysis of catchment areas of Lutheran hospitals in Tanzania showed that about 30% of them have problems of low occupancy due to shrinking catchment areas [112]. Today people tend to use means of public transport and drive to central places for health care services instead of visiting small church hospitals [113]. Therefore, the hospital will have to change its function or fold up. It has to become a service centre for primary health care. However, many church leaders do not have the flexibility to change the function of their hospitals, thus they threaten the *dynamic functional sustainability* of their institutions.

Dynamic functional sustainability will usually require dynamic structural sustainability. An existing hospital, for instance, which is going to be restructured as a service centre for primary health care, will not be in need of a specialized surgeon any more. This means that the change of the function will have to be accompanied by an alteration of the structure.

Costing is a prerequisite to measure structural sustainability. The funds invested into maintenance, re-investment and training are a good proxy for the degree of sustainability of a health care institution or programme. The analysis of the functional sustainability is more difficult and demands precise data on the composition of the clients.

In a nut-shell: effectiveness, quality, participation, affordability and sustainability are important objectives for all health care systems. Health care plans have to define how they will contribute to the achievement of these objectives. *Costing studies are a prerequisite to assess affordability and sustainability. However, they can also be useful for the achievement of the other objectives as they are a precondition for efficiency – the underlying objective of all economic activities.*

Efficiency

Effectiveness/quality, participation, affordability and sustainability are conflicting goals. For instance, affordability calls for low fees for health care services. Consequently, the income of a health care institution is low so that they cannot afford to maintain the existing structures. The result is a poor structural sustainability, i.e., affordability and sustainability are in dissent. Likewise, high quality of care and affordability are conflicting, as the latter calls for low fees, so that the income of the health care institution will not be sufficient to pay for high quality care.

Participation can also be – at least partly – in conflict with the other objectives. Some of the mission hospitals during the colonial era, for instance, provided a high quality of services. All management positions were staffed by Europeans, and the fees were low. After independence, the management of the health care institution was handed over to local staff, and the CBHC concept even called for participation of the local population. In many places the strict, paternalistic management was more effective and led to higher quality of care, at least in a short run. Thus, there was a conflict of goals between participation and quality of care.

Figure 2.5 demonstrates the principle of the conflicts of goals by a model of corresponding pipes filled with gas. If sustainability is increased, all other objectives are reduced, and vice versa. Whenever you press one cylinder, the others will go up. This resembles the conflict, which we always face: If you want to do something for today you might harm tomorrow; if we support the poor, we might not be able to finance our institution.

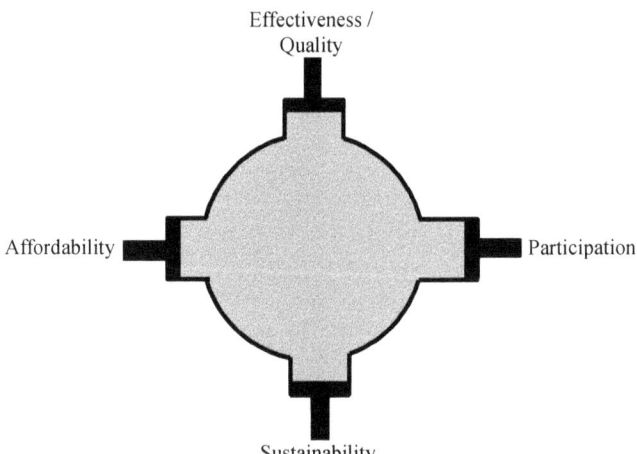

Figure 2.5 Model of conflicts of goals

A simultaneous improvement of several objectives requires that the density of the gas inside the pipe system is increased. *Likewise, managerial conflicts of goals can only be solved by an increase of efficiency* [114]. Efficiency means, that existing resources are made better use of. We can achieve several goals at the same time and to a higher extent, if we use the resources efficiently. Not all objectives can be achieved perfectly, but to a higher extent. *Therefore, efficiency is the art of reconciling conflicting goals.*

Efficiency[2] can be defined as the ratio between inputs and results, i.e.

$$\frac{Result}{Input} \rightarrow Max!$$

As demonstrated in Figure 2.2, the *results* can be outputs, outcomes or impacts. Frequently, managers of health care institutions focus on outputs (e.g. patient days, operations), medical experts on outcomes (e.g. healing of a patient) and public health experts on impacts which can be measured in epidemiological statistics, such as mortality, morbidity, life expectancy, quality of life etc.

The *input* can be measured in quantities, such as labour hours, kg of materials etc. However, as inputs usually have to be bought, it is common to express them with their cost, i.e. the monetary value of the resource consumption. *Therefore, knowing the cost of a programme or institution is a prerequisite for efficiency.* And therefore, costing of health care services is a prerequisite to reconcile the four conflicting objectives.

In a nut-shell: *The principal value of our societies as well as of all health care services is the dignity of man. As unhealth deprives dignity, fighting unhealth is a humanitarian must. This is achieved by striving for effectiveness/quality, participation, sustainability and affordability. However, as this fight against unhealth takes place under the condition of limited resources and as these four objectives are conflicting, efficiency becomes an objective of its own.*

Measuring the achievement of these five objectives is difficult, but knowing the cost of health services is a prerequisite for it. In particular affordability, sustainability and efficiency can be partly expressed by statistics based on cost, i.e., "accurate costing can contribute to the efficient allocation of resources within the health system, and identify where cost reduction is feasible and justifiable. Conversely, misleading or absent cost data can lead to unfair comparisons and flawed policy choices" [115].

2.2 Health Economic Framework

Equity, sustainability and efficiency are difficult terms that need further explanation in order to become fruitful for policy makers. This paragraph develops a health economic framework in order to distinguish different aspects of these basic terms and increase our understanding of their interdependencies.

---

[2] The second chapter of this booklet can only be a short introduction to the essentials of health economics. It is supposed to describe the basic terms and open the door for understanding the importance of costing of health care services in developing countries. Consequently, several aspects can only be touched, important interdependencies between the models have to be neglected, and alternative theoriese are omitted. This includes important concepts such as utility functions, hyperbolic discounting and welfare-economics. For a state-of-the-art analysis see Breyer, Zweifel & Kifmann 2005.

Figure 2.7 (pare 21) exhibits the basic model [15, 17, 18, 116, 117]. It starts with the assumption that demand is usually greater than supply, i.e., the commodities or services to satisfy the needs of people are insufficient to meet the people's needs. This assumption is rather trivial for health services in developing countries, as there is a fundamental shortage of personnel, drugs, functioning equipment and standardised procedures leading into a general under-provision of services with acceptable quality. At the same time transport, funds and time are scarce at the side of the population. Consequently, *scarcity is the underlying principle of all health care activities in this world*. And it is expressed by the simple inequality

$$D > S$$

where D denotes the demand and S the supply.

The supply side can be analysed on two levels. The micro level is the subject of *business administration*, i.e. the transformation of agents of production into health care services in a single health care unit. For instance, human labour, equipment, buildings and materials are used in a hospital to produce operations, beddays or other service units. The macro level is the subject of *health economics*. It analyses the provision of health care services by several health care institutions. For instance, we have to define service levels, such as the traditional health care pyramid consisting of village health care workers, dispensaries, health centres, primary hospitals, secondary hospitals and tertiary hospitals for different spatial units, such as districts and regions. Health care resources have to be allocated to these different levels and spatial units. However, in practical work micro and macro level as well as business administration and health economics cannot be separated.

The demand for health care services is the end-point of a chain of events and filters. It starts with *objective scarcity of health*. This unhealth can be measured by physicians, but the person affected is not necessarily aware of it. For instance, many might suffer from hypertension without their knowledge. Health economists analyse and predict the objective scarcity of health by demographic and epidemiological models. For instance, the model of the demographic transition is used to predict the demand for delivery services [118], whereas Markov models are used to assess the incidence of cancer [119-122].

Unhealth can only result in demand for health services if the sick person is aware of it and experiences the scarcity of health as negative. This subjective experience of scarcity is called a *need*. Health education is employed to make a need out of an objective scarcity of health. Needs can be structured (e.g. physiological needs, security needs, esteem needs, social needs, self-actualisation needs) and prioritized. Health needs are usually physiological needs with a very high priority.

A need exists independently from the good or service that can satisfy the need. For instance, the need to drink is experienced as thirst in China, Africa and Europe. The Chinese will demand some tea, the African some water, and the German some beer. The same need is reflected on different goods or services to satisfy the need. And the need was the same in former times as it is today and will be in future.

2.2 Health Economic Framework

A need that is reflected on a certain good or service is called a *want*. The need of a woman due to deliver is the same in Africa and in Europe, but the want might differ significantly. The European woman wants the support from a gynaecologist in the labour ward of a modern hospital, whereas the woman in rural Africa wants to be supported by a traditional birth attendant. We develop wants out of needs if we know that a certain good or service exists and believe that this commodity or service can satisfy our needs more than any other commodity or service. Consequently, health education has not only to make people aware of their needs, but it also has to convince them that certain goods or services are helpful to satisfy their needs. For instance, an Aids control programme has to explain that Aids is a threat to future life (security need) and has to convince people that condoms can protect them (want). A demand for condoms can only arise, if both steps are successful.

Wants turn into *demand* if the wanting person has sufficient purchasing power, if the supply is accessible, if it is of sufficient quality, and if other commodities or services are not more important for him. Thus, price, distance, quality and priority are filters that prevent wants from becoming a demand [123]. As health needs have a high priority, we can concentrate on price, distance and quality.

Taking for granted that the individual and the household have limited income and wealth, the *price* acts as a filter. The higher the price of a certain good or service, the less likely the person in need will be able to afford it. The *price elasticity* is expressed as the ratio

$$\varepsilon_p = \frac{dq/q}{dp/p}, \text{ with}$$

ε_p price elasticity
q quantity of a good
p price of a good
dq marginal change of quantity
dp marginal change of price

Some cases excepted, an increase of the price will result in a decrease in the quantity demanded, i.e., some people who want a certain good will not buy it, or some sick people with an urgent need of health care services will not be able to afford them. A health insurance is an instrument to reduce the price elasticity. However, the premium is the price of the insurance policy, and there is an elasticity of demand for this policy. Consequently, the higher the price of the insurance, the less is the demand for it.

The price elasticity of demand is closely related to the *income elasticity*, i.e.

$$\varepsilon_I = \frac{dq/q}{dI/I}, \text{ with}$$

ε_I income elasticity
q quantity of a good
I income
dq marginal change of quantity
dI marginal change of income

If the income increases, the demand for commodities or services will usually grow as well. There are very few exceptions to this rule (e.g. for basic food such as potatoes).

Distance is another filter between want and demand. Figure 2.6 demonstrates the friction of distance underlying Figure 2.3. The number of transactions between individuals and groups decreases with distance. However, the friction is not constant, but depends on different variables, such as mobility, gravity and traditions.

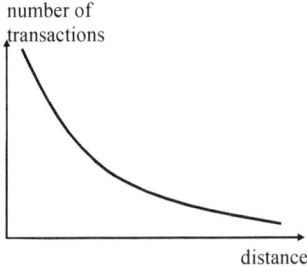

Figure 2.6   Friction of distance

Furthermore, the *quality* of services determines whether wants become a demand. If the quality is not sufficient to satisfy the needs (e.g. does not promise healing) or if it compares unfavourable to the price, the wanting person will invest his funds into other goods or services. Consequently, quality management (including defining and measuring quality) is a major component of health economics.

Finally, demand and supply meet on the *market*. There are many different markets for different levels of health care, in different regions and for different groups. It is generally accepted that health care markets are not equal to markets for other goods or services. This is partly due to the fact that a health care market does not reach "automatically" an efficient allocation of resources, for instance because health care services frequently have external effects. If a hospital heals a TB-patient, the risk of being infected is reduced for many other people. Consequently, the societal utility of healing this patient is higher than the individual utility for the patient. Furthermore, there can be only a limited comparison between the health care market and other markets since health is a basic value of its own. There is no problem if somebody cannot afford brilliants, but if people are not able to afford health care services, basic values of our society are at stake. Consequently, *not every market-solution for health care services is*

2.2 Health Economic Framework

also socially acceptable. Therefore, policy makers have to decide how strongly they influence the health care market. They can interfere directly (for instance by governmental monopolies or by fixing maximum prices), or indirectly (for instance by regulating the approbation).

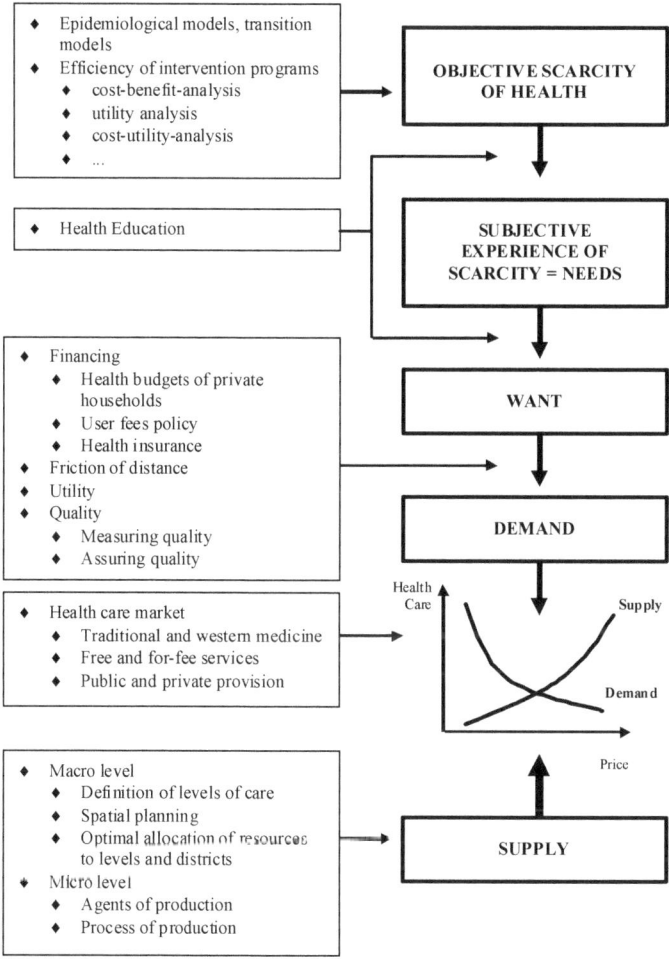

Figure 2.7   Health Economic Framework

The health economic framework can be used to analyse the terms efficiency and equity in more detail. *Efficiency* compares the inputs with the results, i.e., it compares the consumption of resources with the service units produced, with the demand met, the needs satisfied or the health produced. For instance, business administrators compare the input of personnel, equipment, buildings and materials per bed in different hospitals. A hospital is called efficient if it provides a hospital bed with a given quality at a minimum input of these resources. However, this purely technical efficiency might be misleading because it only focuses on the provider side. It might be that the people in need demand something different. In developed countries, for instance, tertiary hospitals might provide efficient and highly professional top-medical services for fatally ill patients, but in reality they just want to die in peace. Demand is not identical with professional service.

Furthermore, policy makers cannot merely analyse the demand for health care services, but they have to look at wants and needs. For instance, a health care system can be based on high-cost hospital services. The patients that come to the hospital and who are able to afford the services receive high-quality, but the majority of the people will not even dare to come because they know that the hospital it too far away from their place of living and too expensive. *From a business administration point of view, the hospital might work efficient, but from a public health point of view the health care system is inefficient because the needs of the majority of the people are not met with the resources consumed.*

Finally, if people are not aware of their diseases, even satisfying their needs might not be sufficient. For instance, people suffering from hypertension might have free access to health care services to satisfy their needs. But many do not know that they require medical support. A health care system that efficiently treats all hypertension patients knowing about their disease but investing no resources to reach those ignorant of their risk is likely to be inefficient.

Equity can also be discussed on basis of the health economic framework [24, 124-126]. Firstly, equity can mean that everybody has the same level of health. This would reflect the basic statement that everybody has the same dignity and the same human right to live a healthy life. However, we all know that this is not possible, just because people are different. Some are born with disabilities that will never allow them to live the same life and experience the same degree of health as others irrespective of societal investments into their health. More important is the fact that people might experience different health conditions quite differently. The satisfaction with a certain living condition, disability or infirmity might differ from person to person, so that total equality of health might lead to inequality of satisfaction.

Therefore, it seems more practical to define equity as the situation in which everybody satisfies their needs to the same extent. However, this would require a technique with which one could measure the utility of a certain condition or the satisfaction with a certain level of health. Practically, this is impossible even if many attempts were made to base health care decisions on subjective measures of the quality of life. They are not reliable or time-constant.

Some have suggested providing everybody with the services they need. This would imply a kind of judge who is able to determine what everybody needs. Furthermore, it

2.2 Health Economic Framework

would require indefinite resources, so that we have to accept that we cannot provide everybody with all services that they need. If equity is interpreted in this utopian way, it becomes invalid for guiding practical decisions.

A fourth alternative would be to give everybody as much as they can afford. From the point of view of distribution, this seems to be very much against the principle of equity. However, some people argue that it is just fair if a hard-working man can afford more and better health care services than a lazy person. *The conflict between these different concepts of justice cannot be solved* [127, 128] *but it can be partly eased by allowing for differences in wealth and income as long as these differences benefit the weakest of the society* [129].

Equity might also be interpreted as the right of equal access to health services. Due to the friction of distance, people living further away from health care services have to overcome a barrier. Equity would call at least for the definition of a maximum distance that should not be exceeded. For instance, Tanzania has a rule that a dispensary should be accessible for every citizen within 10 km of walking distance.

Finally, demand and services rendered are not identical. For instance, the prices of drugs in some developing countries are quite low so that people could afford these goods. However, the drug shelves are empty. The demand is high – but the services are low. Here we might call a system equitable if everybody receives the same services or goods irrespective of his needs and financial ability.

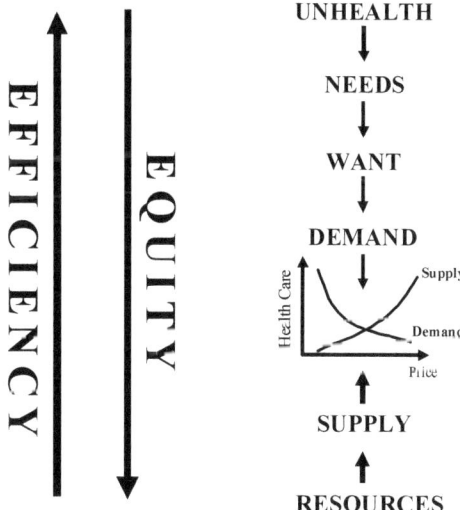

Figure 2.8   Equity and efficiency in the health economic framework

Some authors argue that equity and efficiency are in conflict [130, 131]. This statement must be handled with care, as equity and efficiency can express very different concepts and it is impossible to define them uniquely. We can construct a trade-off between equality and efficiency of a distribution of health, wealth or other goods. But in reality *efficiency is frequently a prerequisite of equity*.

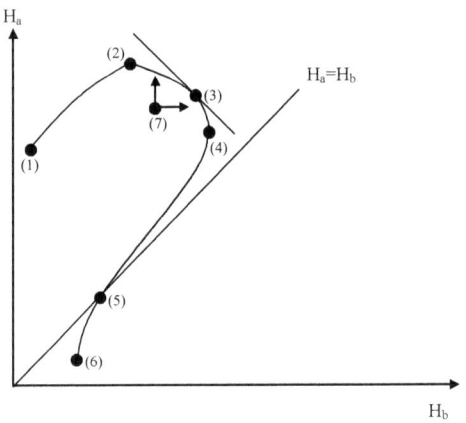

Source: [132]

Figure 2.9   Efficient and equitable allocation of health care resources

Figure 2.9 demonstrates different possibilities of the health status of two persons (A, B). The model assumes that B has a higher natural likelihood of having a lower health status, i.e., his genetic disposition for unhealth is higher. (1) represents the case that nearly the entire health care budget is spent for person A. Consequently, the health of A (H_a) is rather high, whereas the health of B is low. However, if B is rather sick, A cannot enjoy the maximum possible health. For instance, if B has an infectious disease, A might also be infected. Therefore, (1) refers to an inefficient resource allocation. Giving a part of the health care budget of A to B would increase the health of both persons. (2) represents a point which is absolutely dominant against (1), i.e., increasing equality between A and B (B receives more resources, A less) increases efficiency. Equality and efficiency are supporting objectives between (1) and (2).

Radiant from (2), B can only increase his health if the health of A is reduced. All points between (2) and (4) are Pareto-optimums, i.e., the utility of one person can only be increased by reducing the utility of the other person.

Traditional economics has shown a tendency to maximize the total or average of all members of the society, i.e.

2.2 Health Economic Framework

$$Z = \sum_{i=1}^{n} H_i \rightarrow Max! \Leftrightarrow Z' = \frac{1}{n}\sum_{i=1}^{n} H_i \rightarrow Max!$$

For this example we receive (3) as solution for the function

$$Z = H_1 + H_2 \rightarrow Max!$$

No other distribution offers a higher average health than (3), although this point does not guarantee that everybody has the same level of health. Rawls would prefer a distribution where B (= the weakest member of the society) has the highest possible level of health, i.e.

$$Z = \underset{i=1..n}{Min}(H_i) \rightarrow Max!$$

(4) represents the highest possible health for person B. It is preferable to the point of equal distribution (5) as A and B have a higher health status in this point. Total equality might lead to a worse situation than accepting some degree of inequality but with a higher level of health for everybody. The figure also demonstrates that the point of maximum average health (3) and the point of highest health of the weakest (4) are close to each other. The economic solution (3) would provide a higher health for the weakest member of the society than the equal distribution (5).

We can conclude that *the trade-off between efficiency and equity is rather limited, whereas the conflict between efficiency and equality can be huge.* Policy makers have to fight for a distribution of health and health care that accepts the reality of inequality, but still attempts to make the best out of limited resources for the weakest of the society. Consequently, *efficiency with all its different aspects as described above is a prerequisite for most, but not for all aspects of equitable health care.* Wasting resources cannot be accepted. For instance, (7) represents an inefficient use of resources. With the same input, a better health for A or for B can be achieved without changing the situation of the other person.

In principle, the health of both individuals can be increased by investing more resources into the health care system. This could, for instance, be financed by borrowing funds and accumulating a debt for future generations to be paid back. However, as stated before, equity must not be limited to this generation. Inter-generational justice is as important as intra-generational justice, and borrowing money today to invest in the health of this generation implies that future generations will have to pay back these debts and will not have sufficient funds to provide for their own health care. Consequently, *sustainability* is an objective of high importance. Figure 2.10 (page 27) demonstrates a two generational model of inter-temporal allocation. It assumes that resources can be allocated to curative medicine in period t, curative medicine in period t+1 or prevention in period t. Prevention has some negative effects in period t and positive effects in period t+1.

If all resources are invested into curative care for period t, the health status in period t will be high (5). However, the health of period t+1 is poor as no resources are available.

(1) represents the case that all resources are invested into curative care in period t+1, whereas curative medicine in period t and prevention in period t for period t+1 are not financed. Therefore, the health in period t+1 will be rather high, whereas the health in period t is poor.

If a certain part of the two-period health care budget is invested into prevention in period t for period t+1, the health status in period t+1 can be improved (2). This would results in a reduced health status in period t as the prevention might have some negative side-effect in period t (e.g. vaccination damage).

All points on the line between (2) and (5) are Pareto-optimums, i.e., the health status of period t can only be improved by reducing the health status in period t+1. Traditional health economist would maximize the function

$$Z = H_t + \frac{1}{1+r/100} H_{t+1} \to Max!$$

where r denotes the discounting or time preference rate and reflects the importance of the presence compared to the future. The higher the time preference rate, the more important is the presence, i.e., a future health status is highly discounted. Small time preference rates imply that future health has almost the same importance as a good health at the present.

The number of empirical studies to estimate time preference rates is small, and the results are very heterogeneous. Moore und Viscusi [133] calculated individual time preference rates between 2 and 11%. Lipscomb [134] confirms high rates, whereas Cairns [135] finds rates between 0.4 and 3%. Butler, Rabin and Rosser [136, 137] estimate that in some cases time preference rates can even be negative. Studies from developing countries are rare, but the limited insight suggests that future health is usually considered less important than well-being at the present [138, 139].

Based on these time preference rates, different authors suggest diverging discounting rates. Shepard and Thompson [140] propose a rate of between 5 and 15%. Drummond prefers a rate of 5%, and the results of any study should be tested with rates between 2 and 10% [141]. Weinstein and Stason [142] state that future health gains should be discounted with a rate between 4 and 6%. The World Bank discounts the Disability Adjusted Life Years (DALY) with a rate of 3% [143]. Krahn and Gafni [144] analysed 23 cost-benefit-, cost- effectiveness- and cost-utility-analyses in health care which had been published in the journals New England Journal of Medicine, Journal of the American Medical Association, Medical Decision Making ad Medical Care from 1988 to 1991. They found that „where discounting was applied, a baseline rate of 5% was used in every instance" [144]. *In practical health economics a discounting rate of 5% is a good standard, but a sensitivity analysis with rates of 0%, 3%, and 10% is a must.*

2.2 Health Economic Framework

In Figure 2.10 the line [XY] denotes a goal function with r=0. (4) is the maximum average health for both periods which can be achieved if any future health status is appraised as equally important as the present health status and the full impact of prevention can be harvested. With r=∞ all resources will be invested into period t (5). Consequently, all points between (4) and (5) are maximizing the goal function given above subject to different positive time preferences.

If we assume that period t and period t+1 represent different generations and groups of people, (3) indeed seems to be an equitable solution. There is a conflict between equality and the maximum average health. One would expect that (4) is a compromise between these goal functions, i.e., a low time preference is favourable for future generations and sustainability.

However, efficiency and equity are not in conflict. (7) represents an equitable and inefficient solution. With given resources, health in t or in t+1 can be increased without reducing the health of the respective other period. It is obvious that *nothing is as unjust and unsustainable as inefficiency*.

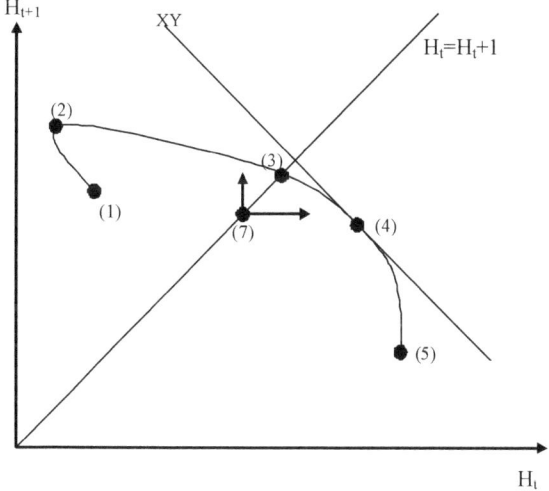

Figure 2.10 Sustainability: basic concept

In a nut-shell: *The health economist contributes to the fight for equity and sustainability by providing instruments to assess the efficiency of health care systems or interventions in order to reduce the waste of scarce resources.* These instruments will be briefly discussed in the next section.

2.3 Economic Evaluation

Efficiency was defined as the quotient

$$\frac{Result}{Input} \to Max!$$

In health economics, the inputs are usually resources whereas the results are related to health. However, as realistic systems have different inputs (e.g. personnel, materials, equipment) and results (e.g. quality of life, incidence, prevalence, morbidity) the simple formula must be widened as

$$\frac{\sum_{j=1}^{m} w_j * x_j}{\sum_{i=1}^{n} v_i * y_i} \to Max! \text{ , with}$$

- x_j Quantity of result j, j=1..m
- y_i Quantity of input i, i=1..n
- w_j Weight of result j
- v_i Weight of input i
- m Number of result factors
- n Number of input factors

In principle, any economic evaluation must record all consumption of inputs and all results. Afterwards, inputs and results must be expressed in one dimension so that a performance measurement can be calculated. This fusion of different dimensions to one measurement is very difficult, as hours of labour, kilograms of food, meters of sutures, square meters of space etc. have to be fused as well as cases, sickness days, death cases, years of life lost and quality feelings. As most inputs have a market price, the fusion of different resources consumed can be done by using the factor price as input weight. The result is the cost of a service or programme, i.e.

$$\frac{\sum_{j=1}^{m} p_j * x_j}{\sum_{i=1}^{n} c_i * y_i} \to Max! \text{ with}$$

- x_j Quantity of result j, j=1..m
- y_i Quantity of input i, i=1..n
- p_j Value of one unit of result j
- c_i Costs of one unit of input i [€]

2.3 Economic Evaluation

    m Number of result factors
    n Number of input factors

Using a monetary expression for the result is more difficult. Some evaluation techniques try to do this. Others restrict the result to one dimension (e.g. life years gained), others artificially combine different results to one statistic according to certain rules. Thus, the degree of fusion differs from one economic evaluation technique to the other. The most important are:

- *Cost minimisation*: The methodology [85, 145] assumes that the result of a health system or intervention is constant so that merely the costs have to be analysed. If we compare alternative services or interventions and if the result is equal to each other, the one with the lowest costs is the efficient service or intervention, the others are inefficient, i.e.

$$Z = \frac{\sum_{j=1}^{m} p_j * x_j}{\sum_{i=1}^{n} c_i * y_i} \rightarrow Max! \Leftrightarrow Z' = \sum_{i=1}^{n} c_i * y_i \rightarrow Min!$$

The disadvantage of this methodology is obvious: In reality different services or programmes will not yield the same results, so that the minimisation of costs cannot be achieved. Frequently the mentality of cost minimisation has led administrators into the temptation to focus on costs only and to disregard the result of the health care activity. Consequently, future chances were neglected even if they were highly efficient because they would have required more resource input.

- *Result maximisation*: Taken a given budget for a certain intervention, the efficient alternative is making the best out of these resources, i.e.

$$Z = \frac{\sum_{j=1}^{m} p_j * x_j}{\sum_{i=1}^{n} c_i * y_i} \rightarrow Max! \Leftrightarrow Z' = \sum_{j=1}^{m} p_j * x_j \rightarrow Max!$$

This methodology [85] can be applied if the budget is without competition to other allocations of funds. In reality, health care or a particular programme or service is always only one possible allocation of funds, i.e., the amount earmarked for this purpose will vary so that this methodology is restricted to few applications within very limited fields.

- *Cost-benefit analysis*: A cost-benefit analysis [145] expresses inputs and results in monetary terms, i.e., not only the costs, but also the incidence, prevalence, life years, death cases and quality of life are expressed in currency units. The efficiency can be expressed by a quotient or a difference, i.e.

$$Z = \frac{\sum_{j=1}^{m} p_j * x_j}{\sum_{i=1}^{n} c_i * y_i} \to Max! \Leftrightarrow \Pi = \sum_{j=1}^{m} p_j * x_j - \sum_{i=1}^{n} c_i * y_i \to Max!$$

The term Π is the profit or surplus. It can also be related to the capital investment (return on investment) in order to calculate the performance of a service or programme. The disadvantages are obvious: It is very difficult to express human life in monetary terms, and all constructions to do so will bear ethical problems. However, the cost-benefit analysis has strong advantages if we want to compare alternative allocations of funds beyond sector borders. For instance, an investment into education and into health care can only be compared if we find a common dimension of results. Money is a weak common dimension, but maybe the only possible one.

- *Utility analysis*: The utility analysis treats inputs and results as one dimension and expresses all quantities in a single utility score [8, 146]. Therefore, costs for resources are not expressed in financial terms but in an ordinal scale (highest, high, lower ...). Seeing the high importance of costs and budgets in the health care sector, this approach is not satisfactory.
- *Cost-effectiveness analysis*: The cost-benefit analysis fuses input and result into one statistic (e.g. surplus). The cost-effectiveness analysis [147, 148] expresses the inputs in monetary terms, but the results are measured in physical units, e.g. number of children immunized. Input and result remain two dimensions, so that this analysis frequently does not produce a single alternative, but a set of alternatives forming an efficiency frontier. Figure 2.11 demonstrates an example of eight health centres in a district offering delivery services. The total costs of this service per health centre are compared with the number of deliveries. It is obvious that health centre 7 has the lowest cost per delivery, it is absolutely efficient. However, if we assume economies of scale, it might be useful to include also unit 2 and 5 as efficient, so that units 2, 5 and 7 form the efficiency frontier.

The units on the frontier are efficient and form the set of benchmarks for the other units, i.e., unit 3 should concentrate on the performance of unit 2. If we assume constant elasticity of scale, only unit 7 is efficient, but for the small unit 3 it is not helpful to attempt at learning from this big health centre.

- *Cost-utility analysis*: This analysis allows that the result is not a single physical unit but an indicator which combines several statistics. For instance, quality of life and life years are combined in the Disability Adjusted Life Year (DALY). The combination will always be artificial and subject to discussion.

2.3 Economic Evaluation

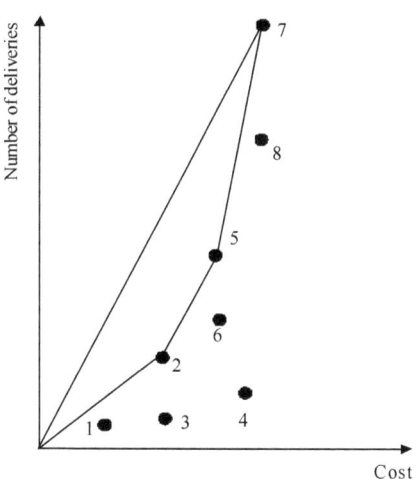

Figure 2.11 Cost-effectiveness analysis

- *Data Envelopment Analysis* (DEA). DEA [149] widens the application of cost-effectiveness analysis to more dimensions of input and result. The weights u_r and v_i are determined with the help of a mathematical programme so that they form an optimum for a particular unit subject to the constraint that the efficiency of each unit must be less or equal to one.

$$h_o = \frac{\sum_{j=1}^{m} w_j * x_{jo}}{\sum_{i=1}^{n} v_i * y_{io}}$$

$$\frac{\sum_{j=1}^{m} w_j * x_{js}}{\sum_{i=1}^{n} v_i * y_{is}} \leq 1 \quad for \ s = 0,1,...,p \ , \text{ with}$$

$$Z = h_o \rightarrow Max!$$

h_o	Efficiency of unit o
x_{jo}	Quantity of result j of unit o, j=1..m
y_{io}	Quantity of input I of unit o, i=1..n
w_j	Weight of result j, j=1..m
v_i	Weight of input i. i=1..n
m	Number of result factors

n	Number of input factors
x_{js}	Quantity of result j of unit s, j=1..n; s=1..p
y_{is}	Quantity of input i of unit s, i=1..n; s=1..p
p	Number of units

In the simple case of one input and one result, DEA leads to the situation shown in Figure 2.11, i.e., the units on the efficiency frontier have an efficiency of one, those under the envelopment have an efficiency of less than one. The advantage of DEA is that multi-dimensional efficiencies can be calculated without being forced to fuse the results into one indicator.

Generally, the cost-benefit analysis dominated the health economic evaluation until the beginning of the 1990s. Since then, cost-effectiveness analysis has become more frequent and is seen as the methodology of first choice by the World Health Organisation [148, 150]. However, both methodologies strongly require a documentation of the resource consumption and the monetary expression of this consumption as costs. *We can conclude that any realistic economic evaluation needs the assessment of costs. Without costing we cannot assess or improve efficiency. Consequently, costing is the prerequisite of affordable, sustainable and efficient health care.*

3 Methodology

The costing methodology will be presented in four steps. Firstly, we provide an overview of the concept of Cost-of-Illness as the frame of all costing studies. Secondly, we discuss the basics of a standard methodology to assess provider costs. The most important difference between costing in developing and developed countries is the problem of incomplete data. This will be addressed in the third section. Finally, the calculation of costs has to provide specific answers to specific questions, so that different concepts of costs become necessary. This will be discussed in the last section of this chapter.

3.1 Concept of Cost-of-Illness

The concept of the Cost-of-Illness (COI) was first developed by Rice [151-153]. It assumes that resources could be used for another purpose if a disease did not exist. Figure 3.1 demonstrates the basic concept of COI. Most health economic studies assessing the total costs of a disease use this methodology [154-167].

Households have direct and indirect costs. *Direct household costs* imply payments for transport to and from the health services, accommodation for the accompanying relative, special buildings for disabled patients (e.g. changed bathroom), costs for diet and the re-education, for instance new training after a paralysis. Private households also have to bear direct payments for user fees and drugs which are an income of the providers. There must be clearing between these components of the Cost-of-Illness in order to avoid double-counting.

Indirect household costs summarize all lost opportunities. During the time of illness, a patient and a caring relative cannot work. Therefore, wage-earners lose salaries as well as the economy production force. Sick parents do not have time to take care of their children so that their education will suffer. Therefore, morbidity leads to indirect costs. The term "socio-economic costs" is used for the total of direct and indirect costs as both have to be shouldered by the society.

Direct and indirect household costs are so-called tangible costs because a monetary value can be attached to them. Pain, psychological pressure, reduced joy of life and social prestige are reductions of the quality of life which do not have a natural monetary value. These *intangible costs* are sometimes evaluated as well and a monetary value is attached to them. For instance, an interviewer might seek the "willingness to pay" of a sick person for being healed [168, 169].

In countries with an existing (social) health insurance system it is usually rather simple do receive a close-to-reality estimate of the *provider Cost-of-illness*. The insurance pays the bills of general practitioners, specialists, hospitals, pharmacies, laboratories etc. so that the total costs per patient can easily be determined. However, in developing countries we cannot receive these data, and sometimes confidentiality regulations do not permit the transfer of insurance data. In this case a sample of patient files has to be analysed with permission of the patients so that the provider costs can be recorded.

The calculation of direct household costs is quite difficult. Firstly, resource consumption is hardly documented, so that patients have to be interviewed or be asked to keep household diaries for all expenditure in connection with their disease. Secondly, it is frequently not easy to allot a certain expenditure to a specific disease. Co-payments for drugs, practitioner and hospital services as well as transport to and from the provider are easily allocated to the COI of this disease. But other direct household costs might be even higher, such as the costs of a special diet, but it is very difficult to analyse whether these costs are really incurred due to this illness. Studies demonstrate that direct household costs might be small in developed countries, but they might make up to 50% of the total COI in developing countries [101].

The calculation of indirect COI can be based on different methodologies, and there is no generally accepted standard for all circumstances [166]. The most common approach to calculate the indirect costs of illness is the human capital method. The loss of welfare of a society in the form of non-generated commodities and services mainly depends on the lost working hours. The method assumes that if a person had not been sick or had not died from a disease, this person could have worked and contributed to the welfare of the society. Therefore, the disease induced a loss of productivity of the factor labour which has to be valued with its marginal contribution to the total production. However, as this is very difficult, most studies use the wage rate as a substitute [152, 153, 158]. The human capital is calculated as the net value of future production of a human being.

The calculation of indirect costs can be based on this methodology if we assume that all patients had a full-time job before they fell sick. However, this is not always the case. Non-paid activities are difficult to consider in this approach, so that the loss of work of – for instance – a housewife suffering from a certain disease cannot be valued easily with the average wage rate. Other concepts of calculating indirect household costs have been developed. For instance, instead of calculating the human capital based on wage rates, one could use the gross national product or the gross domestic product per capita as an indicator of the productivity. However, if patients do not have a wage income (e.g. housewife, pensioner) this approach cannot be applied.

The friction cost method [170] assumes that the human capital approach has a tendency to over-estimate the indirect household costs. If a worker is seriously sick or dies, his job will be vacant for some time until a new person is hired or trained. However, the loss will not be there for many years. Therefore, the loss of human capital is calculated not until the time of retirement, but until the time of replacement. This approach is correct for unskilled labour in a situation of unemployment. It neither fits to a fully employed economy nor to a subsistence farmer society where there is no substitution of a father who died.

Consequently, there is no golden standard of calculating indirect Cost-of-illness, and health economists criticise this approach [171]. The estimates based on different meth-

3.1 Concept of Cost-of-Illness

odologies might differ significantly, and so will the total Cost-of-illness. It is possible to analyse the quality of studies whether all components (such as indirect costs of caring relatives etc.) have been included. Whether the methodology applied is "best", cannot always be determined.

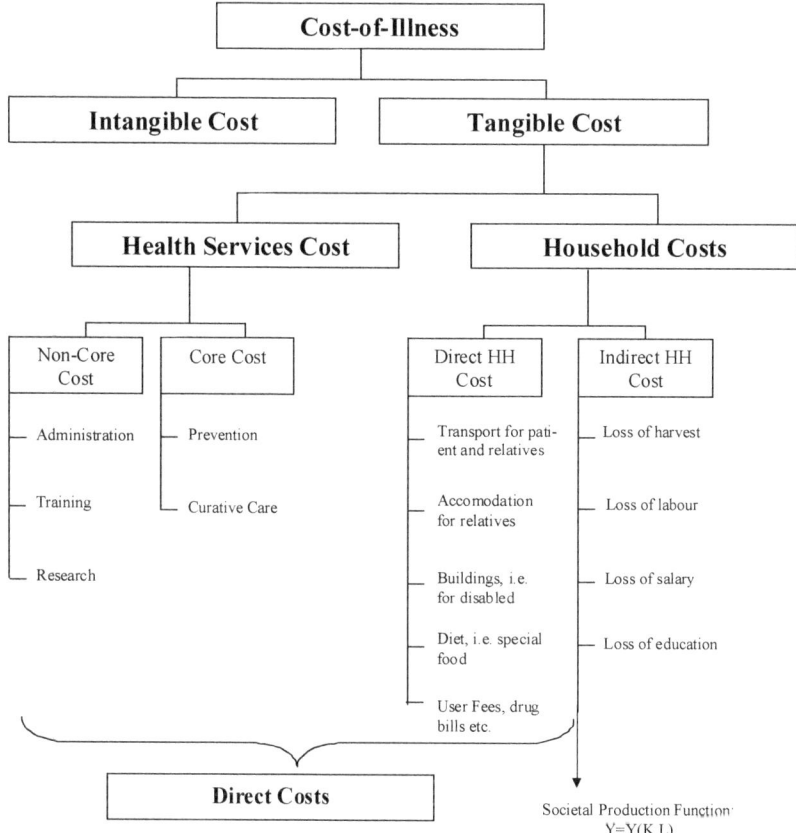

Figure 3.1 Concept of Cost-of-Illness

Even under consideration of these shortcomings, there is no doubt that the Cost-of-Illness concept is useful for the policy maker in developing countries. It demonstrates that the core costs which are usually analysed and which we focus on in this booklet are merely one component of the total costs for the society. *We have to know the core costs – but we have to be humble and confess that provider costs are merely one component of the entire Cost-of-Illness, even if an important one.*

3.2 Provider Cost

This booklet concentrates on the core provider cost, i.e., the cost of the health care services. In principle, provider cost information should be an element of the national health accounts [172-175] and should be retrievable without much effort. *In countries where accounting information is complete and reliable, costing of health care services is a standard.* For instance, Mogyorosy & Smith [115] prepared a detailed literature review of methodological issues in costing health care services in EU states. They conclude that differences in costing methodologies are due to different decision situations and research questions, not due to disagreement on methodology and concepts. Consequently, in these countries costing of health care services is a routine in the hands of professional cost accountants. The literature on general cost accounting [176-182], costing of health services [183-187] and of hospital services [188-197] is enormous.

However, institutions in developing countries (including health care providers in least developed countries) frequently cannot provide the required data for evidence-based decision making, and the national health accounts are often not more than educated guesses. The administration in health care institutions regularly suffers from incomplete records, wrong entries, insufficient number of accounts, poorly trained accountants and a low esteem for accounting work. The situation which Lane describes for Tanzania is similar to the situation in many developing countries: "Perhaps the major problem of any researcher in Tanzania is the lack of data, the almost complete unreliability of what data is available and the absence of any recent data"[198]. This has a strong impact on the achievement of equity, sustainability and efficiency, i.e., „scarcity of information inhibits governments from making informed choices about the allocation of public resources for better health, as well as improvements in the management of publicly provided and/or financed services" [199].

In a situation where wrong or incomplete data is more a rule than an exception, the standards provided by international accounting societies or text books can hardly be applied if we want to base health policy decisions on costing information. *We have to ease the international cost accounting standards so that the costing methodology is applicable for health care institutions in developing countries, and we have to fill the data gap arising from incomplete records.*

3.2.1 Knowledge of Provider Cost

Since the end of the 1980s, a substantial number of papers have indicated the importance of costing health care services in developing countries [200-211]. It is generally accepted that the knowledge of cost is a prerequisite of professional management, equity, sustainability and efficiency, but our knowledge of provider costs in developing

3.2 Provider Cost

countries and in particular in least developed countries is still limited and the quality of studies is heterogeneous.

Vaca, Kreider & Kreider were among the first to cost health care services in developing countries. They conclude „that up-to-date and accurate book-keeping was not followed in many cases. Almost all lacked statistical information on the results of their projects. Among justifications for this were remarks like: ‚We're not working to fill out forms and show statistics.' [...] This would seem to be a common attitude among project staff. [...] Health workers aren't trained as economists and accountants and few projects have the money or inclination to employ such people themselves. It's little surprise that questions of financing sometimes never go beyond the short-term problem of obtaining funding and supplying satisfactory accounts to donors" [212].

This analysis was followed by a number of studies and reviews. In 1990, Mills assessed 30 studies of hospital costs in developing countries and notes that all of them were based on secondary data, i.e., existing accounts from the hospitals were used without consideration whether they were correct or complete [201, 202]. The same approach was followed by the Christian Medical Commission (CMC, Geneva) which sent out questionnaires in order to assess the costs of hospitals. They had to realize that „there were wide variations in thoroughness in use of raw data, analysis and reporting" [213]. The quality of 27 studies on hospital costs analysed by Shepard, Hodgkin & Anthony [206] was higher, but only five of them were from least developed countries.

Meanwhile a number of studies invested effort to check and correct accounting data from health care institutions or programmes and search for missing figures. Our knowledge of costs of hospitals [214-216], districts [217-219] and specific diseases has grown. In particular, the costs of HIV/Aids care and prevention are thoroughly analysed [220-222]. However, the methodologies of these studies strongly differ so that the results can hardly be compared. In particular the allocation of costs and the degree of including fixed assets financed by donations were not standardised.

One attempt to standardise the costing methodology for developing countries is the WHO-CHOICE project which has also contributed to our understanding of health care costs [197, 223]. However, the Costit model of the WHO [224] as the backbone of the WHO-CHOICE project is once more too comprehensive for most practical applications in least developed countries. Consequently, *there is a strong need to develop a simple standard methodology of costing of health care services in situations in which insufficient accounting exists.*

The following pages show the methodology applied in our studies and suggest them as a standard methodology. It is based on some 15 years of costing experiences in developing countries as well as on an extensive literature review, e.g. [188, 189, 192, 194, 195, 197, 206, 214, 218, 225, 226]. We start with basic terms well-known to the accountant or economist. They are merely added here for the readers from another academic background.

3.2.2 Basic Terms

Cost is a financial expression of the consumption of resources [227, 228]. If a system has a certain level of resources and uses them to produce some service or commodity, the quantity and the value of the resources are reduced. Costs express this reduction of value in currency units, such as US$, €, or Shs. In the case of a business unit this is trivial: If a car manufacturer uses a piece of steel to produce a car, the value of this steel is part of his production cost. The consumption of this resource constitutes his cost. In the same way, the use of human labour and the wear and tear of equipment and buildings (depreciation) are costs. Theoretically, we have to distinguish between payments, expenditure and cost. A *payment* is the reduction of cash (cash on hand or bank account). However, this does not necessarily mean a loss of value of the enterprise. If we buy steel for a car production and put it on stock, we do not reduce the value of the enterprise. We pay a certain amount and get steel for exactly the same amount. Therefore, the net value of the enterprise is identical before and after this transaction. If we take the steel out of the stock and use it in the production process, the value of this steel is changed. We do not even know what the value of the car will be. Maybe it cannot be sold, maybe the steel is spoilt during the production process. Therefore, the use of the steel generates cost, not the purchase.

Theoretically, cost is only the reduction of the net worth of an enterprise if this reduction was necessary for the purpose of the enterprise. If a business unit donates to the Red Cross, this reduces its net worth, but it is not necessary for the production process. Therefore, the term *expenditure* covers all reduction of net worth, whereas the term cost means only those expenditures which were necessary for the original purpose of the business unit. For costing health care services in developing countries this difference is not important. Consequently, we will use these terms interchangeable. More important is the fact that costs do not necessarily have to be connected with payments. For instance, the work of the private practitioner does not necessarily lead to a payment as he does not earn a salary in his own practice. However, by working for his own enterprise he loses the opportunity to earn a salary elsewhere. Therefore, the value of a lost opportunity is named *opportunity cost* and has to be included in the total costs, although it is not connected with payments.

A health care institution or programme uses resources in order to produce health services. The most important resources are personnel, drugs, equipment, buildings, water, electricity etc. Therefore we have personnel costs, drug costs, equipment costs, costs of buildings, water, electricity etc. We call these costs the *direct provider costs* because they occur directly in the production process. Salaries and wages, bills for drugs, for water and electricity are, thus, costs. In developing countries we usually do not distinguish payments and costs of these items (although one might argue this for the drug store!). However, in the case of buildings and equipment this must be different. They are established in one year for many other years to come. It would be completely inappropriate to charge all payments to the year of establishment. They are not consumed in this year, therefore only the wear and tear of the first year should be the cost of this

3.2 Provider Cost

year. Consequently, we only take a certain fraction of the original payment as the annual costs. This share is called *depreciation*.

Buildings and equipment do not lead to periodical payments. However, the wear and tear of these items has to be calculated. There are several possibilities. The easiest approach is to divide the original payment by the number of years which the item will be used. Figure 3.2 shows this as a straight line. It might also be possible to reduce the value of the item by a certain percentage every year, so that the annual depreciation is getting smaller every year (declining balance method). Finally, it is possible to include an interest rate for the investment. However, in most cases it is enough to calculate a linear depreciation.

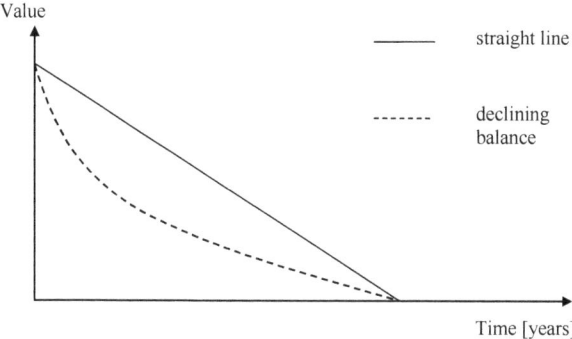

Figure 3.2   Depreciation

The analysis has to distinguish *average cost* per service unit (such as cost per delivery) and *marginal cost* (such as additional cost for one additional delivery).

$$\bar{c} = \frac{C(x)}{x}$$

$$c' = \frac{dC(x)}{dx}$$

with

   $\bar{c}$ unit cost
   c' marginal cost
   $C(x)$ total cost
   x number of service units, i.e. beddays, deliveries, consultancies

The average cost is simply the quotient between total cost and the number of service units. For the calculation of the marginal cost, we have to distinguish between fixed and variable cost. *Fixed costs* do not vary with the volume of activity, whereas *vari-*

able costs increase if we produce more services. Normally, variable costs increase with volume, and the increase can be progressive, linear or degressive. It has to be analysed, furthermore, whether fixed costs are indeed completely constant irrespective of the amount of services, or whether they are *step fixed*, i.e., they are stable until the activity reaches a certain level and then jump to a higher plateau to remain stable there as well. For instance, the costs for salaries of a dispensary are the same, whether a nurse sees 10 or 20 patients a day. However, if the workload increases so much that she cannot do the job alone, a second nurse has to be hired and the costs jump by 100%. For the analysis it will be important to know whether additional demand can be covered by the existing buildings, personnel and equipment.

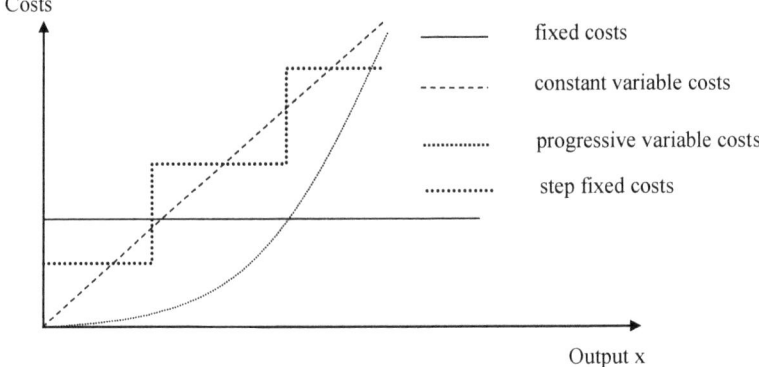

Figure 3.3   *Different cost development pattern*

Assuming a linear cost-function, we receive

$$\bar{c} = \frac{C(x)}{x} = \frac{C_f + c_v \cdot x}{x} = \frac{C_f}{x} + c_v$$

$$c' = \frac{dC(x)}{dx} = \frac{d\{C_f + c_v \cdot x\}}{dx} = c_v$$

with

C_f fixed cost
c_v ;   constant variable cost

Cost can be divided into different *cost categories*. Important categories are salaries and wages, materials and drugs, depreciation, transport, maintenance, etc. Furthermore, costs can be direct and indirect. *Direct costs* can be allocated directly to a service unit. For instance, a certain antibiotic is given directly to one patient. If we want to calculate the costs of this patient, we can allot these costs directly to him. Other costs, such as

3.2 Provider Cost

salaries, buildings or equipment, cannot be traced back to a particular service unit. They are *indirect costs* (*overheads*) and have to be allocated to the service unit in three steps. Firstly, they are allocated to the *cost centres*, i.e. the place where they occur. We have to distinguish between service cost centres and final cost centres. Final cost centres provide services for patients (such as the wards), whereas service cost centres have no direct contact with the costing unit (e.g. administration). Consequently, the costs of service cost centres have to be allotted to the final cost centres in the second step. Thirdly, the total costs of the final cost centres are allotted to the cost unit. Figure 3.3 exhibits this process. As it is quite important for costing of health services, it will be discussed in detail in the next sub-section.

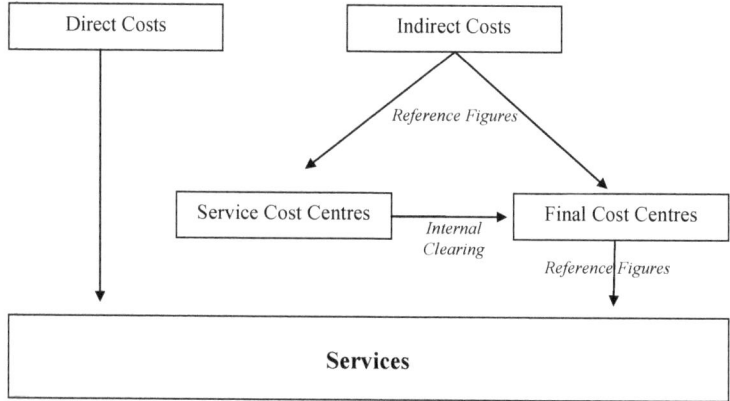

Figure 3.4   Step-down cost allocation

3.2.3   Allocation of Costs

Indirect costs can be *allocated to final cost centres in different ways*:

- *No cost allocation of indirect costs*: Only direct costs (i.e. in the hospital only drugs, materials, infusions and - where applicable - food) are allocated. Overheads are not taken into consideration. It is estimated that overheads make up to 85% of the total costs.

- *Direct allocation*: All cost categories are allocated directly to final cost centres (i.e. the wards). The service cost centres (e.g. administration, laundry, laboratory, X-ray department) are not specifically considered.

- *Step-down allocation*: Costs are allocated step by step to service and final cost centres. The costs of the first service cost centre are then allocated to the other service cost centres and the final cost centres. Afterwards the accumulated costs of the next service cost centre are apportioned in the same way. This procedure is repeated step by step until all service cost centres are allocated to the final cost centres.

- *Step-down with iterations*: As the service cost centres are interdependent the process can step back to cost centres already allocated before and repeat the process a few times (iterative process).
- *Simultaneous allocation*: The interdependencies can be expressed as an inhomogeneous system of equations which are simultaneously solved. This approach requires a high computer capacity for all practical problems.

Most costing studies [211, 229-233] follow the step-down allocation. Table 3.1 demonstrates this methodology.

Table 3.1 Concept of Step-down Costing

	Service cost centre 1	Service cost centre ...	Service cost centre m	Final cost centre 1	Final cost centre ...	Final cost centre n
Indirect costs	XXX	...	XXZ	YXX	...	YXZ
Apportionment						
Total of direct and indirect costs	0	0	0	ZXX	...	ZXZ
Number of service units	0	0	0	a	...	c
Unit costs	-	-	-	$\dfrac{ZXX}{a}$		$\dfrac{ZXZ}{c}$

For this approach the cost accountant has to determine the following *variables*:

- *Outputs*: The final costing units have to be defined. For instance, a hospital can choose the following as output variables: number of outpatient visits, number of inpatients, number of inpatient days, number of operations, number of X-ray procedures, number of laboratory tests.
- *Cost centres*: Service and final cost centres have to be defined. Table 3.2 gives an example of cost centres of a hospital. This table is just for explanatory purposes as most health care institutions in developing countries will not have to distinguish so many cost centres. Instead, the distinction between three cost centres (general services, outpatient department, inpatient department) might be sufficient.

3.2 Provider Cost

- *Cost categories*: The costs of salaries and wages, drugs and supplies, equipment, buildings etc. have to be determined. Most of these figures should be available in basic books of accounts, but some figures (e.g. depreciation) might be missing.
- *Departmental costs*: Costs of all cost categories have to be analysed. Direct costs are directly allocated to costing units, indirect costs are allocated to the cost centres.
- *Step-down costing*: Indirect costs of service cost centres are allocated step by step according to certain keys to the final cost centres. The result are the total costs of each department.
- *Cost per unit*: The total costs per department (as total of direct departmental costs plus allotted overheads of service cost centres) are divided by the number of service units to calculate the costs per service unit.

Table 3.2   Example of cost centres of a hospital

Service cost centres	Director Board, Administration, General Planning, Human Resources, Finance and Accounting, Technical and Material Supplies, Nursing Office, Sterilization, Laundry
Final cost centres	X ray-Image Diagnosis, Haematology, Bio-Chemistry, Microbiology, Consultations, Ophthalmology, Intensive care unit (ICU), General Medicine, Cardiovascular, Digestion, Kidney, Urology, Muscle, Bone, Joint, Clinical Haematology, Endocrine, Neurology, Contagious Diseases, Allergy, Dermatology, Paediatrics, Operating theatre-Anaesthesia, General Surgery, Obstetric and Gynaecology, Traditional Medicine, Gerontology, Psychology, Physical Therapy, Radiation, Poisoning, Dialysis

The step-down approach sounds very simple and precise, but in reality it is quite difficult to determine appropriate keys and receive meaningful results. Frequently, keys can only be guesses. For instance, doctors usually work in the outpatient department and in different wards. Consequently, their costs have to be allocated to different departments. In principle, precise records could be prepared, but in reality we have to rely on questionnaires and interviews where the doctors themselves estimate their time spent in different departments. *All statements based on such a cost allocation model must be handled with care.* Table 3.3 gives an overview of the keys used in our studies.

With this approach the costs per OPD consultation, per IPD day in different wards and per patient can be calculated. If we compare the costs per OPD consultation and per IPD day, we can calculate the number per *equivalent inpatient days* as an estimate of the total workload of a health care institution with in- and outpatient department.

$$n = b + o/e$$
$$e = \frac{C_i}{b} / \frac{C_o}{o}, \text{ with}$$

- n Number of equivalent inpatient days
- e Equivalent costs of an outpatient visit
- C_i Total costs of inpatient department

C_o Total costs of outpatient department
b Beddays
o Outpatient attendance

For instance, if a hospital has provided services for 30,000 beddays and 10,000 outpatient visits, and the cost allocation to IPD and OPD gives figures of 90,000 US$ and 15,000 US$, the equivalent workload is 35,000 beddays.

$$e = \frac{90,000}{30,000} / \frac{15,000}{10,000} = 2$$

$$n = 30,000 + 10,000 / 2 = 35,000$$

The cost allocation and the analysis based on it are of major importance for the allocation of resources, but they should not be over-interpreted as this approach has a number of *short-comings*, e.g.

- *Keys*: Allocation keys are not precise or scientifically sound. They are "best guesses" and therefore subject to changes and different conceptions. Therefore, results are not constant if other cost accountants make a similar calculation with the same data.
- *Apportionment of fixed costs*: The step-down approach linearises fixed costs as if they would increase with growing output. For instance, closing down a department will only change the variable costs, whereas the major share of fixed costs remains unchanged. The step-down approach suggests that the total costs of this cost centre would disappear.
- *Incomplete data*: In developing countries, some data is not recorded and has to be estimated. The most important fields are donations and depreciation.

Consequently, costing studies in developing countries have to invest great effort into overcoming the problem of missing data and handle the results of such an analysis with care. The next subsection discusses some attempts to overcome the problem of missing data.

3.2 Provider Cost

Table 3.3 Allocation keys

	Cost category	Allocation key
Salaries and Wages	Medical doctors, nurses, other ward staff	acc. to time spent in each department, recorded in separate sheets for each member of staff
	Functional staff (x-ray, lab, etc.)	allocation to wards acc. to beddays, allocation to OPD according to lab/x-ray statistics
	Accounting and secretary	50% acc. to floor size, 50% acc. to number of patients
	Medical Recording	acc. to number of files opened
	Laundry	acc. to beddays, no OPD allocation
	Technical department	acc. to floor size
	Training expenditure	acc. to allocation of trained staff to departments
	Other staff expenditure	in proportion to the total of direct staff expenditure
Supplies	Drugs	if possible as direct costs, otherwise IPD/OPD acc. to accounts or sample, to wards acc. to beddays
	Medical materials	IPD/OPD acc. to accounts or sample, to wards acc. to beddays
	Vaccine	OPD
	Infusions	no OPD; to wards according to beddays
	X-ray consumables	acc. to x-ray statistics
	Laboratory supplies	acc. to laboratory statistics
	Domestic supplies	acc. to floor size
	Food for patients	according to patient days (if any food)
	Food for staff	acc. to allocation of staff to departments
	Food for guests	acc. to floor size
	Linen and clothing	only wards, acc. to beddays; private ward increased acc. to estimate
Transport	Depreciation for cars etc.	1/10 of one car allocated to OPD, rest acc. to beddays
	Vehicle running expenditure	1/10 of one car allocated to OPD, rest acc. to beddays
	Cargo transport	acc. to beddays
	Travel expenditure	acc. to beddays
Equipment	Local, cheap	acc. to position of equipment, recorded in a separate equipment sheet
	Depreciation for equipment	acc. to position of equipment, recorded in a separate equipment sheet
	Maintenance and repair	acc. to position of equipment repaired or maintained
Other Expend.	Electricity	acc. to floor size
	Water supply	acc. to floor size
	Postage and telephone	Administration, acc. to floor size
	Printing and Stationary	Administration, acc. to floor size
	Building depreciation	acc. to costs of buildings, building sheets
	Building maintenance	acc. to costs of buildings, building sheets

3.3 Incomplete Data

3.3.1 Donations and Grants

The main problem of the determination of the costs of health care providers in developing countries is the incompleteness of data of the accounting system and medical recording. Book-keeping of most health care institutions in these countries is handwritten, merely payments and receipts are recorded (cash flow accounting). Consequently, costs which are not directly connected with payments are not considered.

The international accounting standard is the so called *accrual accounting*, i.e., a system where the resource consumption is recorded, not the payment. As stated before, the payment for a new hospital building might be in year t, whereas the building will be used for the next 25 years. The loss of value as expression of the resource consumption is not only in the first year, but has to be allotted to 25 years. Accrual accounting safeguards that the resource consumption is a certain share per year (e.g. $1/25^{th}$ with straight line depreciation), whereas cash flow accounting would record the total value in the first year and no charge for all other years.

Therefore, costing of services based on *cash flow accounting* will provide wrong figures and is of limited use for the decision maker. For any meaningful decision support, the cost accountant has to calculate the real costs based on accrual accounting. However, a major share of salaries, buildings, equipment, drugs and other materials are either financed by donations or by grants from the (central) government. In both cases no reliable records are available in the health care institutions or districts.

In principle, all resources consumed by the provision of a service must be recorded and entered into the cost calculation. This includes:

- *Staff*: The costs of staff must be entered into the books of accounts irrespective of whom they are paid. If they are paid by donors, the government or other external sources, the same amount must entered as donation income, e.g., if a nurse is paid by the government with a salary of 10,000 Shs, the entry must be:

    Debit: Salaries and Wages (10,000 Shs)
    Credit: Staff Grants (10,000 Shs)

- *Cash*: If a health care project, institution or district receives cash from external sources without direct consideration, the value should be entered as income and as increase of assets, e.g., if a hospital receives a cash donation of 5,000 Shs, the entry must be:

    Debit: Cash on hand (10,000 Shs)
    Credit: Donation income (10,000 Shs)

- *Equipment and buildings*: If a health care project, institution or district receives a piece of equipment or a building from the government, a donor or another external source, the value of this unit should be entered into the books of accounts as an asset. The same amount is entered as grant so that both balance sheet items cancel each other. In the coming years, asset and grant are written off. For instance, if a piece of equipment has a value of 100,000 Shs and a depreciation period of 5 years, we receive the following entries:

- day of purchase: Debit: Fixtures and fittings (100,000 Shs)
                            Credit: Accumulated grants (100,000 Shs)
- end of year t (t=1..5):   Debit: Depreciation of fixed assets (20,000 Shs)
                            Credit: Fixtures and fittings (20,000 Shs)
                            Debit: Accumulated grants (20,000 Shs)
                            Credit: Depreciation of accumulated grants (20,000 Shs)

- *Drugs*: Drug donations can be handled like cash or like assets. In the first case it is assumed that all drugs donated in period t are consumed in period t. For instance, if drugs with a value of 10,000 Shs are donated, the following entries are made:

    Debit: Drugs consumed (10,000 Shs)
    Credit: Donation income (10,000 Shs)

If we want to be more precise we have to treat drugs like assets. For instance, if drugs with a value of 3,000 Shs. are still on stock at the end of the accounting period, the entries are

- day of delivery: Debit: Drugs on stock (10,000 Shs)
                      Credit: Donation income (10,000 Shs)
- end of year t: Debit: Drugs consumed (7,000 Shs)
                      Credit: Drugs on stock (7,000 Shs)
                      Debit: Donation income (3,000 Shs)
                      Credit: Accumulated grants (3,000 Shs)
- year t+1:   Credit: Accumulated grants (3,000 Shs)
                      Debit: Donation income (3,000 Shs)
                      Credit: Drugs consumed (3,000 Shs)
                      Debit: Drugs on stock (3,000 Shs)

Consequently, merely cash donations increase the surplus of the project, institution or district, whereas all other donations or grants are cost neutral. The advantage of this approach is that the real resource consumption can be calculated so that we receive a realistic picture on the costs of health care services irrespective of their source of income.

3.3.2 Depreciation

The entry of donations and grants assumes that we know the value of the equipment or buildings and of the resource consumption. However, in reality this is not so simple as the value is frequently not known and has to be estimated.

As far as possible the original purchasing or building prices (incl. costs of acquisition, CIF-value) according to the hospital documentation should be used. Where such documentation is not available, estimates from international organisations can be applied. Table 3.4 gives an example for an equipment list based on a publication of the World

Health Organisation [234-236]. Some items require a distinction of levels of health care institutions (e.g. dispensary, health centres, primary hospitals etc.).

Table 3.4 Health care equipment (examples)

Item	Investment Costs [US$]	Maintenance p.a. [US$]	Depreciation Period [years]
hospital beds	100	0	15
basic radiographic system (incl. developing)	20,000	500	10
radiographic system, three phase unit (incl. developing)	100,000	1,000	10
microscope, binocular	700	20	10
centrifuge, mechanical	100	3	10
centrifuge, electrical	500	25	10
incubator (laboratory)	1,500	50	10
spectrophotometer	7,000	400	10
basic laboratory utensils[3]		5%	10
sterilization, autoclave	10,000	800	10
sterilization, steam	2,000	100	10
operating table	8,000	500	15
operating lamp	5,000	500	15
anesthesia, EMO	8,000	600	10
oxygen concentrator	4,000	250	10
sucker	4,000	250	10
diathermy	6,000	300	10
ECG	5,000	200	10
gastroscope	25,000	400	8
basic surgical instruments[4]		2%	15
incubator (baby)	8,000	400	10
slit lamp	5,000	300	10
ultrasound	20,000	1,500	10
dental unit	25,000	2,000	15
generators, 80 kW	17,000	1,400	15
generator, 40 kW	10,000	800	15
generator, 20 kW	7,500	600	15
washing machine, heavy	15,000	750	10
washing machine, household	1,500	75	5
radiocall, incl. antenna	2,500	100	10
refrigerator, electric	800	50	10
refrigerator, kerosene	2,000	100	10
basic workshop equipment	3,000	200	10
basic office equipment[5]		2%	20

---

[3] The original investment costs depend on the level of institution.
[4] Dto.
[5] Dto.

3.3 Incomplete Data

Calculating the equipment costs will always include a complete inventorisation of all pieces of equipment. As inventories are frequently not properly kept, an accountant has to walk with a technician or engineer from cost centre to cost centre and thoroughly record all items. Afterwards, a value has to be attached to them. This list is only the last choice. At first, the accountant should always try to determine the real costs. At second, local experts could be asked for a realistic cost estimate. Only in case that this is not possible or too expensive, such a standard list should be used.

Estimates for buildings are even more difficult than for equipment. Wherever possible, the precise costs of establishment should be retrieved. Only in case that this is not possible, building experts might be asked for advice. They can estimate the current building costs per square or cubic meter of hospital buildings (including water and electricity supply). Afterwards, buildings have to be measured and the original value is calculated. Table 3.5 presents an overview of different constellations. It furthermore distinguishes between two categories of buildings with different costs per square meter. For instance, full buildings have concrete walls, iron sheets, water and electricity supply, whereas primitive buildings are simple constructions (e.g. shelters) without water and electricity. The table furthermore assumes that the costs of a renovation after 25 years are as high as the costs of a new building. Certainly, this assumption can be questioned and the structure of the decision model can be enhanced, but Table 3.5 provides an overview of a possible approach.

Table 3.5 Building depreciation

Age [years]	Original Costs	Renovated	Costs of Renovation	Kind of Building	Actual Depreciation
Buildings is not yet written off ($\leq$ 25 yrs.)	Original value of building is known	Building was renovated within the last 25 years	Cost of renovation known	full	$d = 0.04 \cdot (C_B + C_R)$
				primitive	$d = 0.04 \cdot (C_B + C_R)$
			Costs of renovation unknown	full	$d = 0.04 \cdot (C_B + e_f \cdot m)$
				primitive	$d = 0.04 \cdot (C_B + e_p \cdot m)$
		no renovation		both	$d = 0.04 \cdot C_B$
	Original value of building is not known	Building was renovated within the last 25 years	Cost of renovation known	full	$d = 0.04 \cdot (e_f \cdot m + C_R)$
				primitive	$d = 0.04 \cdot (e_p \cdot m + C_R)$
			Costs of renovation unknown	full	$d = 0.04 \cdot 2 \cdot e_f \cdot m$
				primitive	$d = 0.04 \cdot 2 \cdot e_p \cdot m$
		no renovation		full	$d = 0.04 \cdot e_f \cdot m$
				primitive	$d = 0.04 \cdot e_p \cdot m$
Building is written off (> 25 yrs.)	→original value of building is irrelevant	yes	known	both	$d = 0.04 \cdot C_R$
			unknown	full	$d = 0.04 \cdot e_f \cdot m$
				primitive	$d = 0.04 \cdot e_p \cdot m$
		no		both	$d = 0$

with:

d	Depreciation charge per year
C_B	Building costs according to books
C_R	Renovation costs according to books
e_f	Estimated building costs per square meter for a full building
e_p	Estimated building costs per square meter for a primitive building
m	Square meter of building

The costs of equipment and buildings are frequently neglected in costing of health services in developing countries. As a result, the total costs are under-estimated and future resource allocations will be insufficient. The consequence is a lack of sustainability as future generations will not find appropriate buildings and equipment.

3.3.3 Charity Fund

It should be mentioned that some health care institutions have so called charity funds, i.e. they treats patients who are unable to pay. The costs of subsidizing these patients should be recorded, e.g., an unpaid service of 1000 Shs. should be entered as follows:

Debit: Charity Fund (1000 Shs)
Credit: Patient Fees (1000 Shs)

This short introduction into accounting of incomplete figures cannot cover all aspects. In particular different countries and organisations will demand different concepts. For instance, church-related health care programmes or institutions will have a higher share of donations in the total income than government institutions or programmes. Consequently, dealing with donations might be more important for church-related health care. However, governmental health services frequently have a much higher dispersion of accounting data. Salaries for doctors might be recorded in the central government, salaries of nurses in the regional government, telephone charges in the district and wages for auxiliary staff in the hospital. This makes costing very difficult. In any case, a full and comprehensive picture of the resource consumption must be sought, and missing figures must be retrieved or estimated.

3.4 Concepts of Costs

Although we cannot present a detailed lecture on costing in this small booklet, the reader should have realized until now that *there is not only one concept of costs*. Total costs, average costs, marginal costs and other concepts of costs are related, but their figures differ. This is due to the fact that *cost information should support the managers in decision making, i.e., they should provide specific answers to specific questions*. And different questions will demand different cost calculations. Consequently, the de-

3.4 Concepts of Costs

cision maker first has to define his question. Only then the cost accountant can calculate a meaningful cost figure.

From our experience, the following *questions* might be asked by decision makers in the health care sector:

- What resources do I have to provide in order to keep a certain health care project, an institution or a district at the actual level of quality and scope of services for the next year?
- What resources do I have to provide in order to run a certain health care project, institution or district at the actual level of quality and scope of services for a longer time?
- What resources are actually consumed by a certain health care project, institution or district at the actual level of quality and scope of services?
- What resources do I have to provide in order to keep a certain health care project, institution or district at a level which can be considered a "good standard"?
- What is the cost of a certain department?
- What is the cost per service unit?
- How does the cost per service unit in different programmes or institutions compare?
- How can we increase the efficiency between these units?

The calculation of costs will provide answers to these questions. Consequently, we have to distinguish the following terms:

- *Minimum cost of service*: This statistic presents the monetary expression of the absolute minimum input required to keep the health care project, the institution or the district running for a very limited time (e.g. one year). These costs do not include any donations, maintenance, training or depreciation. Thus, these costs are merely sufficient to pay salaries of local staff and locally bought drugs. This amount is not sufficient to secure viability in a long run. The amount stated in most income & expenditure accounts reflects this concept, i.e., fixed assets are consumed without any cost allocation.
- *Sustainable local cost*: This cost concept assumes that the initial costs of hospital buildings and equipment are and will be financed by donations or grants. However, the local contribution includes all expenses necessary to make the hospital survive in the long run. Therefore, maintenance and the local value of donations are included. Salaries of expatriate staff are accounted for with the equivalent amount which would have to be paid to local staff, if the position of the expatriate was taken over by a national employee with the same qualification and experience.
- *Full cost of services*: This statistic represents the entire input to a service. This includes all donations on the basis of their real value. The amount calculated should be sufficient for indefinite sustainability. In addition to the sustainable local costs, deprecation for equipment and buildings is charged, and expatriates are accounted according to their real costs carried by their sending institutions.

The distinction between minimum cost, sustainable local cost and full cost is mainly a differentiation according to the extent of the local share of costs. Additionally, we should distinguish actual and standard cost.

- *Actual cost*: This statistic is calculated from recent years. We do not ask, whether staff was sufficient, too little or too much. It is not asked, whether some buildings or equipment are missing or need repair. Actual cost does not necessarily represent the figures presented in the income and expenditure accounts of the hospitals because we make use of the system of accrual accounting instead of the cash flow accounting practiced in most of the church hospitals.
- *Standard cost*: This category expresses the amount of cost incurred, if the hospital was run on good standards. The determination of what good standards are is very difficult and certainly a major point of discussion. Donabedian defines standards as "professionally developed expressions of the range of acceptable variations from a norm or criterion" and as "predetermined elements against which aspects of the quality of medical services may be compared" [237]. Heidemann defines standards as "a benchmark of achievement which is based on a desired level of excellence. As such, standards become models to be imitated and may serve, in turn, as the bias for comparisons" [238]. *This actually means that determining standards entirely depends on the local situation and on the judgement of the community by what is desired and/or still acceptable*. This implies that the setting of standards is an ongoing process and the concepts demonstrated here should be reviewed after some time.

In combination we receive a matrix of six cost aspects as presented in Table 3.6.

Table 3.6   Cost matrix

	Minimum Cost	**Sustainable Local Cost**	**Full Cost**
Actual Cost	actual minimum cost	actual sustainable local cost	actual full cost
Standard Cost	standard minimum cost	standard sustainable local cost	standard full cost

Setting a standard is very difficult. Some variables that have to be standardised, and some examples for standardisation are given in Table 3.7. However, the last column must be handled with care. These are merely examples of a particular standard of the hospitals of the Lutheran Church in Tanzania without generalisation.

3.4 Concepts of Costs

Table 3.7 Standards (examples from Lutheran hospitals in Tanzania)

Item to be standardised	Example
Staffing	• 40 occupied beds per physician • 15 occupied beds per Medical Assistant • 20 occupied beds per A-Nurse • 6 occupied beds per B-Nurse • 4 occupied beds per auxiliary nurse
Training	• 5% of pay roll total
Equipment	• Standard equipment list depending on level of health care institution • Standard maintenance: 5% of original value p.a.
Vehicles	• Standard number of vehicles: $1 + round(\frac{beds}{100} + \frac{dispensaries}{10})$ • Maintenance: 10% p.a.
Buildings	• Maintenance: 1-2% of original value p.a.
Occupancy rate	• 85%

In a nut-shell: *Calculating provider costs in developing countries requires a high degree of creativity in order to be able to answer the specific questions of decision makers and provide them with meaningful answers for their particular problem. Only a reliable accounting system in the programmes and institutions as well as the courage to estimate missing figures will provide us with sufficiently precise data to base allocation decisions on. Thus, accounting becomes a prerequisite of equity, sustainability and efficiency of health care services in developing countries.*

4 Case Studies

The methodology presented above was applied to a number of studies in Africa and Asia. In this section we describe four applications. At first, we present the costs of Lutheran hospitals in Tanzania in the year 1995 [112]. At second, we show the findings of a costing study in Dodoma Rural Health District of the year 1998. Thirdly, we analyse the costs of hospitals in Vietnam of the year 2000 [239]. Finally, we present costs of health care institutions in Nouna health district, Burkina Faso, in the year 2005 [240]. The data will not be analysed further since this will be done in the fifth section.

4.1 Costing Lutheran Hospitals in Tanzania

4.1.1 Setting

Hospitals play a key role in the health care system as referral institutions of higher curative care, as training facilities for health care workers and as organizational platforms for primary care activities, including preventive services. It is generally accepted that Primary Health Care cannot be successful without strong support of hospitals at the top of the referral system [241-246]. However, this positive effect of hospitals is paid for by high cost. Hospitals are the largest and most costly health care institutions and require more human and financial resources than any other institution or programme in this sector [247]. Hospitals in developing countries absorb approximately 30-50% of the total health sector expenditure and about 50-60% of the government health sector expenditure, they consume 60-80% of government national health facility expenditures and about 70% of district level health facility expenditures. About 60-80% of hospital expenditure can be absorbed by central and provincial hospitals, the remainder going to district hospitals [201, 202].

The Christian churches in Tanzania have provided hospital services in Tanzania for decades [248]. In 1995, 80 of the 195 Tanzanian hospitals and 11,644 of the 25,834 hospital beds were owned and run by a church. The *Christian Social Services Commission* (CSSC) is an umbrella organisation which is coordinating the church-related health care activities and prepares a bridge to the government and donor agencies. However, the health care institutions are usually directly under the wings of a diocese.

The *Evangelical Lutheran Church in Tanzania* (ELCT) was in charge of 18 hospitals with 2,600 hospital beds and a total staff of about 2,400 in the year 1995. 16 institutions were general hospitals, two were mental hospitals (Irente MH, Lutindi MH) and two health centres (Matema HC, Izimbia HC) were in the process of becoming full hospitals. The hospitals (Figure 4.1) are under the respective diocese, whereas the function of the Medical Department of the ELCT Headquarters is coordinating and consulting.

At the beginning of the 1990s, the financial and managerial situation of Lutheran hospitals in Tanzania became difficult. Donors and church leaders called for equity, sustainability and efficiency of these institutions but there was no methodology to estimate the achievement of these objectives. The costs of providing health care in these institutions were completely unknown. Consequently, the author was requested to conduct a survey and determine the provider costs.

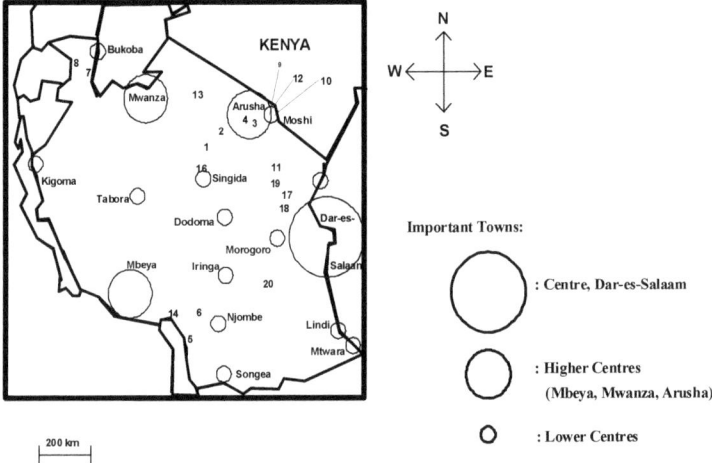

Figure 4.1   Location of Lutheran hospitals in Tanzania[6]

It was decided that the costs of seven Lutheran hospitals of the year 1995 should be calculated.[7] As Table 4.1 shows, 18 hospitals were stratified according to size and region. Hospitals which failed to issue sound data either because of the low information standards (such as Gonja) or because of the bias the status of Designated District Hospital (Bunda, Nyakahanga) brings, were omitted from the sample. In addition, Izimbia and Matema were excluded because they were health centres developing to become general hospitals. Afterwards a stratified random sample was taken of the seven remaining cells of Table 4.1. The following hospitals were selected for a thorough analysis of 10-14 days each: Selian, Karatu, Haydom, Itete, Ilembula, Lugala, Ndolage. All other ELCT general hospitals were visited for 1-2 days respectively and the annual reports of 1995 were analyzed in order to get an up-to-date impression of the condition of the hospital and in order to compare them with the hospitals in the sample.

---

[6] Numbers refer to Table 4.1.
[7] A sample of the questionnaires and forms used is available at http://www.rsf.uni-greifswald.de/fileadmin/mediapool/lehrstuehle/flessa/Appendix_questionnaires.DOC.

4.1 Costing Lutheran Hospitals in Tanzania

Table 4.1   Lutheran hospitals in Tanzania according to size and location

Strata	≤ 80 beds	81-200 beds	> 200 beds
Northern Zone	Karatu (2), Marangu (10)	Nkoaranga (3), Selian (4), Gonja (11), Bumbuli (17)	Haydom (1), Machame (9)
Southern Zone	Matema (15),	Bulongwa (5), Itete (14)	Ilembula (6)
Central Zone		Iambi (16), Lugala (20)	
Western Zone	Izimbia (21)	Nyakahanga (8), Bunda (13)	Ndolage (7)

4.1.2   Findings

4.1.2.1   Costs of Services

The costs of the seven Lutheran hospitals of the year 1995 were analyzed. The second column of Table 4.2 presents the *average cost per equivalent inpatient day*. Applying these figures to all 16 general hospitals of the ELCT we obtain the annual financial needs for Lutheran church hospital services as presented in column three.

Table 4.2   Cost of Lutheran hospital services [US$]: average [minimum; maximum]

Category	Cost per equivalent inpatient day	Total cost for 16 ELCT hospitals
Actual minimum costs	2.79 [1.97; 4.83]	2,272,634 [1,604,691; 3,934,345]
Actual sustainable local costs	2.96 [2.22; 5.17]	2,411,110 [1,808,332; 4,211,297]
Actual full costs	6.43 [4.61; 13.02]	5,237,647 [3,755,141; 10,605,626]
Standard minimum costs	2.76 [2.09; 4.56]	2,536,360 [5,300,994; 3,714,413]
Standard sustainable local costs	3.52 [2.84; 5.28]	3,234,778 [2,313,362; 4,300,899]
Standard full costs	9.62 [7.56; 15.89]	8,840,501 [6,158,105; 12,943,424]

Table 4.2 indicates that the costs of services differ widely according to the cost concept applied. A hospital has to cover the actual minimum costs (2.79 US$ per equivalent inpatient day) if it wants to survive for a very limited period of time (e.g. the next budget period). This figure is closest to the actual expenditure recorded in the cash books. In order to survive in a long run, a Tanzanian church hospital would have to cover the actual sustainable local costs (2.96 US$ per equivalent inpatient day) as capital expenditure of ELCT hospitals (buildings and equipment) is financed by donations. However, a self-reliant health service would have to finance the actual full costs (6.43

US$ per equivalent inpatient day) locally. If the hospitals had to meet the standards defined by the Health and Diaconic Directorate of the Evangelical Lutheran Church in Tanzania, the costs would usually be much higher, e.g., the standard full costs would rise (on average) to 9.62 US$ per equivalent inpatient day.

Table 4.3 shows the *composition of the actual costs*. It is obvious that for all hospitals, salaries and drugs are the most important cost items. However, there are huge differences among the survey hospitals, which is partly due to differences in efficiency of the institutions and partly due to differences in the size of hospitals (economies of scale).

Table 4.3   Composition of actual cost [%]: average [minimum; maximum]

	minimum costs	sustainable local costs	full costs
Salaries	45.72 [41.08; 51.79]	46.77 [39.57; 55.08]	59.04 [29.44; 69.79]
Stores	32.37 [18.26; 42.39]	31.28 [18.36; 41.63]	15.00 [8.70; 33.47]
Transport	6.32 [3.22; 12.86]	5.82 [3.05; 11.75]	2.68 [1.77; 5.20]
Equipment	3.39 [0.71; 11.59]	3.12 [0.64; 9.80]	8.87 [6.52; 15,59]
General Exp.	7.62 [4.10; 12.78]	8.80 [5.54; 12.29]	12.43 [10.12; 18.78]
Projects	4.58 [0.23; 5.45]	4.21 [0.21; 4.49]	1.97 [0.19; 3.48]

Table 4.3 indicates some differences between *actual costs* and *standard costs* per equivalent inpatient day. These differences are partly caused by overspending (e.g. standard minimum costs are less than actual minimum costs). In particular, salaries, drug expenditure and transport costs are higher than necessary. Salaries are the largest cost category. The number of staff of each cadre was analyzed. Table 4.4 shows that the salaries of B-nurses and junior staff (untrained nurses, other staff) make up the largest shares of personnel costs.

In comparison with the standards given by the ELCT headquarters most of the survey hospitals were over-staffed in 1995. The large numbers of non-medical and non-nursing staff seem to have no impact on the quality of services but contribute to the high staffing costs, thus reducing technical efficiency.

The costs of drugs, infusions, x-ray supplies, laboratory supplies, cleaning materials and linen were summarized as stores. Drugs were the most important component (73% of stores costs). The drug expenditure per equivalent inpatient day ranged from 0.38 US$ to 1.90 US$ with an average of 0.80 US$ (1:5). A minor part of this difference can be explained by a different case mix and poor material management and recording. Additionally, in several ELCT hospitals too many drugs are prescribed. In comparison with the WHO standard drug indicators for district hospitals in developing countries [249] ELCT hospitals have a moderate over-consumption of general drugs (26%) but a severe over-use of antibiotics (150%) and injections (60%).

4.1 Costing Lutheran Hospitals in Tanzania

Table 4.4   Staffing (averages and totals of seven ELCT hospitals in 1995)

	Annual costs per employee	% of total personnel cost	Total number of staff actual	Total number of staff ELCT-standard
Physicians	2,452 US$	9.08%	23.5	28
MAs	735 US$	5.79%	50	76
A-nurses	581 US$	4.42%	33	57
B-nurses	586 US$	22.14%	240	190
Untrained Nurses	455 US$	19.03%	266	211
Paramedicals	557 US$	7.20%	82	19-48
Administration	479 US$	4.22%	56	24-63
Other staff	523 US$	14.18%	172	35-37
Training	54 US$	3.96%	-	-
Other staff expenditure	135 US$	9.98%	-	-

The majority of ELCT hospitals had installed an *infusion unit* in order to produce i.v. fluids locally. However, only 37% of these units can break-even, i.e. for the majority of ELCT hospitals the purchase of infusions from the central pharmacy would have been cheaper. The average number of infusions per bedday was 0.43. However, there was a wide range among these hospitals. This range cannot merely be explained by case mix differences. For instance, Ndolage Lutheran Hospital and Haydom Lutheran Hospital provided similar services, but they had very different consumption of infusion fluids (0.075 vs. 0.35 litres per equivalent inpatient day).

Several of the ELCT hospitals are *located* in remote areas. The ELCT Health and Diakonia Directorate expected that the transport costs per equivalent inpatient day would be very high for these remote hospitals as the hospital cars have to drive long distances on bad roads in order to buy necessary supplies in the nearest regional centre. However, the analysis shows that the transport costs per equivalent inpatient day correlate negatively (-0.33) with the distance to the next regional centre. In other words, the more remote a hospital is, the less it spends for transport. Hospitals which are close to the regional centre have short distances per trip, but they drive more often. This indicates that there is potential for reducing the transport costs of these hospitals.

In a nut-shell, the differences between the costs of services in ELCT hospitals are partly due to different technical efficiency of these institutions. Management and administration of several ELCT hospitals are rather unprofessional. Consequently the *technical efficiency* is rather poor and must be improved.

The analysis of the relationship between costs and hospital size indicates that there exist economies of scale. Table 4.5 shows the coefficients of correlation between actual costs and hospital size.

Table 4.5   Correlation between cost and size

	cost per equivalent inpatient day		
	actual minimum	actual sustainable local	actual full
beds	- 0.75	- 0.77	- 0.70
equivalent inpatient days	- 0.59	- 0.70	- 0.69

Several cost categories increase more slowly than the output and, therefore, the unit costs decrease. This is particularly true for the high costs of general staff (administration, laundry, watchmen, gardeners etc.), but also the amount of equipment depreciation per equivalent inpatient day is negatively correlated (-0.65) with the size of the hospital. The coefficient of correlation between the number of equivalent inpatient days and the depreciation for buildings per equivalent inpatient day is -0.61. Bigger hospitals reap economies of scale as the same equipment and building can be used for more patients.

4.1.2.2   Income Analysis

The income of ELCT hospitals consists of government grants, patient fees, project surplus and donations. The income categories reflect the cost categories. Income based on actual minimum costs includes full government grants, patient fees, project surplus and donations in form of drugs and cash. Income based on actual sustainable local costs additionally includes shadow salaries for expatriates. Income based on actual full costs includes all donations for personnel, drugs, cash, equipment and buildings. If the ELCT health care standards were followed, a hospital would need additional donations in order to cover the difference between actual and standard costs. The income based on standard full costs adds these additional donations to the income based on actual full costs. Table 4.6 shows the contribution of the different income items to the total income.

The Tanzanian government supports church hospitals with staff and bed *grants* for an approved number of beds. In 1995 67% of the ELCT hospital beds were accepted by the government, i.e., the government had agreed to support these beds. However, the actual government contribution was on average merely 2.23% of the total income. The Ministry of Health had not fulfilled its financial pledge but owed money to ELCT hospitals. Some hospitals received close to nothing, whereas other hospitals received almost the entire promised grant. No rationale could be found for these differences.

In 1995 the contribution of *donations* to the total income was on average 69%, i.e., the dependency of the hospital based health services of the ELCT on donations was 69%. However, if the 16 ELCT hospitals followed the standards of the ELCT Health and Diakonia Directorate the dependency would increase to 79% and they would need annual donations of about 6,984,000 US$. The annual foreign assistance to the entire ELCT budget was about 3,615,000 US$.

4.1 Costing Lutheran Hospitals in Tanzania

Table 4.6 Income of 7 Lutheran hospitals in 1995 [US$]

Income Item	Actual minimum costs	Income based on Actual sust. local costs	Actual full costs	Standard full costs
Government Contribution	66,614	66,614	66,614	66,614
Patient Fees	793,978	793,978	793,978	793,978
Drug Donations	67,037	67,037	67,037	67,037
Cash Donations	316,173	316,173	316,173	478,488
Expatriate Salaries	0	46,344	1,153,349	2,280,027
Equipment Donations	0	0	279,325	336,190
Building Donations	0	0	202,696	235,407
Other Donations	0	25,241	25,241	26,897
Project and other Income	64,012	64,012	64,012	64,012
Total income	1,307,814	1,379,399	2,968,425	4,348,650

Fees covered between 18% and 61% of the costs. The more comprehensive the cost concept is (actual minimum costs as least comprehensive, standard full costs as most comprehensive), the less important are the fees for the total income. The average fees and subsidy differ between inpatient and outpatient care, as it is shown in Table 4.7 and Table 4.8.

Table 4.7 Cost and revenues of the outpatient department (OPD) in 1995

	average costs [US$]	average fee [US$]	subsidy [% of costs]
actual sustainable local costs	1.70	1.47	13%
actual full costs	4.08	1.47	64%

Table 4.8 Cost and revenues of the inpatient department (IPD) in 1995

	costs per inpatient day [US$]	annual costs per bed [US$]	average fee per inpatient day [US$]	subsidy [% of costs]
actual sustainable local costs	2.88	894	1.52	47.42%
actual full costs	6.09	1,891	1.52	74.98%

The absolute and relative subsidy of the cost per inpatient day was higher than the subsidy of the outpatient department. All outpatient departments visited by the author had a positive marginal contribution to cover a share of the general overheads of the hospital. In some hospitals the OPD even generates a surplus to support the IPD (cross-subsidization). However, since 1991 Tanzanian medical practitioners have the right to open dispensaries and hospitals on their own. Only few private hospitals were founded, but many new private dispensaries attract outpatients. Therefore, the number of outpatients of ELCT hospitals decreased, but the workload of the inpatient department remained almost unchanged. The decrease in OPD cases negatively affects the ELCT hospitals which lose the profitable outpatients and remain with the highly subsidized inpatients.

Some hospitals of the ELCT opened *private wards*. These wards offer higher standards of hotel services in order to attract those patients who are able to pay higher fees. It was the target of the ELCT that these private wards should make a profit in order to subsidize the general wards. However, our analysis shows that in 1993-95 no private ward in ELCT hospitals did have a positive marginal contribution. The subsidy per private bed was always higher than the subsidy per bed in general wards. A more equitable system would require an increase of fees for private wards, but this was not permitted as a major part of the private patients were pastors from the governing dioceses. They have to be given special attention in private wards although they are not able or willing to pay fees which recover full costs. There is some pressure of the diocesan leadership on the hospital management to set low fees in order to make private wards affordable for diocesan employees. This is a kind of subsidy from the hospital to the diocese.

The study of the costs of ELCT hospitals in 1995 strongly supports our argument that costing data can be utilized to measure efficiency and sustainability. In section 5 some of the experiences of ELCT hospitals will be used to demonstrate the utilization of this data.

4.2 Costing a Health District: Dodoma Rural in Tanzania

4.2.1 Setting

The methodology which was originally developed for hospitals in Tanzania can also be applied to dispensaries and health centres as well as to complete health districts. For instance, it was used to cost the health district Dodoma Rural in Central Tanzania, a district with an area of about 10,004 km^2 and a population of about 439,160 (1997). This district is representative in size and population density ($\approx$ 44 inhabitants per km^2) of rural health districts in Tanzania but the average income per capita per annum (17.19 US$) was even lower than the Tanzanian average in 1997.

In the year of the study (1997) the population was served by 57 dispensaries, i.e., one dispensary covered 7,705 inhabitants and 176 km^2 on average. The goal of the Ministry of Health of the United Republic of Tanzania is to have a maximum distance of 10 km and a catchment population of about 10,000 inhabitants per dispensary. A catchment analysis prepared by the District Medical Officer (DMO) showed that in the year 1997 merely 10% of the villages in Dodoma Rural were located outside the radius of 10 km from a dispensary. In some parts of the district, dispensaries of different providers were very close to each other so that the DMO assessed that the number of dispensaries could be reduced to 44 without hardship for the population.

4.2 Costing a Health District: Dodoma Rural in Tanzania

Furthermore, the district was served by six health centres with officially 30 beds each. However, the health centres were not fully accepted by the population. The bed-occupancy in health centres was about 24% and most patients approached the outpatient department of the health centres just as another dispensary. In other words: the health centres did not fulfil their assigned function as intermediate between dispensary and hospital.

The Anglican hospital Mvumi was the only hospital in the district. A catchment analysis demonstrated that a major part of the population lived closer to other hospitals than to Mvumi. In particular the regional hospital in Dodoma City attracts a major part of the population. Thus, a population of about 440,000 inhabitants was served by a district hospital with merely 236 beds, but even for these beds the occupancy rate was merely 61%. A sample taken from inpatient files demonstrated that 70% of the patients covered a distance of less than 25 km.

The demand of the district population for hospital services was lower than one would expect in a rural health district in Tanzania. Based on the study presented in section 4.1 we can assess the admission risk per capita per annum as 4.5%, whereas the admission risk of the catchment population of Mvumi hospital was merely 1.87%. On the other hand, the average length of stay (14.8 days) is about twice as high as in the hospitals studied in 4.1. This can be partly due to the attempt of physicians to increase the occupancy rate by keeping patients longer than necessary. However, it can also be partly due to the fact that patients wait too long to come to the hospital, because they are afraid of the high charges. When they come, they are extremely sick and need a longer stay.

The hospital had an ophthalmology strongly supported by the Christophel Blinden Mission (Germany). Only 10% of the inpatients of the ophthalmology come from within the shortest distance catchment area, 40% from the region and 60% from outside the region. The average distance of travel to the eye-department is 255 km.

The author costed the hospital services in March 1997 and based his calculations on the annual report of the year 1996. The eye-department and training centres were excluded from the analysis as they cannot be assigned directly to the district. Technically, the cost apportionment included these cost centres so that not only the direct costs of the eye-department and the training centres were excluded but also a part of the indirect costs apportioned to these centres. This methodology cannot be used to analyse the impact of closing-down these cost centres as the overheads would remain almost unchanged. It merely gives an answer to the question how high the costs were if these centres had never been established, i.e., the costs of another district without eye-department and training centres.

4.2.2 Findings

4.2.2.1 Costs of Mvumi Hospital

Table 4.9 exhibits the costs of Mvumi hospital in the year 1996. Salaries are the most important cost item, i.e., about 56% of the running expenditure and about 22% of the total expenditure are caused by personnel. In 1996/7, the hospital was over-staffed with junior personnel, especially cooks (12) and watchmen (8). However, there was scarcity of qualified nurses of Grade B.

The equipment of the hospital had an actual value of some 289,800 US$ with an annual depreciation charge of 40,964 US$, i.e. about 14% of the total costs. Almost all equipment had been donated. If all written-off equipment was substituted by new items, the actual value would rise to 597,600 US$ with an annual depreciation of 87,135 US$.

Table 4.9   Total costs of Mvumi Hospital (1996)

Item		Cost [US$]		% of Total	% of Running Expenditure
Salaries			65,648	21.91%	56.47%
Drugs and stores			14,280	4.77%	12.28%
Transport	Running expenditure	6,964		2.32%	5.99%
	Vehicle depreciation	23,000	29,964	7.67%	
Equipment	Equipm. depreciation		40,964	13.67%	
General expenditure	Cleaning, energy, ...	15,747		5.25%	13.54%
	Building maintenance	1,828		0.61%	1.57%
	Building depreciation	119,460		39.86%	
	Office expenditure	8,711		2.91%	7.49%
	Bank charges	272		0.09%	0.23%
	Electricity/telephone.	2,810	148,828	0.94%	2.42%
Total			299,684	100.00%	100.00%

The hospital had (without training centres and eye-department) 5,219 m² of hospital buildings and 5,788 m² of staff houses. As only few members of staff worked entirely for the training departments, all staff houses were allocated to the hospital. If we assume that the hospital has a district function of 140 beds, this makes 37.28 m² per bed. This is higher than the average of ELCT hospitals analysed in section 4.1. The size of buildings for a Lutheran average hospital with 140 beds would be 2,533.74 m² (according to the regression analysis), i.e. 51.45% less. Mvumi hospital is too spacious for its catchment. On the other hand, if one assumes that the hospital actually provides 236 beds (without eye-department), the building space is only 22.11 m² per bed. This is almost identical with Ilembula Lutheran Hospital (21.09 m²). The space of staff houses per bed is rather high (24.53 m²/bed calculated at a hospital capacity of 236 beds), but it is still in range of the other hospitals (e.g. Ilembula: 19.49 m²/bed), especially because Mvumi is a very rural place without a free market for good houses.

In 1997, an architect calculated replacement costs of 1,565,700 US$ for the hospital and 1,736,400 US$ for the staff houses. However, buildings with 1,052 m² had been written off. Therefore, there remains a replacement value of 2,986,500 US$ or an annual depreciation charge of 119,460 US$. In comparison with other Tanzanian hospi-

4.2 Costing a Health District: Dodoma Rural in Tanzania

tals, the proportion of building depreciation in the total costs was quite high. This is due to the fact that the hospital was too huge for the demand of the year 1997, i.e., the hospital had capital costs of a 236-bed hospital, but recurrent costs of a 140-bed hospital. The standard maintenance would be 1% of the replacement costs, i.e. 29,865 US$.

In 1996, Mvumi Hospital had 4,848 outpatient visits, 5,416 admissions and 67,801 inpatient days in the general wards (without eye-department). Table 4.10 shows the costs of the outpatient and inpatient department per service unit. The cost analysis demonstrates that one inpatient day costs as much as 1.49 outpatient visits. Therefore, the hospital had 71,056.18 equivalent inpatient days (4,848/1.49+67,801).

Table 4.10   Cost per service unit of Mvumi Hospital (1996) [US$]

Item	Outpatient department	Inpatient Department
Salaries	0.65	0.92
Drugs and Stores	0.39	0.18
Transport	0.16	0.43
Equipment	0.68	0.56
General Expenditure	0.95	2.13
Total	2.83	4.22

The ratio of 1:1.49 is rather little. For instance, the ELCT-study (4.1) calculated a ratio of about 1:2. This is mainly due to the fact that in 1996/7 the demand for outpatient services was rather low. The outpatient department was staffed with sufficient medical assistants and (part-time) physicians to treat up to 7,500 patients a year. If we assume that the costs of drugs and stores are variable costs, the average cost per outpatient would decline to 1.57 US$ and the cost ratio would be 1:2.66. Thus, the poor occupancy of the outpatient department of about 65% of its capacity leads to high unit costs.

The annual costs per occupied bed were 1,197.27 US$ without expatriates or 1,838.07 with expatriates. Assuming that the hospital serves a population of 140.000 people (see 4.2.1) and an occupancy of 85% is pursued, the annual hospital costs per 1000 inhabitants in the district are 1,408.55 US$ without expatriates and 2,162.44 US$ with expatriates.

4.2.2.2   Costs of Primary Care

Table 4.11 exhibits the total costs of two health centres and five dispensaries in the district. It is obvious that the costs of health centres are much higher than the costs of dispensaries. However, even the total cost and the average cost per outpatient visit in dispensaries differ strongly. The average cost per service unit in all five dispensaries is 1.22 US$, whereas the costs of the two catholic dispensaries (Mlowa and Barabarani) almost double this average. This is mainly due to the fact that they are poorly utilized. It can be assumed that the fees of these institutions prevent patients from seeking help there.

Table 4.11   Total cost of selected health care units in Dodoma Rural (1996) [US$]

Item	Health Centre		Dispensaries				
	Mundemu	Handali	Msisi	Mlowa Catholic	Mlowa Govern.	Barabarani Cath.	Makongwa
Salaries	11,578	11,879	3,548	2,451	2,784	4,358	2,111
Drugs and Stores	3,890	3,343	2563	1,463	2,626	1,296	2,353
Transport	480	468	130	345	234	254	239
Equipment	1,528	1,023	70	780	50	60	132
General Exp.	8,804	16,298	3257	4,499	1,325	2,512	2,360
Total	26,279	33,011	9567	9,537	7,019	8,480	7,194
Per service unit	2.03	2.96	1.12	1.96	0.80	1.96	0.92

As stated before, the District Medical Officer assumed that 44 properly located dispensaries and 3 health centres would be sufficient to cover the entire district. Table 4.12 shows the cost of dispensaries and health centres in the entire district under the assumption that their cost behave like the seven institutions of Table 4.11. With a population of 440,000, a budget of 1.13 US$ p.c. p.a. would be sufficient to provide this level of care for the district population.

Table 4.12   Cost of dispensaries and health centres in the total district (1996) [US$]

Item	Health Centre		Dispensary	
	Total	per equivalent inpatient-day	Total	per outpatient visit
Salaries	35,186	1.15	134,218	0.31
Drugs and Stores	10,095	0.33	132,000	0.30
Transport	1,422	0.05	10,578	0.02
Equipment	3,827	0.13	9,610	0.02
General Expenditure	37,653	1.23	122,776	0.28
Total	88,936	2.91	409,181	0.93

Table 4.13 shows the costs of the district medical team in Dodoma Rural of the year 1996. Again, the biggest amount are the salaries, all other items are almost negligible. This is mainly due to the fact that the buildings, vehicles and equipment of the district management team were almost written off.

Table 4.13   Costs of the district medical team in Dodoma Rural (1996) [US$]

Item	Total cost	Cost per inhabitant
Salaries	427,772	0.97
Other recurrent cost	45,283	0.10
Equipment	1,700	0.00
Buildings	1,965	0.00
Vehicles	37,500	0.09
Total	514,220	1.17

Finally, Table 4.14 exhibits the health care cost per inhabitant in Dodoma Rural in the year 2006. This amount seems to be reasonable, but the average income in monetary terms in Dodoma Rural was only 17.19 US$ per capita in 1997. Therefore, 25.80% of the entire monetary income of the population should be spent for health care in order to fund these basic services. This sum neither includes secondary/tertiary hospitals nor any training institutions. In addition, this amount only reflects the actual costs without depreciation of written-off equipment, vehicles and buildings. In order to maintain the existing standards of care or even to increase them, the financial requirements are even higher.

Table 4.14   Cost per inhabitant in Dodoma Rural (1996) [US$]

Item	Costs [US$/capita]	%
Hospital	2.14	48%
Health Centres	0.20	5%
Dispensaries	0.93	21%
District Health Management Team	1.17	26%
Total	4.44	100%

These few figures should be sufficient to illustrate the use of costing studies for health districts. We can determine the actual costs and provide a basis for future planning. However, we already have to alert the reader here that costs do not behave linearly, i.e., an increase in population or coverage does not necessarily lead to a linear increase in costs as these averages might indicate. This will be addressed in chapter five.

4.3   Costing Governmental Hospitals in Vietnam

4.3.1   Setting

The methodology presented above can be adopted to cost the health care services of governmental hospitals. The following section presents some results of a study done in Vietnam in the year 2002. It is based on data from hospitals of the year 2000, i.e. during the transition period which brought fundamental economic and social change, including strong pressure on existing governmental health care services.

In 1986, Vietnam started a careful but wide-ranging *economic liberalisation* ("Doi Moi") aiming at a so-called "socialist market economy", i.e., „to develop a multi-sector commodity economy towards socialist orientation"[250]. Since then, the Vietnamese economy has constantly grown, and Vietnam has become a booming country with strong private markets, manifold joint-ventures with foreign enterprises and a variety of self-made and imported goods [251]. Doi Moi policy was extended to the social sector as well [252]. User fees were introduced for public hospitals, physicians received the right to open private practices or hospitals, and the pharmaceutical markets were liberalized.

During a transition from governmental planning and omnipresence of the government to market economy, some decision makers tend to believe that governmental and parastatal institutions become obsolete. Governmental health care institutions, public water supply companies or other providers under the wings of the state are frequently seen as inefficient, and privatisation is expected to increase efficiency. However, if we do not want this assessment to be a prejudice, we need to know the costs of governmental institutions and calculate the most efficient allocation of public funds. Therefore, knowing the costs and assessing the efficiency of governmental health care institutions in Vietnam was of high importance for the transition period and for the Doi Moi policy.

The *socialist national health system* was created with the building-up of socialism in Northern Vietnam in the late 1950s, and extended to the whole country after the reunification in 1975. The Vietnamese health care system consists of four levels following the administration structure of the country [253]. The *Ministry of Health* is the highest authority in the health sector. Together with the people's committees at national, provincial, district and commune level, it formulates and executes health policies and programmes nationwide. One important aspect of this policy authority is the fact that the Ministry of Health sets the prices of public health care facilities. In addition, it is directly involved in training of medical and nursing staff, medical research and the production of pharmaceuticals. *Central hospitals* are directly under the Ministry of Health (compare Figure 4.2).

At the second level are 61 *Province Health Bureaus*. Each of these bureaus serves a population from 0.28 to 5.3 million, a population of 1.2 million on average. Planning health services and programmes is a task of province health bureaus, including resource management planning. Provinces prepare annual and multiyear plans on the basis of reports from the districts. In each province there is at least one provincial hospital with 200-1,000 beds that typically has specialist clinical departments, such as internal medicine, obstetrics and gynaecology, surgery, paediatrics, infectious diseases and traditional medicine. Provincial hospitals are intended to be referral centres only. But the referral system does not always work the way it should. In addition to the general hospital, each province may also have one or more specialized hospitals (e.g. TB hospitals).

4.3 Costing Governmental Hospitals in Vietnam

Figure 4.2   Health care pyramid of Vietnam

At the third level, *district hospitals* serve the district population of between 50,000 and 300,000 inhabitants. District hospitals have main clinical departments such as internal medicine, surgery, obstetrics and gynaecology and infectious diseases including a laboratory and X-ray. A unit for maternal and child health (MCH) care and family planning is usually attached to the district general hospital.

At the bottom of the pyramid are *Inter Communal Polyclinics* (ICP) and Commune Health Stations. In 2000, 1,006 ICPs and 9,806 commune health stations were responsible for providing primary care including preventive, ambulatory and inpatient services to a population between 2,000 and 10,000 persons, and for referring complicated cases to upper levels of care. They are expected to implement national health programmes, such as Maternal and Child Health Care (MCH), family planning (FP), Expanded Programme on Immunisation (EPI) etc. In the past, these institutions were supported by village health workers (VHW). These non-professionals were chosen by the villages and provided with very limited training. They dispensed drugs and were the link between the villagers and the health care system. In the last few years this level of health care almost disappeared.

Theoretically, Vietnam has implemented a *referral-system*, i.e., patients have to report at the commune level before they seek help at higher facilities. Only if the medical personnel of the commune level reckons the condition of a patient as too serious, the patient is transferred to the district level. In addition, some cases are always transferred to the district hospital, even before treatment is attempted at a lower level. For instance, if a midwife determines strong risk factors during ante-natal care she will advise the women to go directly to the hospital for delivery without contacting a health centre or polyclinic first. The referral system includes the higher levels of care, i.e., theoretically a patient can only approach a provincial hospital if he is referred by a district hospital, and he can only be admitted at a central hospital after referral from a provincial hospital. However, in reality several levels are by-passed, in particular in towns where distances are no reason to prevent people from seeking health care in higher institutions. At the same time, there is anecdotal evidence that severely sick patients of rural provinces do not go to central hospitals despite referral because of the distances.

Table 4.15 shows the number of hospitals of each level in the year 2000. It is obvious that Vietnam has a sufficient number of hospitals and hospital beds. The majority (76%) are general hospitals. Specialty hospitals include tuberculosis hospitals, leprosy sanatoriums, and psychiatric hospitals as well as some high-tech centres such as cardiology, oncology, etc. In the year 2000, there were only 14 private hospitals with nearly 1000 beds. 75 hospitals with 1415 beds belong to Ministries and agencies other than the Ministry of Health (such as Police, Armed Forces, Transports, Posts and Telecommunications, Agriculture). There is a strong positive correlation between the number of beds per institution and the level of health care.

Table 4.15   Hospitals in Vietnam (2000)

Type of hospital	Facilities		Beds		Average Size
	Number	% of total	Number	% of total	(beds/Facility)
Central (MOH)	30	3.1	11,840	10.1	395
general	10	1.0	6,330	5.4	633
specialized	18	1.9	5,060	4.3	281
traditional	2	0.2	450	0.4	225
Provincial	282	29.1	58,284	49.6	207
general	97	10.0	34,969	29.7	361
specialized	139	14.3	18,815	16.0	135
traditional	46	4.7	4,500	3.8	98
District	569	58.7	41,825	35.6	74
Other Ministries	75	7.7	4,715	4.0	63
Private	14	1.4	898	0.8	64
general	11	1.1	750	0.6	68
specialized	3	0.3	148	0.1	49
Total	970	100	117,562	100	121

Source: [253]

Vietnam faces a growing demand for hospital services. This is due to an ageing population with an increase in chronic-degenerative diseases as well as to a strong increase in accidents with severe traumata [254]. At the same time Vietnam has a growing poverty problem, i.e., the gap between poor and rich and between rural and urban areas in particular has increased [255], so that *cost sharing* places a strong burden on many poor people. The fast growing private markets have sensitized the Vietnamese population that they can demand value for money. At the same time, the government must seek new ways to cover the poor. Therefore, decision makers need cost information. They must know, how high the costs are in a particular institution, how high they are in other institutions and how costs can be saved by curing a disease in another institution.

The following section presents the results of a costing study in one central, two provincial and two district hospitals. The investigated hospitals were not chosen randomly.

4.3 Costing Governmental Hospitals in Vietnam

We selected five hospitals which had shown during the last years that their management and accounting system was reliable. For this purpose we had to rely on the experience of the Ministry of Health and the insight of one of the investigators as servant of this ministry. In addition, some data, such as depreciation, had to be collected by personal field vists in the hospitals, so that only hospitals in Northern Vietnam were investigated.

Bach mai hospital in Hanoi is a 980-beds central hospital. It is the final referral centre for Northern Vietnam and the teaching hospital of Hanoi Medical University. Thai nguyen hospital is the provincial hospital of Thai nguyen province (about 85 km north of Hanoi). It has a capacity of 550 beds. Thai-Binh hospital is the provincial hospital of the province of the same name (about 160 km south of Hanoi). It has 600 beds and is a teaching hospital of Thai Binh Medical School. Van-Dinh hospital is the district hospital of Ung Hoa district, 65 km east of Hanoi. The district comprises a population of 250,000 people, mainly peasants with rice and auxiliary crop cultivation as the main occupation. The hospital has 170 beds. Finally, Binh-Luc hospital is the district hospital of Binh-Luc district about 85 km west of Hanoi. The population of the district consists of some 220,000 people, essentially composed of peasants. The hospital has 100 beds.

All data and information were collected directly in the hospitals and compared with the figures available at the Ministry of Health. Missing figures were collected and calculated (such as depreciation, donations). All results were continuously discussed with the hospital managers and the representatives of the Ministry of Health.

4.3.2 Findings

Table 4.16 shows some *basic activity statistics* for the five hospitals for the year 2000. Thai nguyen provincial hospital is severely over-loaded with an occupancy rate of 132%, i.e., some patients had to stay in emergency beds on the floor or share a bed with another patient. Bin luc district hospital is poorly utilized in both the inpatient and the outpatient department. However, there is a tendency that the outpatient department of higher level hospitals is of lower importance compared with the inpatient department. As expected, the average length of stay correlates positively with the level of the institution, as central hospitals receive severely sick patients requiring a long hospital stay.

Table 4.17 shows the costs for each hospital in the year 2000. In general, the highest costs were caused by personnel (salaries, wages, training etc.; 35% in Bach mai central hospital, 64% in Binh luc district hospital). The second most important cost item are drugs (between 15% and 27%) and other medical materials, including x-ray films, laboratory chemicals, infusions and blood (between 5% in Binh luc district hospital and 19% in Bach mai central hospital). It is interesting to notice that the importance of cost items depends on the level of health care. The costs of personnel are most important for district hospitals (64% and 61% of total). For provincial hospitals the costs only make up 36% or 46% of total costs, whereas they constitute only 35% for the central hospital. Drugs are almost equally important for all hospitals, only in Binh luc district hospital the share of drug costs in total costs is less because of the low utilization. The importance of other medical supplies, however, is highly correlated with the level of services. The central hospital has a high portion of this cost item, provincial hospitals have a lower portion and district hospitals a very small one. In particular the costs of blood transfusions and infusions are almost negligible in district hospitals as these procedures are not regularly done at that level.

Table 4.16   Basic activity statistics (2000)

	Bach mai Central Hospital	Thai nguyen Provincial Hospital	Thai binh Provincial Hospital	Van dinh District Hospital	Binh luc District Hospital	Average
Number of beds	980	550	600	170	100	480
Outpatient visits	240,260	169,701	168,255	80,529	29,342	137,617
Number of inpatients	29,239	21,021	26,518	7,963	3,717	17,692
No. of inpatient days	339,540	266,561	221,097	62,118	23,295	182,522
∅ length of stay [days]	11.61	12.68	8.34	7.80	6.27	9.3
Bed occupancy rate	94.9%	132.8%	101.0%	100.1%	63.8%	98.5%

Table 4.17   Costs of hospital services in Vietnam (2000), [US$;%]

	Bach mai Central Hospital	Thai nguyen Provincial Hospital	Thai binh Provincial Hospital	Van dinh District Hospital	Binh luc District Hospital
Personnel	1,687,997; 35%	510,393; 36%	574,157; 46%	79,159; 61%	58,260; 64%
Drugs	951,106; 20%	318,153; 22%	338,387; 27%	19,416; 15%	16,371; 18%
Other medical supplies	922,856; 19%	159,645; 11%	172,659; 14%	12,788; 10%	4,384; 5%
Energy, water etc.	250,075; 5%	79,795; 6%	67,353; 5%	11,426; 9%	1,478; 2%
Investment, depreciation and maintenance	179,525; 4%	98,000; 7%	36,086; 3%	2,040; 2%	8,237; 9%
Sundry expenses	797,375; 17%	263,440; 18%	47,216; 4%	5,946; 5%	1,844; 2%
Total	4,788,933	1,429,427	1,235,858	130,775	90,573

Table 4.18 shows the calculation of *unit costs* of outpatient and inpatient departments. As expected, the costs per OPD attendance are higher in the central hospital than in the provincial hospitals. At the same time, there is a tendency that the average costs per OPD service unit are lower in district hospitals than in provincial hospitals. However, due to the poor occupancy rate of Binh luc district hospital, its OPD-costs per attendance are higher than for Thai nguyen provincial hospital and at least not significantly

4.3 Costing Governmental Hospitals in Vietnam

lower than for Thai binh provincial hospital. Therefore, poorly utilized outpatient services at district hospitals might be more expensive than highly requested outpatient services at a higher level of the health care system.

The cost per inpatient at the central hospital is three to four times higher than the costs in provincial hospitals and ten to 25 times higher than in district hospitals. This difference is partly due to higher costs per patient day, partly due to higher average length of stay. The duration in the central hospital was double the length of stay in Van dinh district hospital. However, the most important differences are the costs per patient day.

The costs per patient day of district hospitals are significantly lower than for provincial hospitals, which are again lower than the average costs of the central hospital. We found that the costs per patient day of Bach mai central hospital are 16.5 times higher than the cost of Van dinh district hospital. For Thai nguyen and Thai binh provincial hospital the factor is 5.8 and 6.0, for Binh luc district hospital 3.2. Again these *differences* can be due to different reasons. Firstly, the different occupancy might be one cause. Therefore, the costs per inpatient day must be calculated based on a standard occupancy rate for each hospital. Secondly, the differences might be due to higher costs per service rendered per patient day (e.g. per operation, per laboratory test, per x-ray). Thirdly, the variation might be induced by a higher quantity of services per patient day.

The first possible cause of difference is not very convincing. We calculated the average cost per inpatient day under the assumption of an inpatient occupancy rate of 85%. This rate is internationally accepted as a standard allowing hospitals to provide acceptable quality of care. A higher occupancy rate is usually seen as a risk of poor quality as it is likely that patients have to share a bed at least for some days a year. A lower occupancy rate incorporates the risk of not covering the fixed costs. Assuming that the costs for drugs and other medical supplies are variable, the average costs per equivalent inpatient day are still significantly higher at higher levels of health care.

Table 4.18   Unit cost of OPD and IPD in Vietnam [US$]

	Bach mai Central Hospital	Thai nguyen Provincial Hospital	Thai binh Provincial Hospital	Van dinh District Hospital	Binh luc District Hospital
Total OPD-cost	240,261	169,702	168,256	80,529	29,343
Actual total inpatient cost	4,548,672	1,259,725	1,067,602	50,245,	61,230
OPD-cost per attendance	0.86	0.51	0.66	0.27	0.65
Actual inpatient cost per patient	155.57	59.93	40.26	6.30	16.47
Actual cost per inpatient day	13.40	4.73	4.83	0.81	2.62
Cost per inpatient day based on an occupancy of 85%	14.63	7.01	5.69	1.62	2.45

The second possible reason for different costs per inpatient day could be the higher *costs per procedure*. Table 4.19 summarizes the unit costs for some different procedures. Some procedures are cheaper at higher levels of health care than at lower levels because the procedures are done more often. For instance, the costs of x-rays are mainly fixed costs, i.e., the number of x-rays strongly determines the unit costs. Consequently, the costs per x-ray are lower in provincial hospitals than in district hospitals because the volume is higher in the former. The same concept can be applied to most laboratory tests and operations. The official statistics of the Ministry of Health distinguish between operations of complexity I, II and III and so-called "special" operations which can only be performed by sub-specialists. As expected, the average costs depend on the level of operation. They are 133.93 US$ for operations of type I, 90.51 US$ for operations of type II and 36.20 US$ for operations of type III. Special operations cost 170.29 US$ on average. However, there is a wide range. For instance, an operation of type I only costs 37.49 US$ at Thai binh provincial hospital, but 279.82 US$ at Binh luc district hospital. *It is remarkable that the costs of operations done at district hospitals are higher than those of provincial hospitals or even the central hospital.*

Table 4.19   Unit cost of some hospital procedures in Vietnam [US$]

Procedure	Bach mai Central Hospital	Thai nguyen Provincial Hospital	Thai binh Provincial Hospital	Van dinh District Hospital	Binh luc District Hospital
X-ray picture	4.09	1.58	0.48	2.52	4.07
Haematological test	0.33	0.36	0.22	0.27	0.38
Bio-Chemistry test	0.44	0.39	0.23	0.27	0.65
Microbiology test	0.75	0.41	0.06	1.45	1.98
Operation type "special"	251.27	89.32	0.00	0.00	0.00
Operation type I	175.89	62.52	37.49	77.83	279.82
Operation type II	125.63	44.66	26.78	55.59	199.87
Operation type III	50.25	17.86	10.71	22.24	79.95

Finally, the *number of procedures per inpatient day* determines the costs. As Table 4.20 shows, the number of procedures per inpatient day is highest in the central hospital and lowest in district hospitals. *The main reason for the high correlation between costs per inpatient day and the level of health care, thus, is the higher density of services at higher levels.* In particular, the most expensive procedures are superproportionally often performed in hospitals of higher levels. For instance, x-rays are taken 2.5 times as often in the central hospital as in the cheapest district hospital, haematological tests 4.4 times as often, bio-chemistry tests 8.0 times and micro-biological tests 12.2 times as often.

Table 4.20 Quantity of procedures per inpatient day in Vietnam

Procedure	Bach mai Central Hospital	Thai nguyen Provincial Hospital	Thai binh Provincial Hospital	Van dinh District Hospital	Binh luc District Hospital
Image Diagnosis	0.2482	0.1942	0.1955	0.09900	0.0859
Haematological test	2.2861	0.6499	0.6617	0.5173	0.67520
Bio-Chemistry test	1.4762	0.3008	0.8930	0.1847	0.2412
Microbiology test	0.4508	0.1767	0.6489	0.0369	0.0482
Operation type special	0.0058	0.0004	-	-	-
Operation type I	0.0045	0.0038	0.0090	0.00280	0.00047
Operation type II	0.0084	0.0085	0.0068	0.00412	0.00128
Operation type III	0.0018	0.0012	0.0044	0.00616	0.00605

In general, our findings demonstrate that governmental hospitals in Vietnam provide an affordable and rather cost-effective health care. However, costs and efficiency of these institutions differ significantly. The general statement that district hospitals are more efficient than provincial hospitals is as impossible as basing allocations merely on these statistics. As health economists we are mainly interested in outcomes and impact. Assuming that provincial hospitals are too far away for the majority of patients, the technical efficiency in the institution might be high, but the over-all efficiency of the entire health care system might be low if it is strongly based on central and provincial hospitals. Consequently, *assessing the efficiency of hospitals is an important component of estimating the efficiency of a health care system, but it can not be more than a component.*

4.4 Costing a Health District in Burkina Faso

4.4.1 Setting

Burkina Faso is one of the poorest countries in Africa, and the annual public and private health care expenditure of about 8 US$ p.c. [256] is extremely low, even compared to the other sub-Saharan countries ($\varnothing$ 13 US$ p.c., excluding South Africa). 90% of the population of 11 million live in rural or sub-urban areas and mainly relay on subsistence farming. Providing the population with equitable and sustainable health care services of acceptable quality is a real challenge. Decision makers can provide sufficient funds to reach the poor and needy in these areas only if they have knowledge of actual and standard costs of health care services in a rural district.

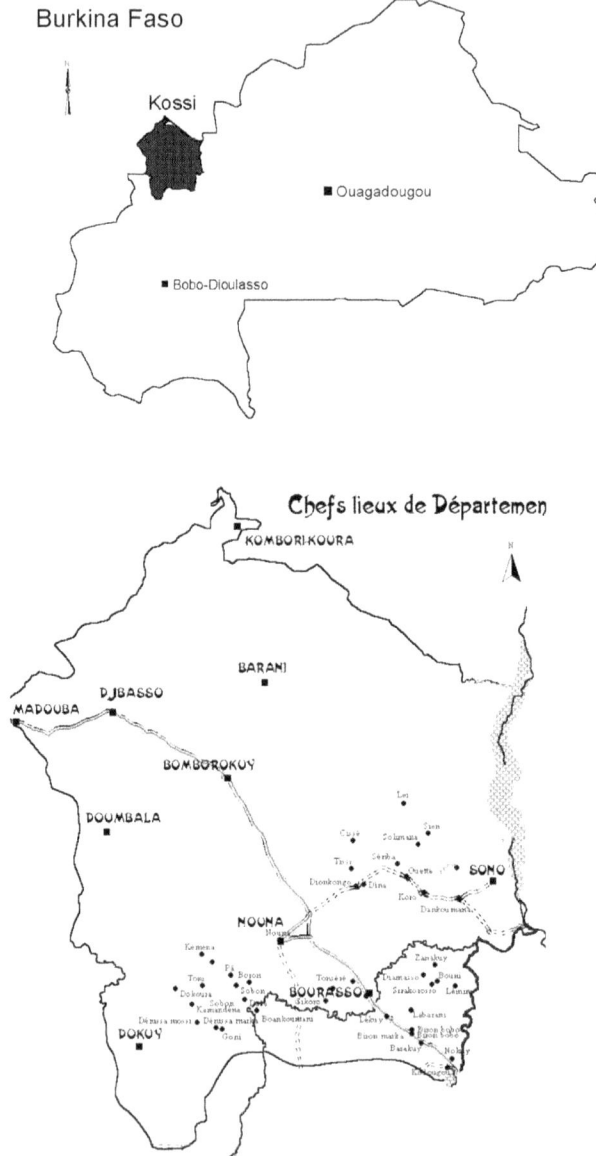

Figure 4.3 Kossi province in Burkina Faso
Source: Map of Western Africa.

4.4 Costing a Health District in Burkina Faso

The costs presented in this section were gathered in one of the poorest districts of Burkina Faso. Nouna is the name of the central town as well as of the health district. Both are situated in Kossi province in the North-East. In 2005, 25 dispensaries (Centre de Santé et de Promotion Sociale, CSPS) and one district hospital (*Centre Medical avec Antenne Chirurgicale*, CMA) provided health care services for the population of 279,730. The basic demographic, epidemiological and socio-economic data is presented elsewhere [257-261].

The utilization of health care services in Nouna health district has declined since the introduction of the cost-sharing concept under the Bamako initiative in 1993 [258, 262, 263] and is rather low. For instance, Sauerborn, Nougtara & Latimer calculate an average of 0.31 contacts with health care services per capita in the year 2000 [264]. For the year 2002, the same researchers found that the average inhabitant of the health district had 0.24 visits to a dispensary and 0.03 visits to a hospital, whereas the Ministry of Health assumes an average number of dispensary contacts of 0.17 p.a. p.c. [265].

The World Bank and the World Health Organisation suggest that one visit to a dispensary per capita and year is sufficient to provide outpatient care in a health district like Nouna. At the same time they propose one hospital bed for 1000 inhabitants [143]. With a standard average length of stay of 7 days and an occupancy rate of 85%, the annual admission frequency is 0.044 per capita. Thus, the demand for dispensary services in Nouna health district is only 24% of this standard, and the hospital admission only 68%. A comparison with our own study in Tanzania (section 4.1) shows that the standards provided by the WHO and the World Bank are quite realistic. Health services were almost free of charge in Tanzania in the year 1995, and the hospital admission frequency was 0.045 and the frequency of visiting a dispensary was 1.1 p.c. p.a. [266].

According to the economic framework model (section 2.2, page 17) the low demand for modern health care services in Nouna health district can have different reasons. Firstly, the population could be unexceptionally healthy, i.e., the objective or subjective scarcity of health could be low. Secondly, it might be possible that people are not aware of the fact that they are sick and need help. Thirdly, filters might prevent people from seeking health care although they need and want it. The most important filters are high costs for the patients, poor quality of services and long distances to the provider.

At first we can state that the population of the Nouna district is not healthier than in other areas. In the study mentioned above, Sauerborn et al. asked a sample of 6431 inhabitants for symptoms. The sample was chosen from a population that is registered in a demographic surveillance system established in this health district. Based on this verbal examination, the objective need for health care was determined by a team of physicians. They realized that on average a person in Nouna health district would have a need for 0.924 dispensary contacts p.a., i.e., 71% of the medical conditions that would require professional treatment never lead to a show-up at the dispensary. At the same time Sauerborn et al. calculated an annual need for major operations requiring hospital admissions of 0.028 p.c., but the hospital statistics showed only few major operations in Nouna hospital. In particular, severe diseases with a strong impact on the well-being of people frequently did not induce a dispensary or hospital visit. Consequently, people were most likely aware of their unhealthy situation but the need never became demand.

Therefore, costs, quality and distance must be responsible for the low demand for health care services. The decision makers realized that there is a great need to know the costs of the district health system in order to overcome these filters. Consequently, a cost information system (see Figure 4.4) was installed. It is an element of the entire health district information system in Nouna district. Its final objective is to provide a solid foundation for a cost-effectiveness analysis of different intervention.

Some basic results of the provider cost information system of the year 2005 are presented in the next section. 25 CSPS and one CMA are included, whereas it has to be noted that three CSPS were inaugurated during this year.

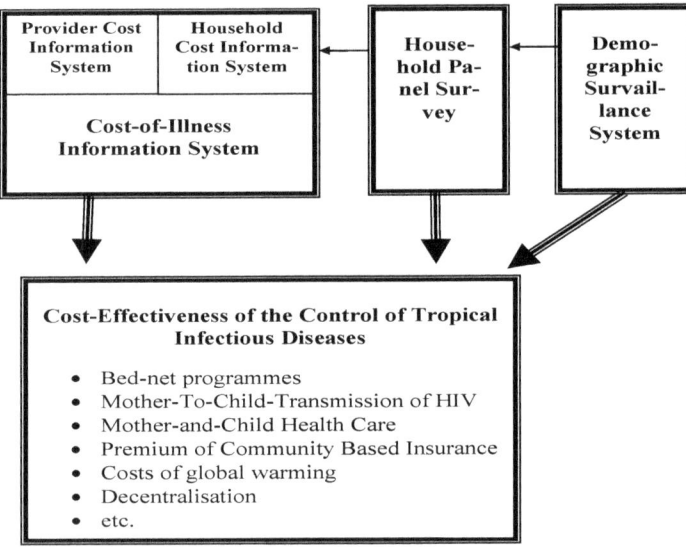

Figure 4.4   Cost information system as basis of evidence-based health care in Nouna

4.4.2   Findings

4.4.2.1   Primary Care

Primary care is mainly provided by 25 dispensaries (CSPS) and by the outpatient department of the hospital. Table 4.21 presents basic figures of the dispensaries. It is obvious that these institutions strongly differ in workload, costs and cost recovery. The cost outlier Dijabasso CSPS used to be a health centre (Centre medical, CM) but it was

4.4 Costing a Health District in Burkina Faso

downgraded to a dispensary. Consequently, it still has the overheads of a health centre resulting in high average cost per service unit.

On average, a dispensary had 2,226 consultations per year (maximum: 4,654; minimum: 825). The staffing, the size of buildings and the equipment should have been sufficient for about 10,000 consultations a year. None of the dispensaries reached this objective, i.e., *even institutions with a workload above the average were strongly under-utilized.*

Table 4.21 Basic statistics of dispensaries in Nouna health district

Cost Centre	Average number	total cost [US$]	unit cost [US$]	cost recovery [%]
Consultation	2,226	4,473	2.01	9
Delivery	369	2,772	7.51	24
Immunisation	7,834	14,683	2.13	0
Pharmacy	2,595	6,145	2.37	125

Most impressive is the wide range of cost between the CSPS. Although all dispensaries are (in principal) built for a population of 10,000 inhabitants, the total costs range between 10,249 US$ p.a. and 100,982 US$ with an arithmetic mean (μ) of 31,271 US$. The standard deviation (σ) was 17,963 and the coefficient of mean deviation 0.57. A major reason for the wide diversity of cost is the different age of buildings and equipment. Newer dispensaries have rather high depreciation charges for these fixed assets whereas some old dispensaries have not seen any major investments for decades. Thus, the total of annual depreciation charges varies between 2,157 US$ (Gassingo CSPS) and 11,068 US$ (Nouna CSPS) with an average of 5,444 US$ (σ=2,500 US$)

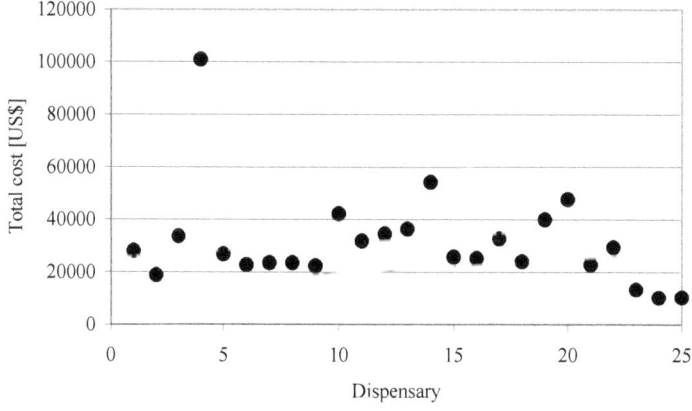

Figure 4.5 Total cost per dispensary in Nouna health district

The total costs of the cost center "general consultation" ranged from 2,460 to 11,491 US$ with an average of 4,473 US$ per institution. The cost per consultation ranged from 0.97 to 4.22 US$ with an average of 2.30 US$. 40.5% of the variance of the average costs can be explained by the different workload. The cost recovery rate was on average 9.36%. The dispensary with the lowest rate recovered 3.82% of the consultation costs, whereas the "best" CSPS recovered 16.9%.

The number of deliveries also varied from one dispensary to the other. Whereas only 40 deliveries were registered in Yevedougou, there were 897 deliveries at Barani, with an average of 369 cases. Unlike the cost centre "general consultation", the cost recovery rate of the cost center "delivery" is much higher. Nevertheless, with 60.6% in Ira and 1.9% in Yevedougou the cost recovery rates differ remarkably between the locations. The amount of the official user fees for normal deliveries as well as for dystocia cases was similar for most facilities.

Immunisations are the most important preventive work done in CSPS, but only 22 of the 25 institutions did immunisations in 2005. The costs of immunisation are quite high, and in contrast to the other cost centres most of the immunisation costs are variable. Even so, the average costs per immunisation range from 0.54 US$ to 10.44 US$ in different facilities with an average of 3.22 US$. The dispensaries of Gassingo, Boni and Yevedougou had not done any vaccinations in 2005, whereas Nian CSPS had recorded 22,826.

The costs at the pharmacies were treated separately as Burkina Faso follows the Bamako initiative. On average, the cost per patient were 2.42 US$ with a minimum of 0.58 US$ (Nouna CSPS) and a maximum of 3.97 US$ (Djiabasso CSPS). The average patient spent 2.97 US$ for pharmaceuticals, but the average patient in Djiabasso spent 5.02 US$ and the average patient in Nouna CSPS spent 0.44 US$. Consequently, the average pharmacy attached to a CSPS had a profit of 1,562 US$, whereas Bagala had a loss of 741 US$ and Djibasso a profit of 5,425 US$.

Table 4.22 shows the cost of consultation in different dispensaries. As stated above, the average cost per consultation was 2.30 US$ but with a standard deviation of 0.96 any statement about averages can be misleading.

The total costs of providing dispensary services in the year 2005 were 31,271 US$ per dispensary. An amount of 1,213 US$ was general overheads per dispensary which was not allocated to different departments, 7,245 US$ were for curative care (consultancy, delivery), 18,428 US$ were for prevention (immunisation, counselling, antenatal care) and 6,145 US$ for the pharmacy. Thus, the total district cost of providing health care at dispensary level in 2005 were 181,132 US$ for curative care, 417,308 US$ for preventive care and 153,622 US$ for the pharmacy, with a total of 781,786 US$ (incl. 30,315 US$ overheads not allocated to different departments of the dispensaries). Thus, the curative and preventive care of the district population at CSPS level cost 2.78 US$ p.c. p.a. The total patient fee for all departments was 219,092 US$ (192,684 for pharmacy, 26,409 for curative care), e.g., 28% of the total cost were recovered by patient fees. Assuming that the government recovered the deficit we can state that the

4.4 Costing a Health District in Burkina Faso

dispensaries of Nouna health district received an annual government subsidy of 563,286 US$ or 2.01 US$ p.c. p.a.

Table 4.22 Consultation services in Nouna health district

Facility	Number of consultations	Annual fixed cost [US$]	Variable cost per consultation [US$]	Average cost per consultation [US$]	Annual total cost [US$]	Adult fee; children fee [US$]	Cost recovery [%]
Bagala	976	2,783	0.05	2.90	2,833	0.19; 0.14	5.79
Barani	3,356	5,325	0.05	1.64	5,506	0.37; 0.37	22.83
Berma	3,018	3,280	0.03	1.12	3,373	0.19; 0.14	14.81
Bomborokuy	4,216	4,029	0.02	0.98	4,131	0.19; 0.14	16.92
Borekuy	1,559	2,589	0.04	1.70	2,644	0.19; 0.14	9.85
Bourasso	3,909	5,252	0.02	1.36	5,328	0.19; 0.14	12.37
Dara	1,398	2,340	0.09	1.77	2,469	0.19; 0.14	9.31
Dembo	2,410	4,998	0.16	2.23	5,385	0.19; 0.14	7.59
Djibasso	4,654	11,172	0.07	2.47	11,491	0.19; 0.14	6.51
Dokuy	1,247	3,858	0.63	3.72	4,643	0.19; 0.14	4.41
Doumbala	2,077	3,079	0.05	1.53	3,187	0.19; 0.14	10.72
Gassingo	919	3,842	0.04	4.22	3,876	0.19; 0.14	3.92
Goni	1,067	2,455	0.00	2.31	2,460	0.19; 0.14	7.12
Ira	2,826	3,177	0.07	1.19	3,369	0.19; 0.14	13.73
Kienekuy	1,904	2,847	0.05	1.54	2,936	0.19; 0.14	10.71
Konankoira	1,445	4,140	0.05	2.92	4,216	0.19; 0.14	5.67
Konkuy Koro	1,511	5,253	0.02	3.50	5,289	0.19; 0.14	4.74
Koro	1,612	5,784	0.06	3.65	5,886	0.19; 0.14	4.51
Lekuy	1,744	4,168	0.06	2.45	4,266	0.19; 0.14	6.67
Nian	2,854	4,040	0.03	1.45	4,135	0.28; 0.14	14.63
Nouna	3,916	8,482	0.03	2.20	8,607	0.37; 0,14	12.61
Sono	1,452	3,990	0.13	2.88	4,177	0.19; 0.14	5.90
Toni	2,972	4,549	0.02	1.55	4,608	0.19; 0.14	10.76
Werebere	1,779	3,591	0.03	2.05	3,652	0.19; 0.14	8.08
Yevedougou	825	3,354	0.02	4.08	3,368	0.19; 0.14	3.82

The total cost of dispensary i can be calculated as

$$TC_i = CF_i + c_i^c \cdot P_i + c_i^d \cdot D_i + c_i^i \cdot I_i + c_i^p \cdot (P_i + D_i) \text{ with}$$

TC_i	total costs of CSPS i
CF_i	fixed costs of CSPS i
c_i^c	variable cost per consultation patient in CSPS i
P_i	number of consultation patients in CSPS i
c_i^d	variable cost per delivery in CSPS i
D_i	number of deliveries in CSPS i
c_i^i	variable cost per immunisation in CSPS i

I_i number of immunisations in CSPS i

c_i^p variable cost per patient in the pharmacy in CSPS i

Table 4.23 shows the results. Again it is obvious that the fixed and variable cost per dispensary differ strongly. In section 4.4.2.3 we will analyse the consequences of the increase in the work load for the total cost.

Table 4.23 Fixed and variable cost

Facility	CF_i [US$]	c_i^c [US$]	P_i	c_i^d [US$]	D_i	c_i^i [US$]	I_i	c_i^p [US$]
Bagala	6,470	0.05	976	0	182	4.20	2,469	1.55
Barani	14,042	0.05	3,356	0	897	0.75	10,231	3,02
Berma	8,905	0.03	3,018	0	789	2.92	6,385	2.30
Bomborokuy	10,561	0.02	4,216	0	397	9.85	1,644	3.31
Borekuy	9,452	0.04	1,559	0	274	3.24	2,712	2.20
Bourasso	14,298	0.02	3,909	0	185	2.63	2,625	1.10
Dara	7,615	0.09	1,398	0	406	1.75	5,990	2.94
Dembo	13,698	0.16	2,410	0	519	2.12	5,483	2.98
Djibasso	34,452	0.07	4,654	0	468	3.38	13,881	3.72
Dokuy	17,478	0.63	1,247	0	237	1.09	10,522	2.45
Doumbala	12,107	0.05	2,077	0	378	2.97	4,475	1.58
Gassingo	7,685	0.04	919	0	42	0.00	0	2.54
Goni	7,652	0.00	1,067	0	74	0.00	0	2.30
Ira	10,984	0.07	2,826	0	761	3.26	7,286	1.38
Kienekuy	7,498	0.05	1,904	0	413	2.73	4,987	1.74
Konankoira	9,720	0.05	1,445	0	249	2.71	3,692	1.72
Konkuy Koro	12,811	0.02	1,511	0	214	2.77	2,648	1.57
Koro	13,523	0.06	1,612	0	391	1.40	7,817	1.69
Lekuy	10,256	0.06	1,744	0	345	3.76	3,082	0.97
Nian	12,670	0.03	2,854	0	318	0.43	22,826	2.92
Nouna	32,780	0.03	3,916	0	779	1.22	10,863	0.31
Sono	15,841	0.13	1,452	0	322	2.91	3,943	2.85
Toni	12,116	0.02	2,972	0	277	2.23	4,320	0.52
Werebere	10,755	0.03	1,779	0	270	3.23	3,474	2.32
Yevedougou	11,247	0.02	825	0	40	0.00	0	2.35

4.4.2.2 Secondary Care

The CMA of Nouna health district is not fully functional as a district hospital. Table 4.24 exhibits the basic service statistics of the year 2005. Based on the official number of 85 beds, the occupancy rate of the entire hospital was 11.4% in 2005. Major surgery was not performed in 2005 as no surgeon was available. The theatre was mainly used for minor interventions corresponding to a very low average length of stay in this department. Merely the psychiatric cases have an acceptable length of stay, all other patients were only admitted for a very short period of time. *This questions the quality as well as the effectiveness and efficiency of the hospital.*

4.4 Costing a Health District in Burkina Faso

Table 4.24 Basic service statistics, CMA Nouna 2005

Department	Outpatients	Official beds	Inpatients	Beddays	Average length of stay [days]	Occupancy [%]
General Medicine	735	24	430	1836	4.27	21.0
Surgery	240	20	79	110	1.39	1.5
Gynaecology, Obstetrics	503	17	621	807	1.30	13.0
Paediatrics	1615	6	154	209	1.36	9.5
Psychiatrics	83	4	18	162	9.00	11.1
Ophthalmology	2746	6	248	550	2.22	25.1
Leprosy, TB	473	8	-	-	-	
ENT[8]	546	0	-	-	-	
Dentistry	424	0	-	-	-	
Total:	7365	85	1550	3674	2.37	11.8

Table 4.25 exhibits the building space per department and the staffing of the year 2005. With a total of 71 members of staff, two doctors, 14 medical assistants and 36 nurses/midwives Nouna hospital seems to be appropriately staffed for an 85-bed hospital in rural Africa. However, compared with the occupancy rate this institution is by far too big and over-staffed. *We can state that it works on the level of a rural health center but with the resources of a district hospital.*

The *ophthalmology department* is an exception. This is mainly due to the fact that this department provides services as referral center beyond Nouna health district and is financially supported by Christophel Blinden Mission. But even this department seems to work more like a major outpatient department of higher quality than like a hospital.

Table 4.26 shows the direct cost per cost center before a stepping-down cost allocation. The personnel costs were divided between the different cost centers according to the self-assessment and questionnaires filled by the members of staff. As expected, salaries and wages are the most important cost categories (48%). The equipment depreciation is rather high (18%), in particular for the laboratory, radiology and theatre. Pharmaceuticals are also of high importance, but compared with other hospitals this amount is not extremely high. The table shows that the majority of buildings were written off so that the building depreciation was zero. This indicates that Nouna hospital urgently needs a major renovation.

---

[8] Ear, nose, throat (ENT).

Table 4.25   Resources of CMA Nouna, 2005

Department		Buildings [m²]	Medical Officers	Medical Assistants	Nurses	Other staff
Wards	General Medicine	80		2	5	2
	Surgery	104		4	9	
	Gynaecology, Obstetrics	106			11	2
	Paediatrics	80	1		4	
	Psychiatrics	51		1	1	
	Ophthalmology	84	1	4		
	Leprosy, TB	27			2	
OPD		240		3	1	
Theatre		40			3	
Laboratory		104				6
Radiology		80				
Administration		74				3
Laundy		36				2
Other		116				4
Total		1228	2	14	36	19

An analysis per cost center shows that the pharmacy is the most expensive cost centre (16%). It is followed by laboratory (12%), theatre (11%) and radiology (6%). The administration costs about 10% of the total expenditure, and all support services accumulate to 18%. However, the most striking result is the total cost of 333,115 US$ for a hospital serving only 7,365 outpatients and 1,550 inpatients. Compared with the findings from other countries (compare section 4.1, 4.2 and 4.3) this cost is extraordinarily high. As we will show in the next paragraph, 13,597 US$ have to be deducted for services provided for patients receiving treatment for eye diseases but who come from outside the district, and 912 US$ have to be allocated to the district administration. However, the remaining amount of 318,606 US$ is still amazing. *Again we can state that Nouna CMA worked as a health centre with the cost of a full hospital.*

The results of Table 4.26 were used to produce the figures of Table 4.27 with the stepping-down allocation method described in section 3.2.3. It includes the clearing of costs that are not attributable to the function of a district hospital. Firstly, Nouna hospital is providing eye services for patients from outside the Nouna health district. Some patients even come from Mali to the eye department. In 2005, 84 outpatients (3%), 114 inpatients (46%) and 286 beddays (52%) could not be allocated to the district function and had to be cleared. Secondly, the laboratory provides services for the Centre de Recherche en Santé Nouna. Consequently, the cost of the work for the research centre had to be deducted. The documentation of the pharmacy does not allow for a proper analysis of cost of in- or outpatient. As Nouna follows the Bamako initiative, the pharmaceuticals have to be bought by the patients in the CMA pharmacy irrespective of their being out- or inpatients.

4.4 Costing a Health District in Burkina Faso

Table 4.26 Cost centers of CMA Nouna, 2005 [US$]

Department		Building depreciation	Equipment/ vehicles depreciation	Salaries & wages	Consumables	Technical services	Fuel	Food	Pharmaceuticals	Total
General Medicine	OPD	0	162	6,355	191					6,708
General Medicine	IPD	0	974	7,795	235					9,004
Surgery	OPD	0	421	5,901						6,322
Surgery	IPD	0	456	3,176						3,632
Gynaecology, Obstet-	OPD	428	1,680	13,969						16,077
Gynaecology, Obstet-	IPD	286	1481	8,193						9,960
Paediatrics	OPD	311	88	4,174						4,573
Paediatrics	IPD	660	385	8,736						9,781
Psychiatrics	OPD	0	207	1827						2,034
Psychiatrics	IPD	0	433	3,316						3,749
Ophthalmology	OPD	0	402	5,874						6,276
Ophthalmology	IPD	0	1362	18,258						19,620
Leprosy, TB	OPD	0	202	2,485						2,687
Leprosy, TB	IPD	0	420	3,729						4,149
ENT		51	544	3,684						4,279
Dentistry		0	3,910	11,052						14,962
Physiotherapy				1,907						1,907
Laboratory		2,166	22,950	10,582	4,245					39,943
Theatre		0	9,469	26,042						35,511
Radiology		0	13,466			4,984				18,450
Pharmacy		196	6	2,239	83				50,655	53,179
Mortuary		68	0							68
Kitchen		0	0					2,062		2,062
Laundry		0	0	450						450
Administration		449	0	6,404	1,121	19,720	4,358	0	0	32,052
Technical services		62	136	3,370	0	2,489	0	0	0	6,057
Transport		0	0	0	0	0	0	0	0	0
Electricity		41	0	0	0	19,582	0	0	0	19,623
Total Cost		4,718	59,154	159,518	5,875	46,775	4,358	2,062	50,655	333,115

Table 4.27 Cost units of CMA Nouna, 2005 [US$]

		Total cost	Cases	Cost per case	Beddays	Cost per bedday
Inpatient	General Medicine	16,244	430	37.78	1,836	8.85
	Ophthalmology	11,241	134	83.89	264	42.58
	Surgery	5,425	79	68.67	110	49.32
	Gynaecology, Obstetrics	22,743	621	36.62	807	28.18
	Leprosy, TB	4,149	-	0.00	-	0.00
	Paediatrics	12,604	154	81.85	209	60.31
	Psychiatrics	4,319	18	239.95	162	26.66
	Total inpatient cost	76,725	1,436		3,388	
	Average inpatient cost			53.43		22.65
Outpatient	General Medicine	19,076	735	25,95		
	Ophthalmology	46,638	2,662	17.52		
	Surgery	11,744	240	48.93		
	Gynaecology, Obstetrics	26,469	503	52.62		
	ENT	12,884	546	23.60		
	Leprosy, TB	10,650	473	22.52		
	Paediatrics	33,944	1,615	21.02		
	Psychiatrics	4,631	83	55.80		
	Dentistry	22,762	424	53.68		
	Total outpatient cost	188,798	7,281			
	Average outpatient cost			25.93		
Total Cost CMA		265,523				
Total Cost Pharmacy		53,082	8,717	6.09	3,388	2.58
Clearing	Eye	13,597				
	Research	912				
Total cost		333,115				

The total cost per outpatient is 25.93 US$ and the total cost per inpatient is 53.43 US$. Compared with other hospitals in developing countries these figures are extremely high. Seeing that the hospital has 82% fixed cost, it is no surprise that those departments have lower unit cost that are better utilized. *The lower the occupancy, the higher is the cost per service unit.* If we deduct the pharmaceuticals, 97% of the total costs are fixed. This is an amazingly high amount, indicating again that the hospital is strongly under-utilized.

The total income of the CMA was 77,024 US$ in the year 2005. This amount does not include about 1,000 US$ income from eye patients from outside the district. The pharmacy contributed 45,941 US$, the inpatient and outpatient department 32,156 US$. The cost recovery rate is very small. Even the CMA pharmacy – which should fully recover all cost under the Bamako initiative – closed the books of 2005 with a deficit of 7,141 US$. The revenues of 45,941 US$ could not even recover the variable cost (50,666 US$). Assuming that the ministry provides the difference between revenues and cost, the government grant for the CMA Nouna of the year 2005 was some 256,091 US$. This amount is not fully correct as some major input was provided by Christophel Blinden Mission. However, the documentation does not allow the assessment of the value of this donation.

4.4 Costing a Health District in Burkina Faso

Table 4.28 Income of CMA Nouna, 2005 [US$]

Department	Outpatients		Inpatients	
	Income	Cost Recovery [%]	Income	Cost Recovery [%]
General Medicine	1,627	9%	4,267	26%
Ophthalmology	6,001	13%	2,774	25%
Surgery	531	5%	676	12%
Gynaecology, Obstetrics	1,349	5%	5,367	24%
ENT	1,208	9%		
Leprosy, TB	1,047	10%	0	-
Paediatrics	3,575	11%	1,315	10%
Psychiatrics	183	4%	218	5%
Dentistry	938	4%		
Total	16,463	9%	15,613	19%
Pharmacy	45,941 (87%)			
Total	77,024 (24%)			

4.4.2.3 Total District Cost

Table 4.29 shows the actual total cost of providing western health care services in Nouna health district in the year 2005. *The cost of dispensary care per capita are 2.80 US$. The respective figures for hospital care and district administration are 1.14 US$ and 0.06 US$ so that the total cost of western health care service per capita are 4.00 US$.*

Table 4.29 Total cost of health care in Nouna Health District, 2005 [US$]

Institution	Cost category	Cost		
CSPS	Overheads	80,429		
	Consultation	111,835		
	Maternity	69,279		
	Immunisation	367,194	628,737	
	Pharmacy		153,662	782,399
CMA	Inpatient	76,725		
	Outpatient	188,798	265,523	
	Pharmacy		53,082	318,605
District Administration				16,159
Total cost				1,117,163

The cost of the district administration mainly consist of personnel (8,553 US$) and depreciation for buildings (2,092 US$) and equipment (5,484 US$). It is quite striking that no running expenditure is documented. There are three possibilities for this finding. Firstly, the documentation is wrong. Secondly, some services are paid for by the Centre de Recherche en Santé. Thirdly, the district administration is not providing the services it is supposed to do.

Compared with other findings (section 4.2) and the literature [143, 267] *the cost of health care in the district are quite low*. However, one should not forget that only 1436 inpatients with 3,0388 beddays and 72,154 outpatients (CMA and CSPS) were treated. Consequently, the total funds of about 1.1 million US$ were utilized by a minority of the population. This calls for further analysis of the possibilities to increase the occupancy of the institutions in order to cover the entire population.

4.4.2.4 Capacity

The actual costs give a fair picture of the monetary value of the resources consumed to produce the service units rendered in the year 2005. However, this figure cannot answer the question of how high the costs would have been if more or less patients had been treated. As stated above, Sauerborn et al. [268] compared the average annual number of CSPS-contacts of an individual with the results of a physical examination of members of the household survey [139]. They demonstrated that on average the actual demand was only 44% of the medically correct need for medical treatment. This under-utilization of health care in Nouna health district was also demonstrated by recent publications of Su et al. [103] and Mugisha et al. [259, 269]. Assuming that the catchment population would be able to utilize CSPS services according to their medical needs, the number of consultations (incl. minor nursing care) with the CSPS would increase by 127% (=100/44-1) to cover those medical needs.

Furthermore, we can also assume that the number of deliveries attended by CSPS is lower than the actual need. Assuming a birth rate of 4.2% [270], we would expect some 11,750 deliveries in the district. It is the objective of the MoH to have all deliveries attended by professional midwives in dispensaries or hospitals. In the year 2005, 9,227 deliveries were professionally attended. Therefore, full coverage would mean an increase of the number of deliveries at CSPS by 27% (11,750/9,227-1).

Assuming that this additional demand for consultation and deliveries is proportionally distributed among the existing health centres, Table 4.30 shows the number of consultations and deliveries after adjustment (consultations with factor 2.27, deliveries with factor 1.27). If an average consultation takes 12 minutes, a facility has a capacity of 10,000 consultations a year (5 consultation per hour • 8 hours per day • 250 working days per year). Thus, merely Djibasso would come to its capacity limit if the medical needs were satisfied. Furthermore, assuming that one mid-wife can attend a maximum of 4 deliveries a day, a CSPS has a maximum capacity of 1,460 deliveries p.a. (4 deliveries per day • 365 days per year).[9] Thus, the increase to cover all deliveries in modern facilities does not bring the CSPS to their capacity limit. This statement is also true if we consider the fact that Yevedougou was inaugurated in May whereas Gassingo and Goni were opened in June 2005. Even doubling their service load after adjustment would not bring them close to their capacity limits.

---

[9] Deliveries cannot be limited to working-days.

4.4 Costing a Health District in Burkina Faso

Table 4.30   Consultations and deliveries after adjustment

Facility	Consultations		Deliveries	
	Actual	Adjusted	Actual	Adjusted
Bagala	976	2,216	391	497
Barani	3,356	7,618	182	231
Berma	3,018	6,851	237	301
Bomborokuy	4,216	9,570	468	594
Borekuy	1,559	3,539	270	343
Bourasso	3,909	8,873	249	316
Dara	1,398	3,173	406	516
Dembo	2,410	5,471	277	352
Djibasso	4,654	10,565	274	348
Dokuy	1,247	2,831	397	504
Doumbala	2,077	4,715	318	404
Gassingo	919	2,086	519	659
Goni	1,067	2,422	789	1,002
Ira	2,826	6,415	897	1,139
Kienekuy	1,904	4,322	185	235
Konankoira	1,445	3,280	413	525
Konkuy Koro	1,511	3,430	322	409
Koro	1,612	3,659	345	438
Lekuy	1,744	3,959	761	966
Nian	2,854	6,479	779	989
Nouna	3,916	8,889	214	272
Sono	1,452	3,296	378	480
Toni	2,972	6,746	40	51
Werebere	1,779	4,038	42	53
Yevedougou	825	1,873	74	94

According to national vaccination figures from UNICEF's routine information system of the coverage of 1-year-old children immunized in 2004, Burkina Faso has satisfactory values with BCG (99%), DPT1 (99%), DPT3 (88%), Polio (83%) and measles (78%) [271]. It cannot be assumed that these figures could be strongly increased, so that additional costs cannot be calculated. In addition, additional immunisation coverage would most likely be refinanced by UNICEF or other international donor organisations. Consequently, we will not consider it here.

Assuming that the fees per patient remain stable and the number of consultations and deliveries is increased by 127% respectively 27%, Table 4.31 shows the cost and cost recovery after the adjustment. If we assume that the clients are not able to pay any additional fees, the government subsidy of Nouna Health District will have to increase by 157,132 US$ or 6,285 US$ per CSPS. This implies an increase of the government subsidy by 28% but it can cover the cost of an increase of consultations by 127% and of deliveries by 27% as the majority of cost are fixed! *If we assume that the revenues from consultation and deliveries increase proportionally to the number of clients, the additional grant would have to be only 137,999 US$.* If the patients are also able and willing to pay for the increased demand for pharmaceuticals proportionally, i.e., if the rules of the Bamako initiative are thoroughly followed, the government grant could even be reduced as the pharmacies sell the drugs above their purchasing price. However, this scenario is rather unrealistic because the high price elasticity of demand is one reason why patients cannot seek health care [101].

Table 4.31   Cost and cost recovery in CSPS after adjustment [US$]

Facility	Total cost (adj.)	Additional government grant, no additional revenues from fees	Additional government grant, additional revenues from fees for consultation and deliveries	Additional government grant, all revenues from fees increase proportionally
Bagala	20,987	2,098	1,790	-310
Barani	64,069	9,859	7,783	-5,914
Berma	46,054	9,640	8,584	-6,790
Bomborokuy	60,508	18,336	17,264	-7,346
Borekuy	27,011	4,654	4,197	-2,334
Bourasso	31,419	5,622	4,687	-4,090
Dara	29,459	5,834	5,322	-2,177
Dembo	44,748	10,193	9,325	-4,611
Djibasso	124,058	23,076	21,809	-8,783
Dokuy	38,730	5,090	4,703	-1,875
Doumbala	33,993	4,538	3,900	-4,395
Gassingo	13,295	3,046	2,830	-1,049
Goni	13,480	3,191	2,929	-1,211
Ira	45,609	5,608	4,610	-3,505
Kienekuy	29,908	4,598	3,978	-2,499
Konankoira	26,194	3,420	2,941	-2,289
Konkuy Koro	26,120	3,189	2,757	-3,305
Koro	31,889	3,847	3,259	-2,478
Lekuy	26,476	2,392	1,846	-1,019
Nian	42,910	11,057	10,054	-5,595
Nouna	49,534	1,812	-592	-2,907
Sono	38,543	5,843	5,324	-1,266
Toni	25,701	2,109	1,329	-1,311
Werebere	32,401	5,568	5,049	-3,458
Yevedougou	15,823	2,511	2,322	-1,619
Total	938,918	157,132	137,999	-82,136
Average	37,557	6,285	5,520	-3,285

The hospital in Nouna had a capacity of 85 beds, the occupancy rate was 11.8% (9.95 occupied beds!) and the average length of stay was 2.37 days in the year 2005. As

4.4 Costing a Health District in Burkina Faso

stated before, one bed per 1,000 inhabitants, an average length of stay of seven days and an occupancy rate of 85% are international standards [143]. Thus, a district population of 279,730 would require a hospital of about 280 beds. If we assume that the average length of stay remains as it was in 2005, a hospital with 95 beds would be sufficient. As stated before, Sauerborn et al. found that the average medical need for major operations was 0.03 visits p.c. p.a. With an average length of stay of 2.37 days this would call for a surgical department of 54 beds and with an average length of stay of 7 days for a surgical department of 171 beds.

The extremely low occupancy rate is caused by three factors. Firstly, a part of the population lives too far away from the hospital and cannot reach it (see section 5.1.2). Secondly, the medical risk of admission does not lead to a demand of the same rate. Assuming a risk of admission of 0.044 p.c. p.a. (see section 4.4.1) one would expect a workload of 12,308 admission per year in the total district. However, quality, distance, priority and price filters lead to a demand which is merely 13% of the medical need. Thirdly, even those patients who come to the hospital stay there only for a short time. *Again we can state that Nouna CMA is not fulfilling its function as a district hospital.*

If we assume that the number of outpatients remains stable and the number of inpatients increases to an occupancy of 85% of the current capacity, the total cost increase from 333,115 US$ to 438,037US$. However, the increase of variable cost of the core CMA without the pharmacy would be 49,725 US$, whereas the increase of cost of the pharmacy would be 55,187 US$. Thus, the main increase occurs in the pharmacy. The Bamako initiative assumes that patients are able to pay for drugs so that merely 49,725 US$ would have to be spent additionally to increase the occupancy to 85%.

This calculation assumes that the capacity is sufficient to treat all inpatients if the hospital is fully occupied. This can be assumed as the staffing (see Table 4.25) is calculated for a 85-bed hospital.

In a nut-shell: *Costing of health care services in developing countries gives deeper insights into the monetary value of resources consumed to produce these services. The actual costs of the entire institution or district, of the cost center and of the service units allow conclusions about efficiency, sustainability and quality. The comparison between income and expenditure helps to assess the viability of the institution and the population's hardship to pay for these services.* However, knowing these facts is usually not sufficient to gear policy-making and further calculations must follow. The next section exemplifies the utilisation of costing data for decision-making.

5 Utilizing Costing Studies

In the second chapter of this booklet we argued that costing of health services is a prerequisite for an equitable, sustainable and efficient health care system. The third and fourth chapter presented the methodology and some results of costing studies which we undertook under the condition of incomplete original documentation. Finally, we would like to demonstrate how this information can be used to safeguard the provision of sufficient resources, efficient resource allocation, equal access of the poor and sustainability.

This chapter consists of four sections. In the first section we calculate the budget required to finance a district health care system. The calculation is based on the assumption that the entire population is covered at a certain level of quality. The health care structure and in particular the allocation of funds is considered as a constraint and is not subject of decision. This might reflect the reality in most health care districts.

In the second section the optimum allocation of given resources to different health care services is calculated. It is based on a linear programme and computes the budget given to different institutions and services. On the level of the health district this approach might be difficult, but on a national level it is feasible.

In the third section we calculate the premium of a community based health insurance subject to certain assumptions. The rationale behind this calculation is the supposition that the ability to pay is low for poor people in developing countries [101, 103, 104] and the price elasticity of demand is rather high [264, 272]. Consequently, a health insurance can increase the affordability of health services and thus contributes to the achievement of equitable health care services. However, this is only true if the insurance is viable itself. Therefore, the analysis presents the break-even point of the health insurance premium where viability of the insurance and affordability for the insured find a compromise.

Finally, the last section demonstrates the conditions of inter-temporal equity. Based on a non-linear programme we provide an insight into the rationale of sustainability, thus opening the discussion platform for other studies, for instance for sociological research on time preference rates in developing countries.

In all four sections our arguments are based on the costing studies presented in the fourth chapter.

5.1 Estimating Standard Costs

One of the most important duties of a health economist is the determination of the resources and the computation of the cost of resources required for a planning unit in order to maintain an agreed-on standard. Such a decision making unit can be a health care institution, a health district, a disease control programme, a region, or an entire nation. In the following we calculate the standard costs of two health districts based on the actual cost in Tanzania and Burkina Faso. The model includes variables for the most important prices (e.g. salaries) and quantities (e.g. minimum staffing) so that it can be adapted to other situations.

The computation faces two major problems: First we have to determine the cost per institution at a given work-load, and second we have to determine the number of institutions necessary to cover the entire population with certain assumptions of accessibility and acceptable maximum distances. The model assumes that each institution is technically efficient, i.e., the quality of services provided fulfils at least a minimum standard and no resources are wasted.

The total costs per institution at a given workload are

$TC_i = CF_i + SF_i(d_i) + d_i \cdot \bar{c}_i$, with

TC_i	Total costs of health care institution i
CF_i	Fixed costs of health care institution i
SF_i	Step-fixed costs of health care institution i at a given demand of d_i
d_i	Service units rendered at health care institution i
$\bar{c}_i$	Average variable costs per service unit

Under normal conditions in developing countries, the depreciation and maintenance charges for buildings and equipment of the health care institutions are fixed costs. Likewise, the costs of the management of the institutions are fixed. Salaries and wages are step-fixed. For instance, if we assume that a nurse or medical assistant needs 10 minutes on average, one member of staff has a capacity of 48 consultations per day or about 10,000 consultations a year. If the number of consultations goes beyond this figure, the dispensary will require a second person. The variable costs per service unit comprise drugs and other consumables as well as other proportional overheads (e.g. cost of a patient file).

Secondly, the number of health care units of different levels has to be determined. Under the condition of a resource poor country it can be assumed that the need for health care services of a particular institution is proportional to the population living in its catchment area. Consequently, the calculation of the catchment population becomes crucial for the calculation of health care costs. For our analysis we assume that one district hospital is situated in the centre of the district and can cover the entire population, i.e., everybody in the district lives within a distance acceptable for him. The number of beds is proportional to the population of the district. The number of dispensaries is a function of the acceptable distance, the size of the district and the population density. Thus, the calculation of the catchment area and the costs of the health care district strongly depend on the calculation of the number and capacity of dispensaries necessary to cover the population.

5.1 Estimating Standard Costs

The next sub-sections will calculate the number of health care units, the resources required and the costs of these resources. This is done in two alternative ways. Firstly, we assume a plainly distributed population, i.e., there are no villages, but everybody lives on his little farm. This is, for instance, the case in some areas of Tanzania. Secondly, we assume a population pattern with villages and wide areas without any population as it is in Nouna health district.

5.1.1 Costing a Pattern Health District in Tanzania

A health district must be small enough to allow the participation of the local population and big enough to safeguard efficient planning and controlling of all curative, preventive and health promotion activities [273]. The WHO Global Programme Committee defines "a district health system based on primary health care is a more or less self-contained segment of the national health system. It comprises first and foremost a well-defined population, living within a clearly delineated administrative and geographic area, whether urban or rural" [274]. Consequently, providing accessible and affordable health care for the entire population irrespective of their place of living is a crucial element of the district health care system.

The number of health care units in a health district depends on the population density and on the maximum distance people are able or willing to travel to this institution. If the population is homogenously distributed, the entire area can be covered by a number of catchment areas equal in size and in the shape of hexagons (Figure 5.1).

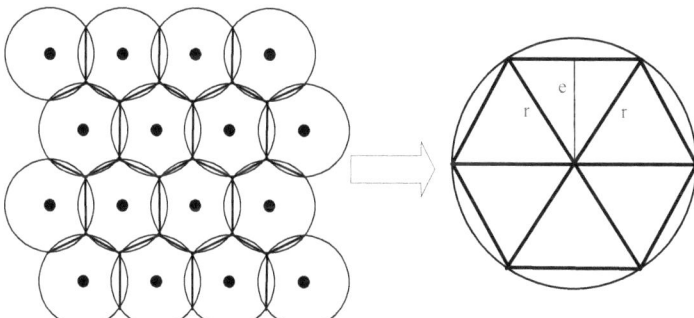

Figure 5.1 Hexagons as ideal catchment areas

Each hexagon has an area of $3 \cdot r^2 \cdot sin(60)$, whereas r denotes the maximum distance a person is willing to travel to this institution. Thus, we receive:

$$Catch_l = 3 \cdot r_l^2 \cdot \sin(60)$$

$$num_l = Max\left[1; round\left\{\frac{Catch_3}{Catch_l}\right\}\right]$$

$$Pop_l = \frac{pop\_d \cdot Catch_3}{num_l}$$

$$con = Pop_1 \cdot dem_1$$

$$b_l = Pop_l \cdot bed\_dens_l$$

$$b\_day_l = 0.85 \cdot b_l \cdot 365$$

$Catch_l$	Catchment area [km^2] of a health care institution of level l, l=1..3
l	Level of health care: l=1: dispensary; l=2: health centre; l=3: hospital
r_l	Maximum distance for a health care institution of level l, l=1..3
num_l	Number of health care institutions of level l in the district, l=1..3
Pop_l	Catchment population of a health care institution of level l, l=1..3
pop_d	Population density [inhabitants/km^2]
bed_dens_l	Beds required per capita of a health care institution on level l, l=2,3
dem_l	Demand per capita for service units of level l, l=1..3
b_day_l	Number of beddays in a health care institution on level l, l=2..3
b_l	Beds of a health care institution on level l, l=2..3
con	Number of contacts with a dispensary

Tanzania, for instance, has an area of 942,799 km^2. In the year of the study (see section 4.1) there were 175 non-private general hospitals that served (at least) in the function of a primary hospital. If they were located in order to guarantee equal maximum travelling distances, the maximum distance (r) would be 45.54 km with an average distance of 26.29 km. The average distance between two *hospitals* would be 78.88 km. As most patients still approach the hospital without a vehicle, a maximum distance of 12 hours walking (40-50 km) seems to be acceptable.

The district health plan allocates a number of health centres to the district hospital. According to our experience, most people are not willing to walk more than 4 hours to a *health centre* and not more than 2 hours to a *dispensary*. Consequently, the number of health centres (and dispensaries) can be calculated by dividing the area of the health district by the catchment area of each health centre (and dispensary) subject to the maximum distance.

Table 5.1 shows the basic district parameters representative for a pattern district in Tanzania. Making used of these constants we can calculate the catchment areas and the number of institutions. A health district with a maximum distance of 40 km has an area of 4,156.92 km^2. Assuming a population density of 38.5 inhabitants per km^2, the district has a population of 160,041. Thus, the hospital needs a capacity of 160 beds for

5.1 Estimating Standard Costs

7.091 admissions (admission risk: 0.044 p.c. p.a.), and with an average length of stay of 7 days 49.640 beddays.

Table 5.1 Costing model: basic district parameters

Parameter	District	Dispensary	Health Centre	Hospital
Maximum distance (r_l)		10 km	16 km	40 km
Population density (pop_d)	38.5 person/km^2			
Bed density (bed_dens_l)			0.8 beds/1000 inhabitants	1 bed/1000 inhabitants
Average length of stay			3 days	7 days
Demand (dem_3)		1 contact p.c. p.a.		
Standard occupancy			85%	85%

Source: [275]

The number of health centres is determined as the quotient of the entire district area and the catchment area of one health centre at a given maximum distance of 16 km (665.11 km^2). With this population density, we receive a need for 6 health centres with a catchment population of 26,674 inhabitants each. With the given risk of admission, each health centre has 2,214 admissions annually and 6,642 beddays provided by 21 beds per health centre.

16 dispensaries can cover the entire district at a maximum walking distance of 10 km. With the given population density, each dispensary has a catchment population of 10,003 inhabitants, i.e., each dispensary has 10,004 patient contacts every year.

It is obvious that this approach is rather rough. However, it gives a first idea of the number of health care institutions needed and the resources required. In Tanzania it is a good proxy for district planners.

Table 5.2 shows the staffing standards in Tanzania in 1996. The number of staff depends on the service units (beddays, beds, outpatient contacts, admissions), but a certain minimum standard always has to be guaranteed (for instance not less than two physicians per hospital irrespective of its number of beds). Consequently, the number of staff of category s in a health care institution on level l is calculated as

$$St_{s,l} = S\_Min_{s,l} + Max\left[0; Trunc\left\{SU_{s,l} / N_{s,l} - S\_Min_{s,l}\right\}\right]$$

$$Sal_l = \sum_{s=1}^{7} basic\_S_{s,l} \cdot St_{s,l}$$

$St_{s,l}$ Number of staff of category s on level l, s=1..7, l=1..3

s   s=1: medical officers; s=2: clinic officers; s=3: nursing officer; s=4: trained nurse; s=5: paramedicals; s=6: administrative staff; s=7: other staff

$S\_Min_{s,l}$	Minimum of staff of category s on level l, s=1..7, l=1..3
$SU_{s,l}$	Number of service units on level l relevant for staff category s, s=1..7, l=1..3
$N_{s,l}$	Norm of service units per member of staff of category s on level l, s=1..7, l=1..3
Sal_l	Total salary for a health care institution on level l, l=1..3
$basic\_S_{s,l}$	Salary of one member of staff of category s on level l, s=1..7, l=1..3

It is obvious that the number of staff categories and levels of health care can be altered for different countries and situations. For the basic scenario we receive a demand for hospital staff of 120 with annual costs of 120,320 US$. This is equivalent to personnel costs of 2.08 US$ per bedday or 14.57 US$ per admission. The number of personnel in health centres is 16 per unit with annual cost of 15,360 US$. Consequently, the cost per patient is 6.94 US$ and the cost per beddays 2.31 US$. We need 5 members of staff per dispensary and annual resources of 4,800 US$ for salaries and wages. The personnel cost per contact run to 0.48 US$. We will discuss some scenarios later.

Table 5.2 Staffing standards

Parameter	Salary p.a. [US$] ($basic_S_{s,l}$)	Dispensary ($N_{s,1}$; $S\_Min_{s,1}$)	Health Centre ($N_{s,2}$; $S\_Min_{s,2}$)	Hospital ($N_{s,3}$; $S\_Min_{s,3}$)
Medical officers (physicians)	1800	-	-	40 beds/medical officer; Minimum: 2
Clinical officers (medical assistants)	1200	-	20 beds/clinical officer; Minimum: 3	15 beds/clinical officer; Minimum: 4
Nursing Officer (A-Nurse)	1200	10,000 contacts/nursing officer; Minimum: 1	20 beds/nursing officer; Minimum: 1	15 beds/nursing officer; Minimum: 4
Trained Nurse (B-Nurse)	720	5,000 contacts/trained nurse; Minimum: 2	6 beds/trained nurse; Minimum: 2	4 beds/trained nurse; Minimum: 12
Paramedicals	600	15,000 contacts/paramedical; Minimum: 1	50 beds/paramedical; Minimum: 2	60 beds/paramedical; Minimum: 6
Administration	960	15,000 contacts/admin. staff; Minimum: 1	400 admissions/admin. staff; Minimum: 2	400 admissions/admin. staff; Minimum: 8
Other staff	600	-	200 beddays/other staff; Minimum: 2	1500 beddays/other staff; Minimum: 10;

5.1 Estimating Standard Costs

Furthermore, we distinguish different categories of the size of institutions to model buildings, equipment and overheads and develop thresholds for step-fixed costs. Hospitals are divided into three strata. Small hospitals (< 100 beds), medium-sized hospitals (100..199 beds) and big hospitals (> 199 beds) have a different demand for buildings, equipment and general services which cannot be linearised. The same is true for health centres (small: < 20 beds; 20..39 beds; > 39 beds). For the buildings of dispensaries we distinguish small, medium and big dispensaries (< 7500 contacts; 7500..12499 contacts; >12499 contacts), whereas we just divide between big and small (< 10000 contacts, > 9999 contacts) for the equipment. The initial costs and the depreciation period depend on the quality of buildings and equipment, i.e., hospitals, health centres and dispensaries might have different standards. Table 5.3, Table 5.4 and Table 5.5 show the basic parameters.

Table 5.3   Building standards

	Fixed space [m^2] ($FF_{l,z}$)	Space per bed [m^2] (Fv_l)	Building costs [US\$/m^2] (IC_l)	Depreciation period [years] (bd_l)	Maintenance (bm_l)
Small hospital	400	12	250	25	5% of original value
Medium hospital	600				
Big hospital	800				
Small Health Centre	200	8	200	25	5% of original value
Medium Health Centre	250				
Big Health Centre	280				
Small Dispensary	200	-	150	15	5% of original value
Medium Dispensary	250				
Big Dispensary	280				

Table 5.4 Equipment and overheads standards

	Minimum equipment [US$] ($EF_{l,z}$)	Additional equipment per service unit (Ev_l)	Depreciation period [years] (ed_l)	Maintenance (em_l)	Minimum overheads [US$] ($OF_{l,z}$)	Additional overheads per service unit [US$] ($Ov_{l,z}$)
Small hospital	50,000	1000 US$ per bed	8	5% of original value	10,000	0.10 US$ per bedday
Medium hospital	75,000				12,000	
Big hospital	90,000				14,000	
Small Health Centre	15,000	500 US$ per bed	8	5% of original value	2,000	0.10 US$ per bedday
Medium Health Centre	20,000				2,500	
Big Health Centre	23,000				2,800	
Small Dispensary	10,000	-	8	5% of original value	800	0.10 US$ per contact
Big Dispensary	12,500					

Table 5.5 Materials and transport standards

Parameter	Dispensary	Health Centre	Hospital
Materials ($drug_l$)	0.35 US$ per contact	0.60 US$ per bedday	1.30 US$ per bedday
Minimum number of vehicles (VF_l)	-	1	1
Additional number of vehicles (Vv_l)	-	1 per 100 beds	1 per 100 beds
Initial value of vehicle (IV_l)	-	30,000 US$	50,000 US$
Depreciation period (vd_l)	-	5	5 years
Maintenance (vm_l)	-	10% of original value	5% of original value

Thus, the building depreciation and standard building maintenance p.a. are calculated as

$$B\_D_l = \frac{IC_{l,z}}{bd_l} \cdot \{FF_{l,z} + b_l \cdot Fv_l\}$$

$$B\_M_l = bm_l \cdot IC_{l,z} \cdot \{FF_{l,z} + b_l \cdot Fv_l\}$$

5.1 Estimating Standard Costs

B_D_l Building depreciation p.a. on level l [US$], l=1..3

B_M_l Standard building maintenance of a health care institution on level l, l=1..3

bd_l Building depreciation period [years] in a health care institution on level l, l=1..3

$FF_{l,z}$ Fixed space [m²] of a health care institution on level l and capacity category z, l=1..3, z=1..3

Fv_l Variable space [m²] per service unit of a health care institution on level l, l=1..3

IC_l Building costs [US$] per m² in a health care institution on level l, l=1..3

bm_l Standard building maintenance rate in a health care institution on level l, l=1..3

with

$$z = \begin{cases} 1 & if \quad (b_3 \leq 99) \vee (19 \leq b_2) \vee (con \leq 7499) \\ 2 & if \quad (100 \leq b_3 \leq 199) \vee (20 \leq b_2 \leq 39) \vee (7500 \leq con \leq 12499) \\ 3 & if \quad (b_3 \geq 200) \vee (b_2 \geq 40) \vee (con \geq 12500) \end{cases}$$

The equipment cost and the other cost are calculated as

$$E\_D_l = \begin{cases} \dfrac{EF_{l,z} + b_l \cdot Ev_l}{ed_l} & if \quad l = 2,3 \\ \dfrac{EF_{3,z}}{ed_3} & if \quad l = 1 \end{cases}$$

$$E\_M_l = \begin{cases} em_l \cdot EF_{l,z} + b_l \cdot Ev_l & if \quad l = 2,3 \\ em_3 \cdot EF_{3,z} & if \quad l = 1 \end{cases}$$

$$O\_T_l = \begin{cases} OF_{l,z} + b\_day_l \cdot Ov_l & if \quad l = 2,3 \\ OF_{3,z} + con \cdot Ov_3 & if \quad l = 1 \end{cases}$$

E_D_l Equipment depreciation p.a. on level l [US$], l=1..3

E_M_l Standard equipment maintenance of a health care institution on level l, l=1..3

ed_l Equipment depreciation period [years] in a health care institution on level l, l=1..3

$EF_{l,z}$ Minimum equipment [US$] of a health care institution on level l and capacity category z, l=1..3, z=1..3

Ev_l Additional equipment [US$] per service unit of a health care institution on level l, l=1..3

O_T_l Other costs [US$] in a health care institution on level l, l=1..3

$OF_{l,z}$ Minimum overheads [US$] of a health care institution on level l and capacity category z, l=1..3, z=1..3

$Ov_{l,z}$	Additional overheads per service unit [US$] of a health care institution on level l and capacity category z, l=1..3, z=1..3
em_l	Standard equipment maintenance rate in a health care institution on level l, l=1..3

Differing from above the definition of z for equipment calculations is

$$z = \begin{cases} 1 & if \quad (b_3 \leq 99) \vee (19 \leq b_2) \vee (con \leq 9999) \\ 2 & if \quad (100 \leq b_3 \leq 199) \vee (20 \leq b_2 \leq 39) \vee (10000 \leq con) \\ 3 & if \quad (b_3 \geq 200) \vee (b_2 \geq 40) \end{cases}$$

The transport and materials costs are calculated as

$$V\_D_l = \begin{cases} IV_l \cdot \dfrac{VF_l + trunc(b_l \cdot Vv_l)}{vd_l} & if \quad l = 2,3 \\ 0 & if \quad l = 1 \end{cases}$$

$$V\_M_l = \begin{cases} ev_l \cdot IV_l \cdot (VF_l + trunc(b_l \cdot Vv_l)) & if \quad l = 2,3 \\ 0 & if \quad l = 1 \end{cases}$$

$$C\_M_l = \begin{cases} b\_day_l \cdot drug_l & if \quad l = 2,3 \\ con \cdot drug_l & if \quad l = 1 \end{cases}$$

C_M_l	Material costs [US$] in a health care institution on level l, l=1..3
V_D_l	Vehicle depreciation [US$] in a health care institution on level l, l=2..3
V_M_l	Standard vehicle maintenance of a health care institution on level l, l=2..3
$drug_l$	Material cost [US$] per service unit in a health care institution on level l, l=2..3
VF_l	Minimum number of vehicles in a health care institution on level l, l=2..3
Vv_l	Additional number of vehicles per bed in a health care institution on level l, l=2..3
IV_l	Initial value of vehicle [US$] in a health care institution on level l, l=2..3
vd_l	Depreciation period [years] of vehicles in a health care institution on level l, l=2..3
vm_l	Standard vehicle maintenance rate in a health care institution on level l, l=2..3

With the help of these parameters we can calculate the total costs of the health care district and per service unit.

$$Total\_C = \sum_{l=1}^{3} num_l \cdot \begin{pmatrix} Sal_l + B\_D_l + B\_M_l + E\_D_l + E\_M_l \\ + O\_T_l + D\_M_l + O\_T_l + C\_M_l + V\_D_l + V\_M_l \end{pmatrix}$$

$$CPC = \frac{Total\_C}{Pop_3}$$

5.1 Estimating Standard Costs

Total_C   Total costs of health care [US$] in the district
CPC   Cost per capita [US$] in the district

Table 5.6 shows the results for this basic scenario based on the data of Table 4.2, Table 4.4, Table 4.7 and Table 4.8 (section 4.1). The proposed staffing, building, equipment and materials standard can be reached with an input of 5.15 US$ in a district with a population density of 38.5 inhabitants per km^2 and with the given basic costs (e.g. 1,800 US$ per medical officer p.a.). As Figure 5.2 demonstrates, the majority of these costs is formed by salaries and wages as well as drugs (materials). However, the standard costs of the other categories are about 50% of the total costs. If a health district only provides for actual running expenditure (personnel, materials, transport running expenditure and other costs), 3.11 US$ would be sufficient, i.e., 40% of the total costs are not financed. In a long run, the structure is used up so that the health care provision is not structurally sustainable.

Table 5.6   *District costs: basic scenario [US$]*

Cost category	Dispensaries	Health Centres	Hospital	Total district	Cost per inhabitant
Personnel	76,800	92,160	103,320	272,280	1.70
Materials	56,017	23,911	59,568	139,496	0.87
Building depreciation	40,000	20,064	25,200	85,264	0.53
Building maintenance	30,000	25,080	31,500	86,580	0.54
Equipment depreciation	25,000	22,875	29,375	77,250	0.48
Equipment maintenance	10,000	9,150	11,750	30,900	0.19
Transport capital exp.	0	36,000	10,000	46,000	0.29
Transport running expenditure	0	18,000	5,000	23,000	0.14
Other costs	28,805	18,985	14,964	62,754	0.39
Total	266,622	266,225	290,677	823,524	5.15
%	32%	32%	35%	100%	

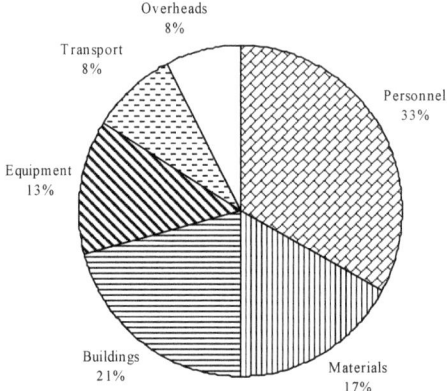

Figure 5.2   Cost categories: basic scenario

It is worthwhile noting that this scenario suggests an almost equal distribution of funds to dispensaries, health centres and hospitals. In reality, hospitals still receive the lion share of district health care budgets. This leads to an inefficient allocation of health care resources and to lower accessibility to health services.

Figure 5.3 shows the results of a scenario with different population densities. It is obvious that the resources required per inhabitant to safeguard the standards defined above strongly depend on the population density. As we have incorporated step-fixed costs, the cost curves are not perfectly monotonous. The curves underline a basic ethical conflict which we discussed in the second chapter: A health care district with a lower population will require a higher health care budget per capita to provide the same accessibility and service quality as a district with a higher population density. Consequently, *equity and equality are in conflict.* Equality ("everybody gets the same") calls for the same input to different districts, whereas equity of needs calls for the same service level for everybody, even if this means that some might receive higher resources. This conflict has to be addressed, but it cannot be completely solved.

Finally, Figure 5.4 demonstrates some results of other simulations. Scenario "Standard" was described above and represents the data from the study of 1996/97. "PD20" assumes a population density of 20 inhabitants per km^2. "PD100" assumes a population density of 100 inhabitants per km^2. "MD50" assumes a maximum walking distance to a hospital of 50 km, whereas "MD30" assumes a distance of 30 km. "SAL2" assumes double salaries, and "MD2" simulates doubled salaries for medical officers only. T2007 proposes salary and material standards as they might be applicable to Tanzania in the year 2007 (see Table 5.7).

5.1 Estimating Standard Costs

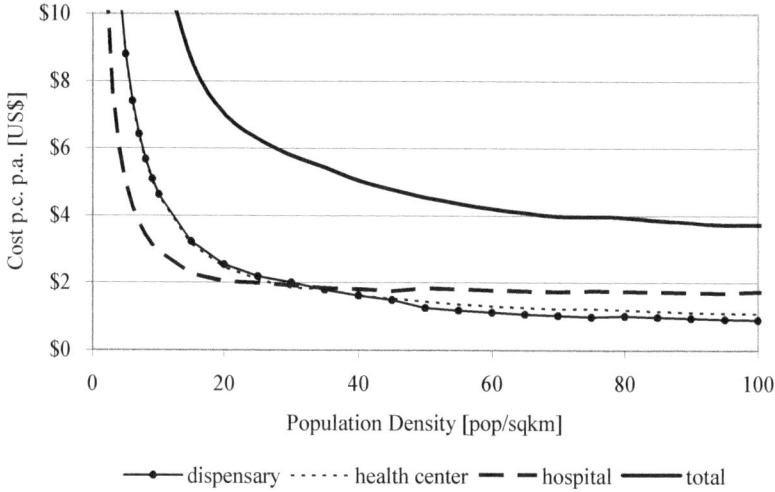

Figure 5.3 Costs and population density

Table 5.7 Scenario T2007

Parameter		Salary p.a. [US$]
Salaries	Medical officers (physicians)	7200 p.a.
	Clinical officers (medical assistants)	3600 p.a.
	Nursing Officer (A-Nurse)	3600 p.a.
	Trained Nurse (B-Nurse)	2160 p.a.
	Paramedicals	1800 p.a.
	Administration	1920 p.a.
	Other staff	1200 p.a.
Materials	Dispensary	0.70 per contact
	Health Centre	1.20 per bedday
	Hospital	2.60 per bedday
Additional Overheads	Dispensary	0.20 per contact
	Health Centre	0.20 per bedday
	Hospital	0.20 per bedday

As discussed before, a lower population density (PD20) leads to higher health care expenditure per capita, and a higher population density (PD100) induces lower unit cost. A decrease in population density of 48% increases the costs per capita by 36.5%, whereas an increase in the density of 160% leads to a decrease in costs per capita by 27.7%. Materials remain stable, as the amount does not depend on the size and occupancy of the institutions. The biggest difference is seen for vehicle costs (depreciation and maintenance). A hospital with 83 beds (PD20) needs one vehicle as well as a hospital with 160 beds (Standard). The 416-bed hospital (PD100) would require 4 cars according to our calculation. Thus, a reduction of the population density by 48% will result in no or only minor reduction of fixed costs, whereas an increase in the population density will lead to a moderate increase in fixed costs.

A district with a low population density will have a lower proportion of dispensary costs, whereas the hospital costs strongly contribute to the total health district costs. The scenario PD20 produces a share of dispensary costs of 36.1% and of hospital costs of 29.0%. The respective figures for the scenario Standard are 32.4 and 35.30, and for the scenario PD100 24.2 and 46.5%. This is due to the fact that the model assumes that a dispensary has rather high fixed costs, but only minor step-fixed and variable costs. Consequently, a higher workload due to an increasing population will increase the hospital costs to a higher extent than the dispensary costs.

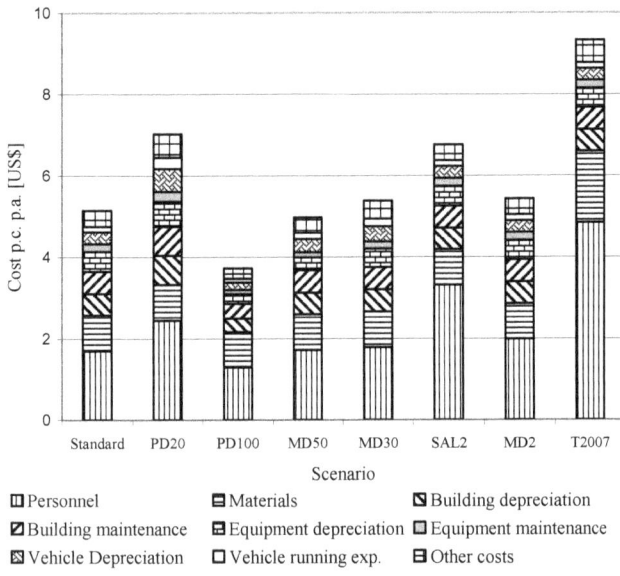

Figure 5.4   Cost per capita [US$], different scenarios

5.1 Estimating Standard Costs

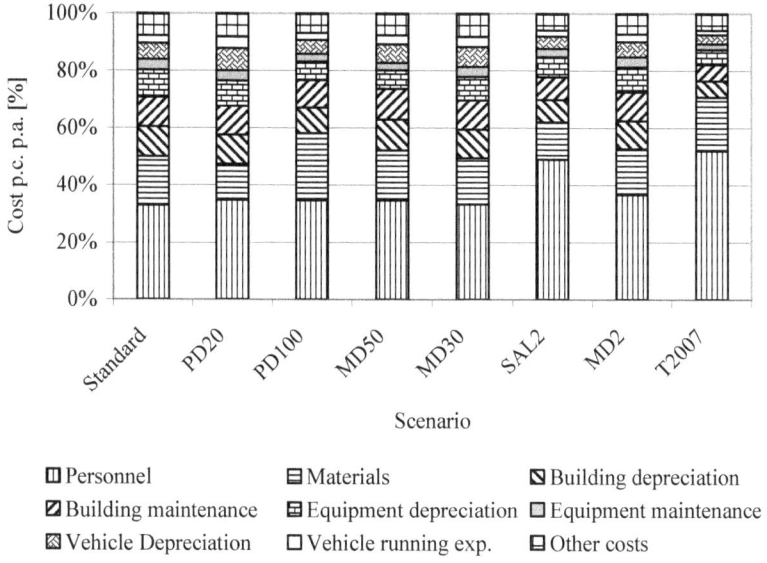

Figure 5.5 Cost per capita [%], different scenarios

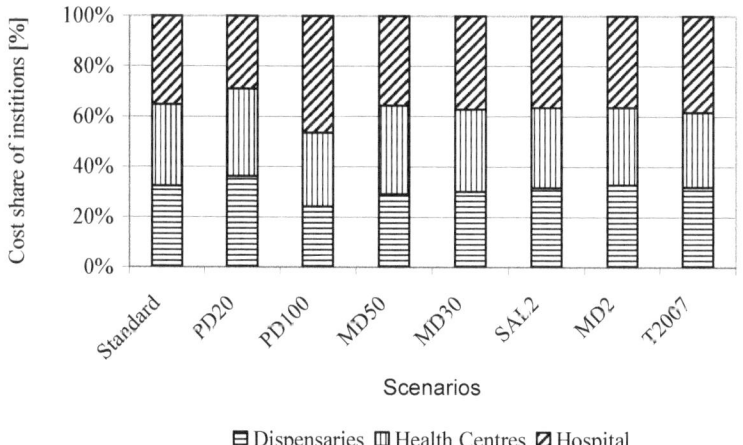

Figure 5.6 Cost share of institutions [%], different scenarios

If the maximum acceptable distance is increased, the cost per capita decreases whereas a reduction of distance leads to increasing health care expenditure per capita. As expected, *accessibility and efficiency are in a trade-off situation*. However, we should not forget here, that the health care institution costs merely present one component of the entire cost-of-illness. The household costs are at least as important and behave inversely, i.e., an increase in the maximum distance will definitely lead to higher household costs. The contradicting development of provider and household costs is a major goal conflict in health care planning.

This problem can only be overcome by a better infrastructure. Currently, the model assumes that 40 km can be covered by the population on foot within one day. If private and public transport can be improved, household and provider costs can be reduced. There are examples that building a road over a river, setting up a public transport line or simply preparing a road have a very high impact on the efficiency of the district health care system.

Changing salaries does naturally only impact the personnel costs. Their portion increases from 33% (Standard) to 49% (Double) or 37% (MD2). The salary changes stronger affect hospitals with their professional staff and a higher share of personnel costs in total costs, so that increasing salaries will also increase the portion of hospital costs in the total health district costs. The scenario MD2 must be handled with care. It leaves the impression that doubling the salaries of medical doctors does hardly have any impact. However, managerial consequences might be much more important than financial impacts: Doubling the salary of one staff category will most likely demotivate other members of staff – an aspect that is not reflected in this model.

Finally, scenario T2007 reflects the situation in a Tanzanian health district in the year 2007. The model assumes, that 9.32 US$ would be sufficient to finance institutional health care in this country. However, this amount does not include preventive services and the costs of health care administration. In chapter 5.2 we will discuss a model that includes the costs of preventive medicine and suggests, that prevention should make up for at least 33% of the total health care costs, i.e., a health district in Tanzania would require at least 14 US$ p.a. p.c.

It is obvious, that this calculation is more for insights than for numbers [276]. A health planner will have to calculate the costs for each district individually. However, the basic simulation and scenarios demonstrate that a simple spreadsheet model can be developed that gives a deep insight into standards and flow of funds. Staffing, building, equipment and accessibility standards have a major impact on the costs per capita. District health managers should be aware of these consequences and analyse them for their districts.

5.1.2 Costing a Pattern Health District in Burkina Faso

The model presented in section 5.1.1 assumed that the population is equally distributed over the entire district. This assumption is acceptable for many districts in Tanzania, but it is unacceptable for the health district of Nouna, the study-site of the costing research presented in section 4.4. The vast majority of the inhabitants of this district

5.1 Estimating Standard Costs

lives in villages, and health care institutions can only be situated in these villages. In Tanzania, dispensaries, health centres and hospitals are sometimes built without considering the existing village structure. In particular churches have frequently built their health care institutions in unsettled locations. This is not the case in Burkina Faso, so that another approach must be sought.

Figure 5.7 demonstrates the basic model. Five villages (i=1..5) with a respective population of P_i have to be covered by a set of health care institution. The model assumes that the distance from village i to village j is equal to the distance from village j to village i, an assumption which is correct for rural Burkina Faso. If the villages have the same population and only one health care facility has to be located, the problem is rather simple. If villages have a different number of inhabitants and if more than one institution can be built, the problem becomes more difficult.

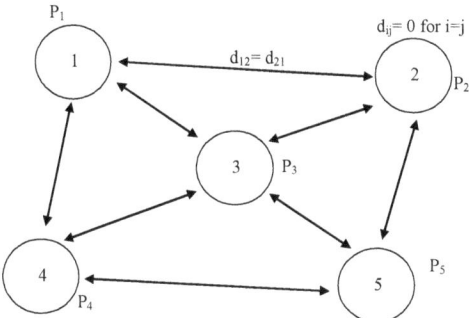

Figure 5.7   Location problem

Depending on the goal function, two types of models can be distinguished. The *covering model* tries to cover a given part of the population within a given maximum distance with as few institutions as possible. This means that the model determines the number of dispensaries and their position in the district so that all inhabitants of the district have to walk less than 10 km to reach a dispensary.

The *median model* locates a given number of health care institutions, so that the average distance to the institution is minimized. For instance, a health planner in Nouna might ask where the existing CSPS in Nouna health district should have been located in order to minimize travelling distances.

Figure 5.8 demonstrates the distribution of villages and existing dispensaries in the health district of Nouna [277] in 2005. The village distribution highly correlates with the population density. In this year, the average travel distance to a dispensary was 7 km but the maximum distance was 35 km. Each dispensary was set up for a catchment population of about 10,000 inhabitants but served a theoretical catchment population of 3,700 to 22,900 people. 8 dispensaries had a distance of less than 10 km between each other, whereas two dispensaries were 60 km away from each other.

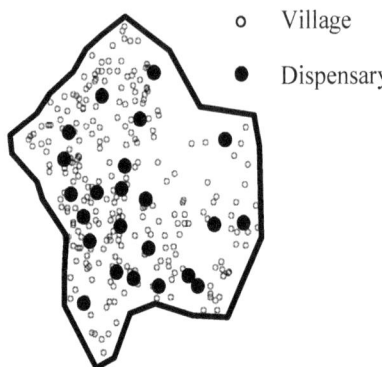

Figure 5.8   Distribution of villages and dispensaries in Nouna health district

The objective of the first model is to maximize the part of the population living within a distance of 10 km from a dispensary. Likewise we would like to minimize the distance to a dispensary of that part of the population living outside this radius. We assume that dispensaries can only be located in existing villages and the capacity of the dispensaries is a constraint. Furthermore, we make the assumption that travelling distances are Euclidean distances. In the semi-arid climate and the flat relief of Nouna, this assumption is appropriate.[10] For this model we define the following variables and constants:

$$x_{ij} = \begin{cases} 1 & \text{village i is covered by dispensary j} \\ 0 & \text{else} \end{cases}$$

$$z_j = \begin{cases} 1 & \text{a dispensary is located in village j} \\ 0 & \text{else} \end{cases}$$

a_i Population in village i
w_{ij} Distance between village i and village j
n Number of villages
p Number of dispensaries
C_j^{max} Maximum capacity of dispensary j
C_j^{min} Minimum capacity of dispensary j

Thus, we receive the following model:

---

[10] We are aware of the fact that some villages cannot be reached during the rainy season. The question how these villages can be covered by health care services has to be addressed, but it is not considered here.

5.1 Estimating Standard Costs

$$Z = \sum_{i=1}^{n}\sum_{j=1}^{n} w_{ij} \cdot a_i \cdot x_{ij} \rightarrow Min!$$

s.t.

$$\sum_{j=1}^{n} x_{ij} = 1; \quad for\ i = 1..n$$

$$x_{ij} \leq z_j; \quad for\ i = 1..n;\ j = 1..n$$

$$\sum_{j=1}^{n} z_j = p;$$

$$\sum_{i=1}^{n} a_i \cdot x_{ij} \leq C_j^{\max}; \quad for\ j = 1..n$$

$$\sum_{i=1}^{n} a_i \cdot x_{ij} \geq C_j^{\min} \cdot z_j; \quad for\ j = 1..n$$

Figure 5.9 sets a contrast between the existing position of dispensaries in mid-year 2005 and the optimum positions. We realize that the areas surrounding Nouna city have an over-proportionally good coverage, i.e., optimizing the distribution of dispensaries would lead to a transfer of dispensaries towards peripheral areas of Nouna health district. Here, *efficiency and distribution fairness are identical, but a better coverage of peripheral areas without additional resources is only possible if the privileged areas around Nouna city receive a lower share of the dispensaries of the health care district.* In 2005, about 75% of the population lived within a radius of 10 km from a dispensary (Table 5.8). If the 23 dispensaries[11] that were fully functioning in mid-year 2005 had been built in different locations, 97% of the population could have been covered within the same distances. The average distance of the population living outside this area was 15.5 km but this figure could have been 13.1 km if the same number of dispensaries had been located differently. The average travel distance could decline from 7.0 to 5.7 km, and the maximum travel distance could be reduced from 35.2 to 15.2 km.

The existing distribution of dispensaries cannot be changed. We can regret the inefficient allocation of institutions, but for practical health care planning it is much more important to determine where the next dispensary should be built and what consequences this will have. Figure 5.10 demonstrates that eight additional dispensaries have to be built in order to cover the same population within a distance of 10 km as it would have been if the 23 existing dispensaries had been built in their optimum location (97%). In other words: The inappropriate location of the existing health care institutions requires the initial and running costs of 8 new dispensaries to make good for

---

[11] The number of 23 dispensaries that were fully functional in the midyear 2005 is not contradicting with the 25 CSPS by the end of the year 2005 given in section 4.4. Two dispensaries were inaugurated in the second half of 2005. According to generally accepted accounting standards the rate of depreciation of buildings and equipment of institutions that were opened in the second half of the year is 50% of the annual rate.

this mistake. If 14 new institutions were established, the population could be covered by 99.4% and the maximum distance could be reduced to 13.4 km. Figure 5.11 shows the location of these new facilities.

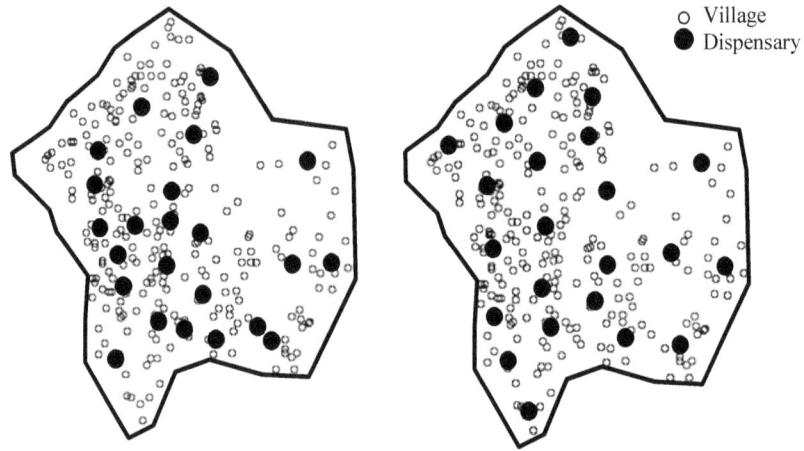

Figure 5.9   Distribution of dispensaries in Nouna health district: Status quo and optimum

Table 5.8   Existing and optimum distribution of 23 dispensaries

	Population within 10 km	Ø distance of population > 10 km	Ø distance of total population	Maximum distance
Status quo	75%	15.5 km	7.0 km	35.2 km
Optimum	97%	13.1 km	5.7 km	15.2 km

The Ministry of Health had decided to eliminate the level of health centres, i.e., the district hospital in Nouna and the dispensaries shoulder the entire work load. Figure 5.12 exhibits the part of the population living within a certain distance from the hospital for the year 2005, i.e., 42.7% of the population had no access to the hospital if we assume a maximum travel distance of 40 km and 28.1% with a maximum distance of 50 km. The population-weighted average distance is 36.7 km but the maximum distance from Gani to the hospital was 85.7 km. Realizing that public transport is – in particular for severely sick people – a major obstacle, a number of villages have no access to any hospital services at all.

5.1 Estimating Standard Costs

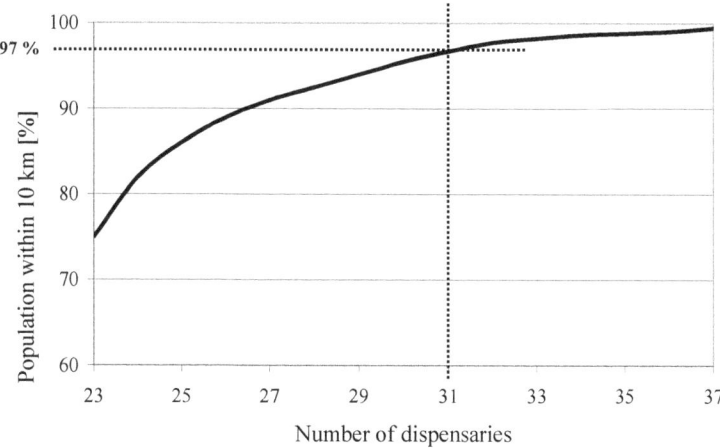

Figure 5.10   Population within a distance of 10 km

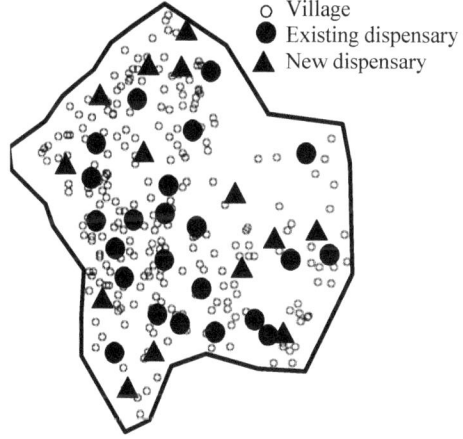

Figure 5.11   Optimum distribution of 37 dispensaries

At the same time, the hospital capacity of 85 beds is very limited compared with the catchment population of 157,062 (at a maximum distance of 40 km) and a total health district population of 279,730. Being aware of the fact that no health centres exist, we can talk about a strong under-provision of inpatient services in Nouna health district. As discussed before, the international standards of one dispensary visit a year and an admission risk of 0.044 p.a. p.c. reflect the real need of health care services. In Nouna health district the majority of people do not demand these services. The possible reasons for a low demand in comparison to the need were discussed in the second chapter of this booklet. Poor quality, high fees and long distances in particular are the most important filters preventing wants to become demand.

It is worthwhile to estimate the total costs and the costs per capita needed if the entire population were covered with health care services. Based on the cost-of-illness information data base in Nouna district, we can determine the costs of a dispensary with a capacity of 10,000 contacts p.a. and of a hospital with a capacity of 280 beds. Table 5.9 shows the results. The calculation assumes that the support centers of Nouna hospital (e.g. theatre, laboratory, administration, kitchen etc.) are sufficient to support a bigger hospital so that merely the number of beds in the wards would have to be increased. This could be questioned and our figures might under-estimate the real cost. In particular building a second hospital to cover those areas that are too far away from Nouna would strongly increase the cost.

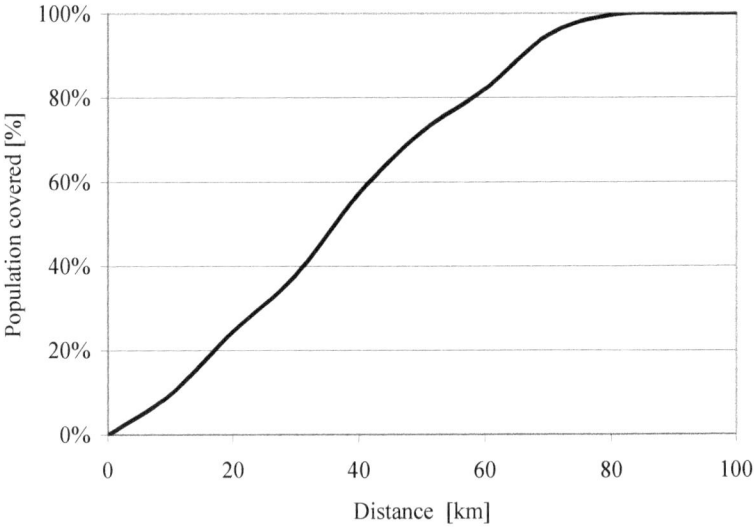

Figure 5.12   Catchment area of Nouna hospital

5.1 Estimating Standard Costs

Table 5.9   Cost of health care services in Nouna health care district 2005 [US$]

	Initial building cost	Initial equipment cost	Annual fixed cost	Variable cost
Dispensary	58,000 per CSPS	17,000 per CSPS	12,985 per institution	1.92 per consultation[12]
Hospital	2,700 per bed	200 per bed	274,523	4.76 per bed-day[13]

Consequently, covering 97% of the population within a CSPS-distance of 10 km would require 6 new dispensaries or an initial input of 450,000 US$ for buildings and equipment. If we take the international standard of one dispensary contact a year, the variable cost for deliveries and consultations would be 537,139 US$. In section 4.4.2.3 we assumed that the immunisation coverage does not change so that the variable immunisation cost remain 320,462 US$. Finally, the fixed cost would increase to 402,535 US$, so that the total curative and preventive cost of providing dispensary care would be 1,260,136 US$ or 4.50 US$ p.c. p.a. Compared with the current input, this would be 61% more. However, the increase is due to an improved coverage of the population. The existing institutions hardly need any more resources to provide more services as they are strongly under-utilized and the strongest share of cost is fixed.

The establishment of further 195 beds in addition to the existing hospital would require building and equipment cost of 565,500 US$ so that the annual depreciation would increase to 24,960 US$. With an admission risk of 0.044 and an average length of stay of seven days Nouna health district would demand 86,240 patient days, i.e., the variable cost for food, consumables and pharmacy would increase from 58,592 to 410,448 US$. However, assuming that the staffing is appropriate for an 85% occupied hospital, the increase in bed-capacity to 280 beds would also increase the salaries and wages from 159,518 US$ to 525,471 US$, i.e., the total cost of the hospital would grow from 333,125 US$ to 1,075,894 US$. In other words: full coverage with hospital services would cost 3.84 US$ p.c. p.a. This would be 742,769 US$ more than the current input. If we assume that the patients are able to pay for drugs, the additional funding would decrease by 88,314 US$.

Consequently, we can state that the real problem of Nouna health district is the poor provision of hospital services. This has to be addressed – and does not seem to be a financial problem only. Knowing costs and financing them is meaningless unless the managerial capacity is sufficient to produce worthwhile health services with these resources.

In a nut-shell: Costing studies are strongly required to calculate the total cost of providing health care services in a district and to predict the development subject to

---

[12] Variable cost for consultation, delivery and pharmacy. It is assumed that the immunisation coverage does not change.
[13] Variable cost for consumables, food and pharmacy. It is assumed that the number of outpatients of the CMA remains stable.

changes of different variables. Unless the health care planner has a profound knowledge of the development of cost, he cannot allocate resources efficiently and will finally waste some of his resources. In the next section we will discuss some insights of a resource allocation model based on the data presented here.

5.2 Resource Allocation

5.2.1 Modelling Resource Allocation

The allocation of health care resources is done in three steps. Firstly, individuals, organisations and the government have to divide their resources between various goods of different sectors (*inter-sectoral allocation*), e.g., private and public resources have to be divided between food, clothing, education, health care, security, investment etc. On a national level, different stakeholders try to influence this political process [278] to receive a higher share. We will neglect this level of allocation and assume that the individual and public health care budget is fixed. However, the reader should be aware that health care is merely one possible way to increase personal utility and national welfare, and the health sector is in strong competition for resources.

Secondly, health care resources have to be allocated to different spatial and hierarchical units (*intra-sectoral allocation*). This includes the allocation to different regions and districts, but also the allotment to prevention and cure as well as to different levels of the health care pyramid. The allocation decision is reflected by the share of the budgets for prevention, for dispensaries, for health centres, for district hospitals and for higher-level hospitals in the total health care budget. It is obvious that any allocation decision under the condition of scarcity means *rationing*. Resources allocated to a certain prevention programme will not be available for another programme or institution. Thus, the consumption of resources will always entail opportunity costs in the form of reduced service units of another service.

Thirdly, the *scope of services* has to be determined on each level of health care. This includes a decision which diseases are cured and for which diseases prevention programmes are launched. It is usually impossible to finance all possible preventive and curative interventions against all kinds of diseases. Consequently, someone has to decide whether the hospital funds should be used to cure malaria cases, treat patients requiring a dialysis or provide brain surgery.

The model presented in the next sub-section will solve the allocation problem of the last two levels. The health care budget is assumed to be constant, i.e., the inter-sectoral allocation is fixed. It assumes a rational decision-making process. In reality, however, the intra-sectoral allocation is also frequently a political decision. Important stakeholders, such as physicians, rich urban minorities, army representatives etc., attempt to influence the allocation so that their own interest group receives a higher share of the health care resources. Frequently, this has resulted in a strongly curative health care system with big hospitals in a few major cities. This advantage for these pressure groups is usually a disadvantage of the poor and needy without a voice. Thus, *equity calls for fair and transparent decision-making based on a clear objective system.*

Mathematical programming allows the optimisation of the allocation of health care resources. Boldy [279], Heidenberger et al. [280, 281] and Harfner [282] discuss linear and non-linear models of resource allocation in the health care sector. They conclude that older attempts to allocate health care resources based on a Linear Programme (LP) were not very successful, as the computer capacity did not allow realistic models. Recent models did not fight with this problem any more, but frequently they lacked data and had to rely on fictive parameters. It is obvious that *costing studies are most important to make resource allocation models relevant for real-life decision making.*

Only few allocation models were designed for developing countries [283-286]. The objective of these models was the optimum portfolio of disease control strategies, usually as an element of vertical disease control projects. A complete health care system was not incorporated into these models. In order to be a worthwhile decision-support system for health planners and policy makers, the incidence and prevalence of the most frequent diseases as well as the supply of health care services must be incorporated into the model.

5.2.2 Model

Basic structure of the model

The model calculates the annual incidence and prevalence of a number of diseases in a developing country. It is mainly based on the situation analysis of Tanzania discussed in section 4.1. It allows for co-morbidity and recurrent morbid episodes. The model assumes a population with 80 age-groups (age 0 to 79) and 25 different diagnosis groups, as indicated in Table 5.10. These groups are chosen in such a way that the top-four infectious diseases (malaria, acute lower respiratory infections, sexually transmitted diseases and anaemia) represent 89% of all morbidity and 62% of all mortality in a typical country in the first phase of the epidemiological transition. The most important chronic diseases represent 65% of the morbidity (hypertension, chronic respiratory infects, mental disorders, occupational diseases) and 76% of the mortality (coronary heart disease, hypertension, cerebrovascular diseases, diabetes) in a country in the fourth phase of the epidemiological transition.

Table 5.10   Diagnosis groups

Infectious diseases		Chronic-degenerative diseases		Other conditions	
j	Diagnosis group	j	Diagnosis group	j	Diagnosis group
1	Malaria	11	Hypertension	22	Accidents
2	Acute lower respiratory infections	12	Chronic Respiratory Infects, Asthma	23	Malnutrition
3	STDs, excluding AIDS	13	Mental and psychological disorders	24	Ordinary deliveries
4	Anaemia	14	Arthritis	25	Pregnancy disorders
5	Amoebiasis	15	Occupational diseases		
6	Measles	16	Diabetes		
7	Pertussis	17	Glaucoma		
8	Tuberculosis	18	Coronary heart disease		
9	Diarrhoea	19	Rheumatic fever		
10	AIDS	20	Cerebrovascular disease		
		21	Other heart diseases		

The model assumes four levels of institution-based health care (Table 5.11). Resources allocated to curative medicine reduce the mortality and average length of sickness. In addition, resources can be allocated to preventive programmes to reduce the incidence of diseases.

Table 5.11   Levels of institutional health care

k	Institution	k	Institution
1	Dispensary	3	primary hospital
2	health centre	4	regional hospital

Variables, constants and constraints

The basic service units are outpatient contacts for dispensaries and beddays for other levels of care. A given health care budget is allocated to the different levels of health care in order to minimise number of deaths, lost life years, cases, morbidity days or lost quality of life. Thus, the following decision variables are defined:

Pr_{ij} Annual number of people of age i receiving preventive services against morbidity in diagnosis group j

P_A_{ijk} Annual number of service units delivered at level k to patients of age i in diagnosis group j

L_{ijk} Annual need for treatment at level k by patients of age i in diagnosis group j

W_{ijk} Annual number of patients of age i in diagnosis group j that require treatment at level k but are treated at a higher level

5.2 Resource Allocation

A_{ijk} — Annual number of patients of age i in diagnosis group j that are rejected at level k
x_{ij} — Number of cases in a year in diagnosis group j at age i
T_{ij} — Number of death cases in a year of people of age i in diagnosis group j
C_prev — Annual costs of preventive health services
C_cur — Annual costs of curative health services

The following constants are used:

BEV_i — Number of people of age i in the population
l_{ijk} — Proportion of patients of age i in diagnosis group j that require treatment at minimum level k
d_p_{jk} — Number of days per annum of morbidity (chronic disease) or infection (infectious diseases) for a patient in diagnosis group j and treated at level k. k=5 indicates that the patient is not treated.
d_{jk} — Number of service units at level k required by a patient in diagnosis group j
cP_j — Annual per capita cost of preventive services against morbidity in diagnosis group j
c_k — Unit cost of service at level k
$Budget$ — Annual health care budget for the population
mor_normal_{ij} — Annual per capita morbidity rate for patients of age i in diagnosis group j that do not receive preventive services
mor_schutz_{ij} — Annual per capita morbidity rate for patients of age i in diagnosis group j that receive preventive services
r_j — Quality score for morbidity in diagnosis group j
$mortal_{ij}$ — Annual per capita mortality rate for patients of age i in diagnosis group j that do receive treatment
$mortal\_abge_{ij}$ — Annual per capita mortality rate for patients of age i in diagnosis group j that do not receive treatment

The LP models define the following constraints and equations:

Preventive services: $Pr_{ij} \leq P_i$ for i = 0,...,79; j = 1,...,25

Demand at each level of care:
$L_{ij1} + W_{ij1} = l_{ij1} x_{ij}$ for i = 0,...,79;
$L_{ij2} + W_{ij2} = l_{ij2} x_{ij} + W_{ij1}$ j = 1,...,25
$L_{ij3} + W_{ij3} = l_{ij3} x_{ij} + W_{ij2}$
$L_{ij4} = l_{ij4} x_{ij} + W_{ij3}$

Number not treated: $A_{ijk} = L_{ijk} - \dfrac{PA_{ijk}}{d_{jk}}$ for i = 0,...,79; j = 1,...,25; k = 1,...,4

Cost $Cc + Cp \leq B$

Cases: $x_{ij} = n_{ij} \cdot (P_i - \Pr_{ij}) + s_{ij} \cdot \Pr_{ij};$
for i = 0,...,79 for j = 1,...,25

Death cases:
$$T_{ij} = m_{ij} \cdot (x_{ij} - \sum_{k=1}^{4} A_{ijk}) + g_{ij} \cdot \sum_{k=1}^{4} A_{ijk}$$
for i = 0,...,79; j = 1,...,25

Objective functions

The objective function of a linear programme expresses the priorities of the decision maker. As seen in the second chapter, a different value system will lead to different priorities and objective systems. Therefore, five different objective functions are employed which represent common priorities of decision-makers in health care systems.

Goal 1: Minimisation of number of deaths. The number of death cases is minimised.

$$Mortality\_Rates = \sum_{i=0}^{79}\sum_{j=1}^{25} T_{ij} \to Min!$$

Goal 2: Minimisation of lost life years. The model has a population structure of 80 age-groups (i=0,...,79) and assumes that everybody is born and dies – on average – on the 30th June, i.e. midyear. Therefore, 79 is the maximum age. Every year which a person dies earlier is a lost year. Therefore, the following objective function minimises the number of lost life years. The model does not discount years.

$$Lost\_Years = \sum_{i=0}^{79}\sum_{j=1}^{25} (79-i) * T_{ij} \to Min!$$

Goal 3: Minimisation of cases. The following objective function minimises the number of cases.

$$Incidence = \sum_{i=0}^{79}\sum_{j=1}^{25} x_{ij} \to Min!$$

Goal 4: Minimisation of morbidity days. The following objective function minimises the morbidity days. The weight for the rejected patients (A_{ijk}) of age i with condition j at level k is directly the average length of sickness (d_p$_{j5}$) of a rejected patient with condition j. The variable P_A$_{ijk}$ is not the number of patients, but the number of service units. Therefore, P_A$_{ijk}$ must be divided by the average number of service units required for the treatment of a patient with condition j at level k (constant d$_{jk}$) before it can be weighted with the average length of sickness of a patient with condition j at level k (d_p$_{jk}$). The result is the days of sickness.

$$Prevalence = \sum_{i=0}^{79}\sum_{j=1}^{25}\sum_{k=1}^{4} \frac{d\_p_{jk}}{d_{jk}} * P\_A_{ijk} + \sum_{i=0}^{79}\sum_{j=1}^{25}\sum_{k=1}^{4} d\_p_{j5} * A_{ijk} \to Min!$$

5.2 Resource Allocation

Goal 5: Minimisation of lost quality of life. The concept of prevalence does not consider the different loss of quality of life which different conditions mean for the diseased. The calculation of quality of life weighs the prevalence with a quality score. Additionally, it is possible to include the loss of life in this calculation, as death has a quality score of 0. Again we assume that the death occurs on the 30. June, i.e. midyear.

$$Lost\_Quality = \sum_{i=0}^{79}\sum_{j=1}^{25}\sum_{k=1}^{4}(1-r_j)*d\_p_{jk}*\frac{P\_A_{ijk}}{d_{jk}} + 182.5*\sum_{i=0}^{79}\sum_{j=1}^{25}T_{ij}$$
$$+ \sum_{i=0}^{79}\sum_{j=1}^{25}\sum_{k=1}^{4}(1-r_j)*d\_p_{j5}*A_{ijk} \rightarrow Min!$$

The impact of these different objective functions and different budgets on the allocation process are analysed by comparing the results of 90 LPs. In principle, the model is also applicable to countries with higher health care budgets. However, here we will concentrate on least developed countries. The data set was taken from the study presented in section 4.1.

5.2.3 Results

The morbidity pattern of the population in the district will dependent on the health care budget and the selected goal function. This is demonstrated in Figure 5.13 which expresses the incidence of infectious diseases as percentage of all morbidity (without conditions 22-25). It expresses the priorities of preventive and curative medicine because a higher share of infectious diseases – ceteris paribus - shows that a major share of the budget went into prevention and cure of chronic diseases.

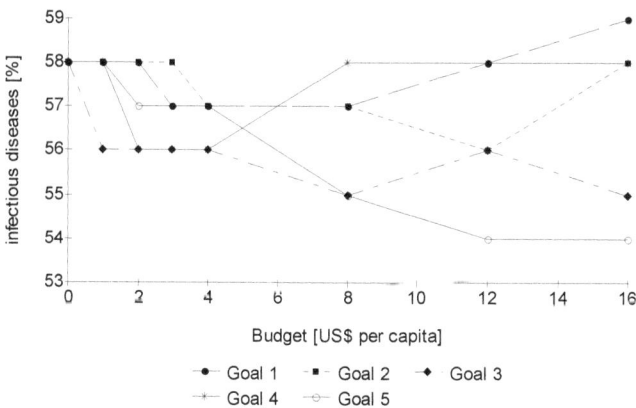

Figure 5.13   Share of infectious diseases in morbidity

The analysis shows that *the optimal allocation of health care funds is highly dependent on the goal function*. Additionally, the curves are not monotonous, but there are ups and downs. This shows that *health policies must not apply a "golden rule" but consider the health care priorities of a particular region and the available budget.*

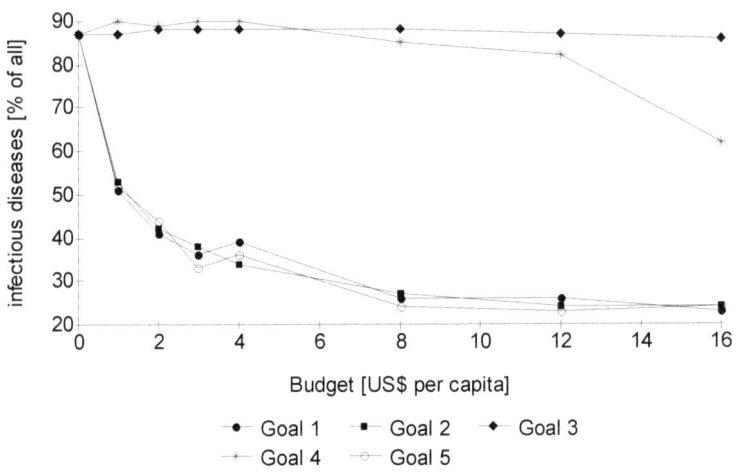

Figure 5.14 Share of infectious diseases in mortality

Figure 5.14 shows the mortality due to infectious diseases as a percent of the total mortality (without conditions 22-25). The goals 1, 2 and 5 are minimising mortality rates and their curves are almost identical. Without any health care budget the mortality due to infectious diseases is 87%. Infectious diseases have a very high mortality rate, if no measures to prevent and treat them are taken. This mortality can be easily reduced by prevention and cure of infectious diseases, i.e., the efficacy of interventions against infectious diseases is high. Therefore, if a health care system follows goals 1, 2 or 5 and the health care budget is rather low, this budget is mainly spent for the prevention and cure of infectious diseases. Thus, the mortality rate goes down. If the health care authorities follow goals 3 or 4 they will not spend very much on fighting mortality.

Again, the curves are not monotonous and differ even more than for the morbidity. Therefore, the efficient health care policy is quite complex and highly dependent on the health care resources and the goal function.

Figure 5.15 shows the optimal allocation of health care resources to preventive health care activities. The rest of the health care resources is spent for curative medicine.

5.2 Resource Allocation 123

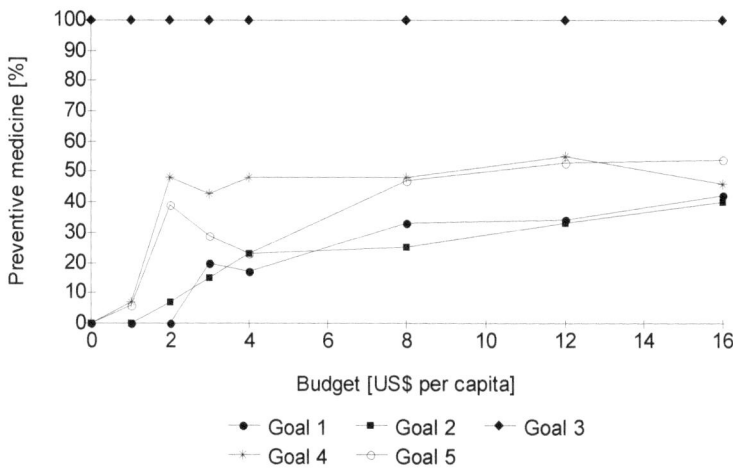

Figure 5.15 Importance of preventive health care [% of total budget]

Goal 3 leads to a complete allocation of all health care resources to preventive services, i.e., any budget increase leads to a linear increase in expenditure for preventive medicine. Even for the other goals it is obvious that preventive medicine is an important part of the entire health care system. However, the efficiency of this type of health care is increasing with health care budgets, i.e. *the share of the health care funds allocated to prevention grows with increasing budgets. That means that an increase in economic strength of a country or district must lead to an absolute and relative increase in preventive medicine.*

It is obvious that the share of expenditure for preventive medicine in the total health care budget is not a monotonous function. The curves for goal 1 and 2 start rather late to allocate resources to preventive medicine, i.e., curative medicine seems to be more efficient to reduce the mortality with such low budgets. Goal 2 emphasises the health of children, as their loss of years of life is higher if they die. Therefore, prevention of diarrhoea is introduced earlier than with goal 1.

However, an annual health care budget of less than two US$ per capita is so small that hardly any meaningful work is possible. The curve of goal 4 (prevalence) reaches a high level of preventive medicine rather early. The World Bank suggests that about 33% of the annual health care budget of 12 US$ per capita should be spent for prevention programs. Our model confirms this data for goal functions 1 and 2, i.e., if mortality rates are minimised. For other health care priorities and for other budgets this proposal cannot be supported. The share of preventive medicine does definitely depend on the budget and the goal function.

Additionally, also the allocation of the prevention budget on different programmes (and diagnostic groups) depends on the total budget and the goal function. Table 5.12 shows the first, second and third condition which are incorporated into the prevention program.

Table 5.12   Conditions targeted by prevention programs

	First condition	Second condition	Third condition
Goal 1	TB	Diarrhoea	AIDS
Goal 2	TB	Diarrhoea	Measles
Goal 3	STDs	Malnutrition	Acute lower respiratory infection
Goal 4	STDs	TB	Hypertension
Goal 5	TB	STDs	Hypertension

Goal function 1 prefers prevention against conditions with a high mortality and a high efficiency of prevention. At the same time the impact of curative care on mortality should be low. This is the case with TB as this infectious disease is highly fatal, treatment is expensive and many patients are dying even under proper therapy. Therefore, prevention is most important. Mass-screening of suspected before they are so sick that they demand health care services as well as treatment are highly efficient. Diarrhoea is most severe with children and mortality is high. It can be reduced by provision of clean water and proper latrines.

Goal function 2 emphasises the survival of children, i.e., childhood diseases are more efficient to prevent than conditions which influence adults. Therefore, the prevention of measles which affect only children is more important than the prevention of AIDS which has mainly impact on adults. Goal function 3 minimises the incidence. Therefore, those diseases are part of the prevention programme which have a high incidence and a high efficacy of prevention. Sexually transmitted diseases can be easily prevented and are quite common in many developing countries. At the same time there are many malnourished children and those suffering from acute lower respiratory infection (ALRI). As these conditions are easily prevented, they receive a high priority. Goal function 4 minimises the prevalence, i.e., those diseases will be of high priority which have a long period of sickness. Therefore, resources will be allocated to the prevention of TB and hypertension.

Goal function 5 minimises the loss of quality of life. It combines goals 1 and 4, which is reflected by the conditions of high prevention priority. TB is the first disease to receive a part of the prevention budget. This was the same with goal function 1. STDs and hypertension are also of high importance, as it was the case with goal function 4.

As there is no natural demand for the majority of preventive services, the share of the health care budget of the Ministry of Health which is allocated to preventive services must be much higher than the figures given above.

Figure 5.16 shows the share of the curative budget allocated to dispensaries. It is obvious that the importance of dispensaries decreases with increasing health care budgets.

5.2 Resource Allocation

With very low budgets almost all resources should flow into dispensaries as they are most efficient. With increasing budgets the absolute expenditure for dispensaries increases until it reaches a level of about 2.78 US$ per capita. However, as the total budget increases, the relative share of dispensaries in the total cost of curative services decreases. The World Bank suggests that from a total health care budget of 12 US$ per capita 7.80 US$ should be spent for curative services [143]. Our model proposes that at a budget of 12 US$ per capita about 2.60 US$ (or 33% of the curative budget) should be spent for dispensaries.

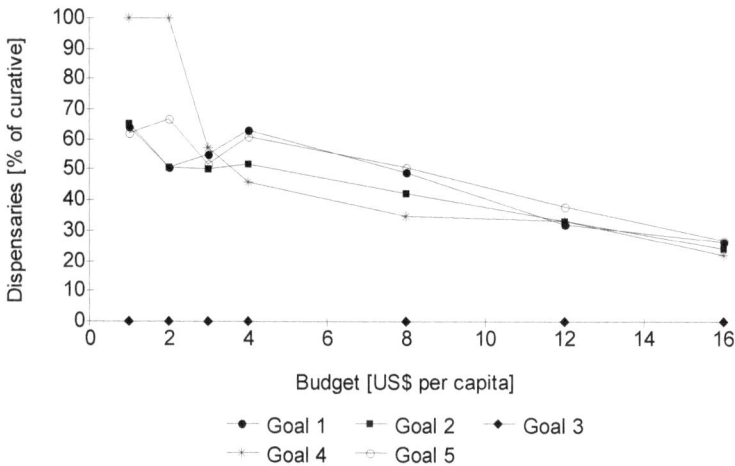

Figure 5.16   Importance of dispensaries [% of curative budget]

It is obvious that the share of the curative health care budget allocated to dispensaries is not a monotonous function of the budget. Therefore, policy-making is a difficult task. Goal 3 gives no budget to curative medicine so that the share of dispensaries is zero.

Figure 5.17 shows the share of the budget of health centres in the total budget of curative medicine. The allocation to health centres depends very much on the goal function. Goal 4 does not provide any health centres with resources if the total curative health care budget is less than 3 US$ per capita. Then it jumps to an allocation of 43%. At this level funds are sufficient to treat patients with chronic diseases in dispensaries, so that resources can be allocated to health centres. At a health care budget of 12 US$ per capita, 1.90 US$ (goal function 1), 1.68 US$ (goal function 2), 0.00 US$ (goal function 3), 1.52 US$ (goal function 4) and 1.42 US$ (goal function 5) are allocated to health centres. Therefore, the amount spent for health centres depends much more on the goal function than the amount spent for dispensaries.

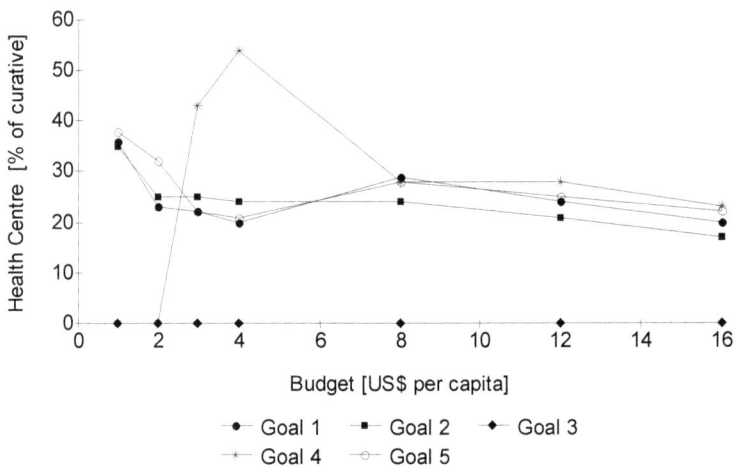

Figure 5.17   Importance of health centres [% of curative budget]

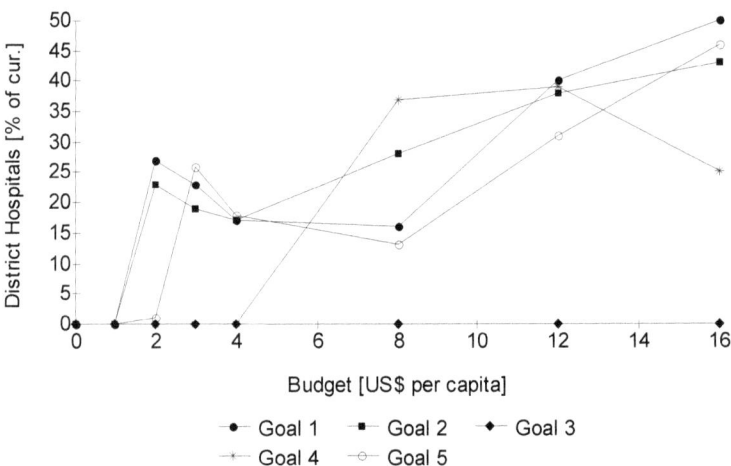

Figure 5.18   Importance of district hospitals [% of curative budget]

The share of the curative health care budget which is allocated to district hospitals is even more dependent on the budget and the goal function. This is shown in Figure

5.2 Resource Allocation

5.18. It is obvious that the function is not monotonous. For low budgets the curves of goal 1 and 2 are not as close together as they are for higher budgets.

Figure 5.19 shows the importance of the regional hospital. It demonstrates that the minimum budget which is necessary to allocate any resources efficiently to the regional hospital depends on the goal function. If the reduction of infant mortality (goal 2) is the main target of the health care policy a regional hospital can be run which provides mainly paediatric services.

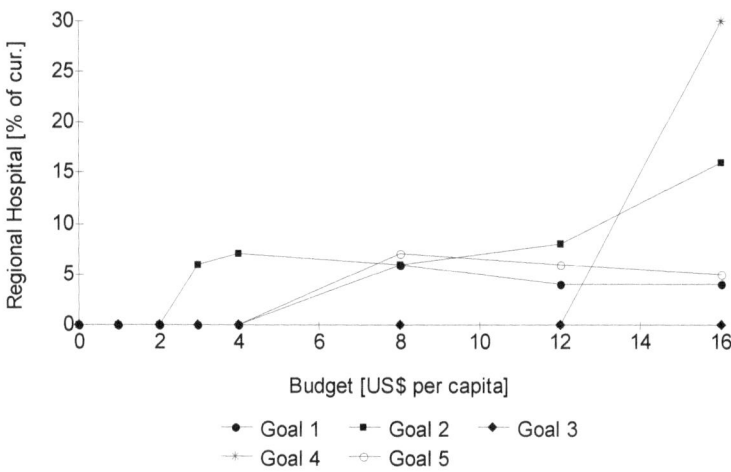

Figure 5.19   Importance of regional hospital [% of curative budget]

The differences between the curves are stronger than for the other institutions of health care. Therefore, *a detailed analysis is required to allocate the funds efficiently to the different levels of health care. These non monotonous functions will place a severe burden on decision-makers.*

Table 5.13 gives a recommendation how to spend the "magic" 12 US$ recommended by the World Bank, whereas Table 5.14 demonstrates the same for a health care budget of 4 US$ p.c. p.a. The tables underline the statement given above that the allocation of health care resources strongly depends on the objective function chosen and the budget.

Table 5.13   Allocating 12 US$ p.c. to different levels [US$ per capita (% of curative)]

	Prevention	Curative	Dispensaries	Health Centres	District hospitals	Regional hospital
Goal 1	4.09 (34%)	7.91 (66%)	2.53 (32%)	1.90 (24%)	3.16 (40%)	0.62 (4%)
Goal 2	3.97 (33%)	8.03 (67%)	2.65 (33%)	1.69 (21%)	3.05 (38%)	0.64 (8%)
Goal 3	12 (100%)	0	0	0	0	0
Goal 4	6.57 (55%)	5.43 (45%)	1.79 (33%)	1.52 (28%)	2.11 (39%)	0
Goal 5	6.32 (53%)	5.68 (47%)	2.16 (38%)	1.42 (25%)	1.76 (31%)	0.34 (6%)

Table 5.14   Allocating 4 US$ p.c. to different levels [US$ per capita (% of curative)]

	Prevention	Curative	Dispensaries	Health Centres	District hospitals	Regional hospital
Goal 1	0.68 (17%)	3.32 (83%)	2.52 (63%)	0.80 (20%)	0.68 (17%)	0
Goal 2	0.92 (23%)	3.08 (77%)	2.08 (52%)	0.96 (24%)	0.68 (17%)	0.28 (7%)
Goal 3	4 (100%)	0	0	0	0	0
Goal 4	1.92 (48%)	2.08 (52%)	1.84 (46%)	2.16 (54%)	0	0
Goal 5	0.92 (23%)	3.08 (77%)	2.44 (61%)	0.84 (21%)	0.72 (18%)	0

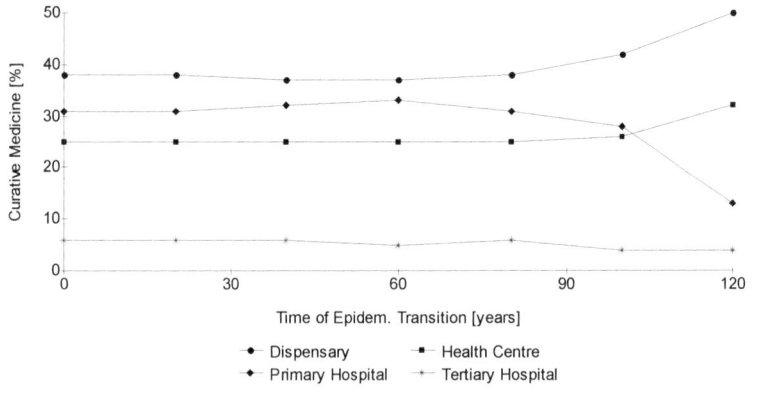

Figure 5.20   Curative medicine and transition: Budget = 12 US$ p.c. p.a.

Finally, the age structure influences the allocation scheme. Figure 5.20 exhibits the share of dispensaries, health centres and hospitals in the total budget of curative medicine for different years of the epidemiological transition [118] for goals function 5. The model assumes that the second phase of the transition starts in t=20 with a declining mortality at given fertility. At t=60, the population reaches the third phase where fertility also begins to decline. At t=100, the transition has reached the fourth phase where fertility and mortality are almost equal (about 1% p.a.).

As long as the population is rather young, the changes of the epidemiological transition have only minor impact on the allocation scheme. *However, an aging population with a strong share of chronic-degenerative diseases calls for a higher share of district hospitals as these diseases cannot easily be treated in dispensaries.* At a budget of 12 US$ p.c. p.a., the funds are not sufficient to invest much in regional hospitals. But district hospitals are an appropriate provider for chronically sick patients of higher age.

5.2.4 Policy Implications

The allocation of health care resources is painful. We have to be aware of the fact that the recommendation to allot a certain budget share to a certain level of health care or disease implies that this amount cannot be spent at another level or for another disease. Any US$ that flows into prevention cannot be invested in curative medicine. Any US$ that is allocated to a dispensary is not available at a regional hospital. And the treatment of one malaria patients takes away the funds for treating an arthritis patient. It is banal, but the consequences are immense: *Resources are limited and any programme or treatment entails opportunity costs in the form of lost opportunities to rescue other lives, health other patients or increase other quality of life.*

We must be aware of this existential dimension of the allocation of health care resources. The model presents the most efficient allocation, i.e. the minimum of death cases, of life years lost, of new cases and of sickness days or the maximum of quality of life in a certain population. But "is efficient sufficient?" [287]. *We might deviate from an efficient allocation of funds to increase equity or for political reasons. But policy makers should make their values and the decision making processes leading to this deviation transparent.*

Health planning and decision-making are complex as there is no "golden rule". The efficient allocation of funds strongly depends on the objective system, the available budget and the age structure of the population. The value system which we discussed in the second chapter has an extraordinary influence on the allocation process. Priorities must be stated clearly and health care visions have to be formulated precisely in order to be able to produce optimum allocation schemes for health care budgets. Up to now, most of the health care objectives formulated by the World Health Organisation, Ministries of Health, regional health management teams and development agencies are not very specific. Because of that, it has been very difficult to take action to attain these objectives or measure the performance of these measures. Even the famous Alma Ata declaration has not provided a precise and measurable goal system.

For all objective functions, however, one result is clear: *A reallocation of health care resources from curative to preventive medicine and from hospitals to dispensaries and health centres is urgently needed.* The model proves that an increase in the share of the health care budget allocated to primary care would increase the efficiency of the health care system in most developing countries. At the same time, the results illustrate that Primary Health Care is not the "medicine for the poor", because its efficiency will increase with growing health care budgets. Economic development and increasing budgets must lead to an increasing share of primary care if a health district wants to attain a highly efficient health care system. A "basic package" of health care – as recommended by the World Bank [143] – will include preventive services for the most important infectious diseases, treatment at dispensaries and health centres for the most common conditions (including deliveries) and referral services at district hospitals for diseases with public health consequences (e.g. TB). This could indeed be financed with 12 US$ per capita per year – an amount far too high for many health districts in developing countries.

The 30 years after Alma Ata were filled with hopes that the implementation of Primary Health Care (PHC) could be achieved without reducing the existing hospital-based health services. For instance, the strategic health care plan of 1981 of Zimbabwe was made with scientific consultancy of the Institute of Development Studies at the University of Sussex. It was believed that health care budgets would grow steadily during the following years. Therefore, the focus on primary health care simply meant distributing a greater share of the *additional budgets* to primary, rather than secondary, health care. This was expressed with the words: "Reshaping resource distribution is less a redistribution of existing resources than the allocation of new resources in accordance with PHC priorities" [288]. It was suggested that the budgets of dispensaries should grow by 17% per annum (deflated), whereas the budgets for hospitals should only grow by 5% per year. In other words: the allocation of the old funds should remain unchanged, whereas the allocation of additional funds would still allow the regional hospital to grow. The different growth rates would change the ratio between primary and secondary health care without facing negative consequences from reduced budgets.

Until the end of the 20th century it has become clear that neither development aid for health nor local funds per capita had grown in most developing countries, especially not in very remote areas. Many developed countries signed the Alma Ata declaration and pledged to pay more development aid for health care services. However, "no increase in aid flows has occurred" [289]. The economic crises of many developing countries made it impossible to have growing health care budgets, so that the adoption of the primary health care innovation stands and falls with the re-allocation of resources. The new millennium has seen great pledges from the international community for the health care in developing countries. However, most of these funds are invested in fighting specific disease (in particular Aids, Malaria, TB) without a major impact on the entire health care system. The general problem of under-funding and the necessity of re-allocating resources remain unchanged in this new century.

The consequent implementation of the decisions of Alma Ata would definitely increase the efficiency of the health care system. This requires the re-allocation of funds: from curative to preventive, from regional and district hospitals to dispensaries and health centres, and from specific diseases to the entire health care system. Primary Health Care cannot be achieved without a sacrifice.

Finally, the age structure has a major impact on the allocation. Based on this rather simple model one would expect that the share of district hospitals in the curative health care budget would increase. However, this assumption is too simply as the demographic situation of many developing countries is complex. Urban areas reach the third or sometimes even the fourth phase of the transition while rural areas are still in the first or second phase with a very young population. Thus, allocating health care resources also means to consider different development and transitional levels in the same country with very different needs.

In a nut-shell: *We urgently need the ethical discourse on values and objectives. We need increasing budgets and a wide understanding of the impacts of the epidemiological transition. And we require decision-support systems that allow the computation of the optimum allocation scheme for a particular health district. But first of all, we need the parameters required by these models, e.g. the constants d_{jk}, cP_j and c_k. Costing studies provide a major share of this data and build the foundation for equitable and efficient health care services.*

5.3 Setting a Premium for an Insurance Scheme

The establishment of health insurance schemes is frequently seen as an instrument to increase equity in health care [290-296]. In particular, the burden of catastrophic household expenditure is reduced [101, 297-299]. Positive examples from other countries [108, 109, 300-303] induced the development of so-called community based health funds (CFHF)[14] in Tanzania [304-308] and Burkina Faso [290, 309-316]. For instance, the health district of Nouna introduced a community health fund in the year 2005.

However, most of these funds still suffer from low utilization [105, 317, 318]. The overall coverage rate is about 8.2% of the target population [319] and community-based or initiated schemes have even lower enrolment rates [319]. Thus, the objective of increasing equity has not yet been fully achieved. At the same time, the economic solvency of these funds is at stake. There seems to be a major conflict between affordability and sustainability. Affordability calls for low premiums, whereas sustainability requires higher contributions so that the risk of going bankrupt is lower. The main question is: how high should the premium be so that the insurance can survive and that as many poor people as possible can afford it? The following model attempts to give an answer to this question based on the data from Nouna health district in the year 2005 (see section 4.4).

---

[14] In this paper we will use the terms health fund and health insurance interchangeable. For a more detailed analysis of different terms see the literature given above.

5.3.1 Basic Model

The calculation of a premium of a community based insurance (CBI) is based on four assumptions. Firstly, we assume a *negative price elasticity* of demand for CBI, i.e., the number of people insured decreases with an increasing premium. This assumption has been frequently discussed. Dong, Kouyate & Sauerborn [311] proved for Nouna that the willingness to pay for CBI correlates negatively with the premium.

Secondly, we assume that the demand for health care services will increase after a household or an individual will be covered by the insurance. This increase has two reasons: backlog and luxurious demand. Most inhabitants of rural districts in developing countries demand much less health care services than medically necessary. They are sick, they need help – but they cannot afford these services. Therefore, this *backlog demand* will be satisfied after they are insured, i.e., insurance increases demand for health care. In addition, some people might demand even more health care services than medically necessary. They have the feeling that "if I pay something, I want to have something". According to our experience this approach is not very strong in Nouna, the backlog demand will prevail. Both aspects are commonly summarized under the term *moral hazard*, but it is necessary to notice that moral hazard is not necessarily immoral. Frequently, people with a severe disease did not have the financial resources to demand health care services before the insurance was introduced. It is not immoral if they demand additional health care services to satisfy these needs after subscribing to a health insurance.

Thirdly, poor people will have a greater additional demand than rich people. We can assume that the demand for health care is *income elastic* because most people in rural areas of developing countries have to spend almost their entire income on food. They cannot afford to buy all health care services they wish to and which are medically appropriate. If the income increases, the demand for health care will increase as well. However, it is likely that the poorest stratum of the population has the highest difference between actual demand and medically necessary demand. Consequently, Sauerborn, Nougtara & Latimer [320] found that households with a high income spend more on health care than households with low income. Furthermore, the arc price elasticity of the richer population is lower than the one of the poorer population (-1.44 for the lowest quartile and -0.12 for the highest quartile). Therefore, *introducing CBI will increase the demand for health care of the poor to a higher extent than the demand of the rich*.

Fourthly, we can assume that the demand for health care depends on many *stochastic variables* so that the health care cost per insured are not deterministic. If we knew exactly the number of cases per year, the drugs consumed and the number of beddays, we could calculate an average premium. However, reality is not deterministic. In one year we might have a malaria epidemic increasing the demand by factor two, in another year the weather is dry so that the health care institutions are half empty. One patient with an appendectomy leaves the hospital after 3 days, the other requires 14 days. Therefore, the unit costs of health care are stochastic.

5.3 Setting a Premium for an Insurance Scheme

The *model* defines the following variables:

d	Average increase factor of demand for all insured
d_ind	Increase factor of demand of an individual
$Expenditure\_H$	Expenditure of health care services [US$]
$Expenditure\_I$	Expenditure of CBI [US$]
$Income\_H$	Income of health care services [US$]
$Income\_I$	Income of CBI [US$]
NS	Number of insured [households]
p	Premium [US$]

Furthermore, the following constants are defined:

c	Capitation [US$ per household]
d_max	Maximum increase of demand of an individual
EH_f	Fixed expenditure of health care services [US$]
EI_f	Fixed expenditure of CBI [US$]
f	Average fee [US$ per household]
IH_f	Fixed income of health care services [US$]
II_f	Fixed income of CBI [US$]
p_max	Maximum premium [US$ per household]
Pop	Total population [households]
v_i	Variable costs per insured [US$ per household]
v_n	Variable costs per non-insured [US$ per household]

The implementation of a CBI can only be seen as a success if both the insurance and the health services are financially sustainable. Therefore, the sum of fixed and variable income must not be less than the sum of fixed and variable expenditure.

$$IH_f + II_f + p \cdot NS + f \cdot (Pop - NS) - \{EH_f + EI_f + v\_n \cdot (Pop - NS) + v\_i \cdot d \cdot NS\} \geq 0$$

NS, the number of insured, is a function of the premium p. Based on data of a willingness to pay (WTP) study [311], we assume that NS grows linear with the catchment population, but develops negative exponential with the premium.

$$NS = Pop \cdot e^{-0.045 \cdot p}$$

The increase of demand of the individual and of the entire population are a function of the premium. d_max denotes the maximum increase of demand for a household which will only join if the premium is zero, i.e. $d\_ind(0)=d\_max$. p_max is the maximum premium at which no increase will occur, i.e. $d\_ind(p\_max)=1$. Figure 5.21 exhibits the increase of demand in respect to the premium. On theoretical grounds, one would expect a negative exponential function. However, as no data can support this assumption, we assume a linear function which might slightly overestimate the increase of demand, i.e., a linear function leads to a conservative estimate.

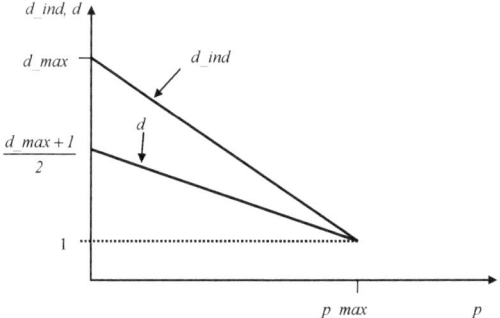

Figure 5.21   Increase of Demand in Respect to Premium

The average increase of demand for all insured (*d*) can consequently be expressed as

$$d = \frac{1}{2} \cdot \left[1 + d\_\max - p \cdot \frac{d\_\max - 1}{p\_\max} \right]$$

Table 5.15 summarizes the basic data of the model. It is assumed that a CBI will finally cover the entire population (279,730 inhabitants, 34,967 households, ∅ 8 inhabitants per household). If we assume that the accessibility is increased (97.5% within 10 km to a dispensary) and the hospital capacity is enlarged to 280 beds, the annual cost of health care in Nouna health care district would be 1,488,204 US$. This figure assumes the same service-seeking behaviour as before, e.g., prices and quality are unchanged. On the assumption that the additional bed capacity and spatial accessibility of dispensaries were financed by the government, the fixed income would be 1,192,033 US$ and the patient fee per household would be 8.47 US$. Fixed income is mainly provided in the form of government grants and some donations from overseas. It is assumed that fixed income, fixed expenditure, variable costs per household and fees per non-insured household will not change after introducing CBI.

Furthermore, we assume that an insurance scheme will require two employees, an office, office equipment depreciation (incl. one computer), a motor bike and marketing costs. We assume that a fixed expenditure of 5,000 US$ p.a. would be sufficient to run the CBI.

Finally, we calculated the need of health care services in Nouna health district and compare it with the current demand. We found that the maximum increase (d_max) will be 5.6. The maximum premium which is still acceptable is 25 US$.

5.3 Setting a Premium for an Insurance Scheme

Table 5.15 Data for the premium calculation

Constant	Content	Value
d_max	Maximum increase of demand	5.6
EH_f	Fixed expenditure of health services	1,308,823 US$
EI_f	Fixed expenditure of CBI	5,000 US$
f	Fee per household	8.47 US$
IH_f	Fixed income of health services	1,192,033 US$
p_max	Maximum willingness to pay of household	25 US$
Pop	No. of households	34,967
v_n	Variable costs per non-insured household	5.13 US$
v_i	Variable costs per insured household	5.13 US$

5.3.2 Results

As Figure 5.22 shows, the premium per household must be 13.95 US$ in order to break-even. 18,665 households (53%) would join the insurance. The demand increase is about 2.0. If the premium is lower, more people will join, but the demand will increase considerably so that the district health services run into a loss.

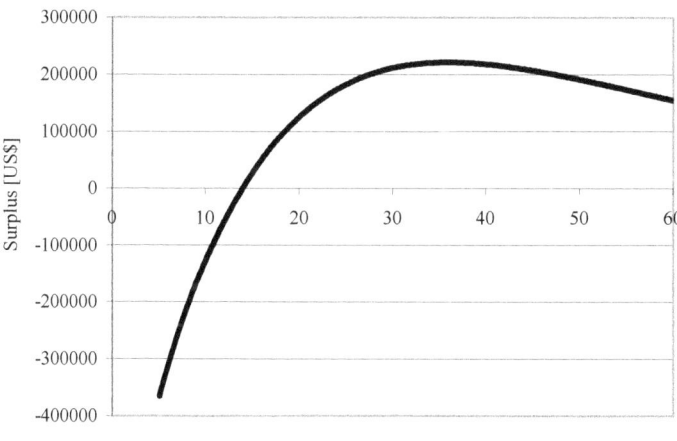

Figure 5.22 Break-Even analysis: Basic scenario

The following scenarios attempt to answer the question: What will happen if the real values of the constants given in Table 5.15 increase or decrease? This will finally demonstrate the reliability of the analysis.

5.3.2.1 Fixed Income

The number of insured is a function of the subsidy. In the year 2005, the health district of Nouna received a fixed income of 835,536 US$. If the government had recovered all cost needed to provide accessible health care for all medical needs, the fixed income would rise to 1,192,033 US$. Assuming that the government or a donor would also cover the overheads of the insurance, the respective amounts are 840,536 US$ and 1,197,022 US$. Figure 5.23 demonstrates that the health district (incl. CBI) cannot break-even without additional subsidies by the government if the entire population should be reached.

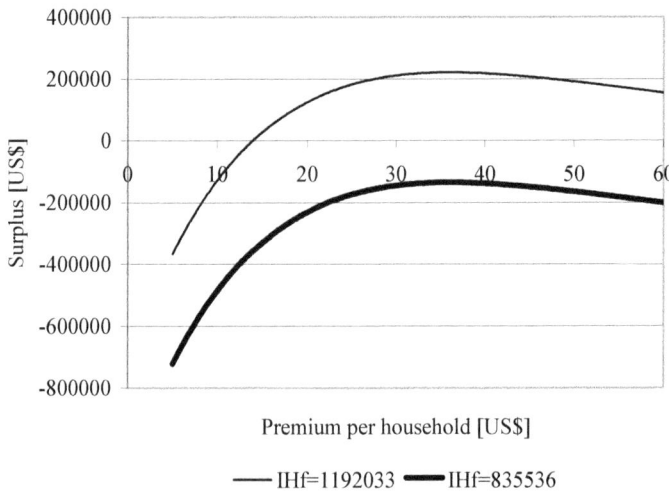

Figure 5.23 Break-Even analysis, different fixed income

If the subsidy is increased, the number of insured can be increased as well (Figure 5.24). For the basic scenario (IHf=1,192,033 US$), an additional subsidy of the fixed costs of the insurance (5,000 US$) would allow 93 additional households to join the insurance. If the additional donations were 713,746 US$, all households could join. This means that a total fixed income of 1,905,779 US$ (i.e. 54.50 US$ per household or 6.81 US$ per capita) would be required to cover the entire population. Currently there is no source available which could provide these funds so that *CBI will be no solution for the poorest in Nouna health district.*

5.3 Setting a Premium for an Insurance Scheme

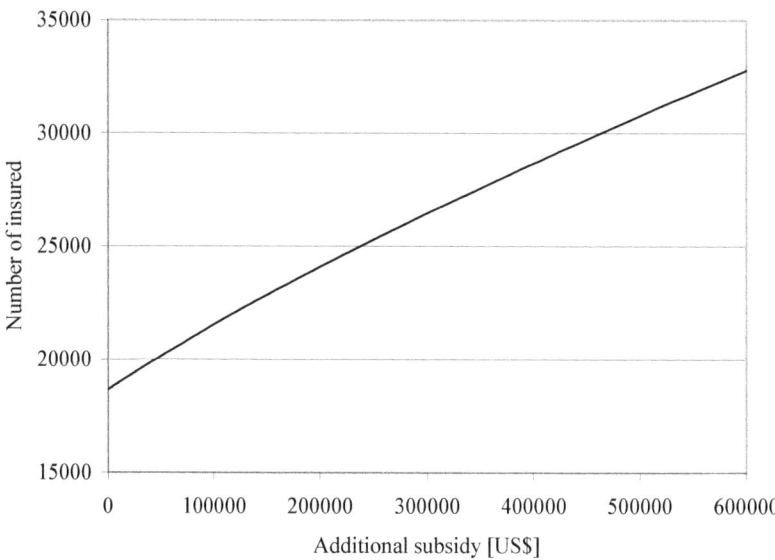

Figure 5.24   Number of Insured as a function of increase in subsidy

5.3.2.2   Non-linear Demand Increase

The following scenario assumes a non-linear demand increase. Figure 5.25 shows the original linear and the following degressive function.

$$d = \frac{d\_max+1}{2} \cdot e^{\frac{\ln(d\_max+1)-\ln(2)}{p\_max} \cdot p}$$

As Figure 5.26 shows, the premium must be about 12.80 US$ in order to break-even if the increase in demand is exponential. The demand increase would be 1.86 and 20,377 households would join the insurance. A comparison with the linear model (premium = 13,95 US$, 18,665 households, demand increase about 2.0) shows that the linear model is more pessimistic.

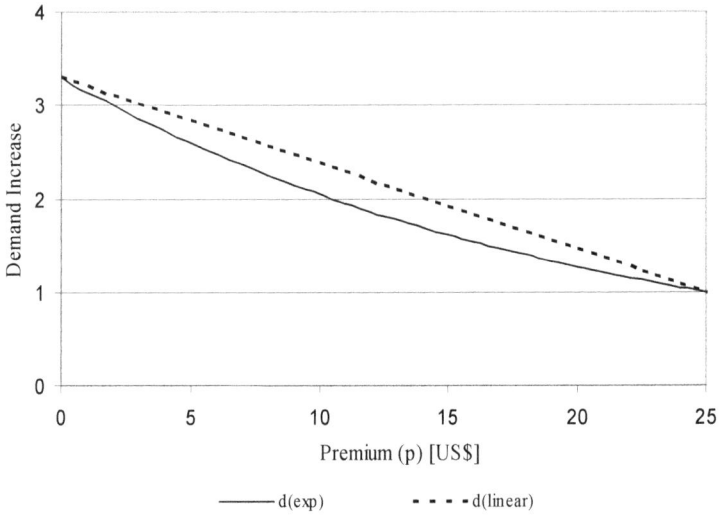

Figure 5.25   Scenarios of Demand Increase

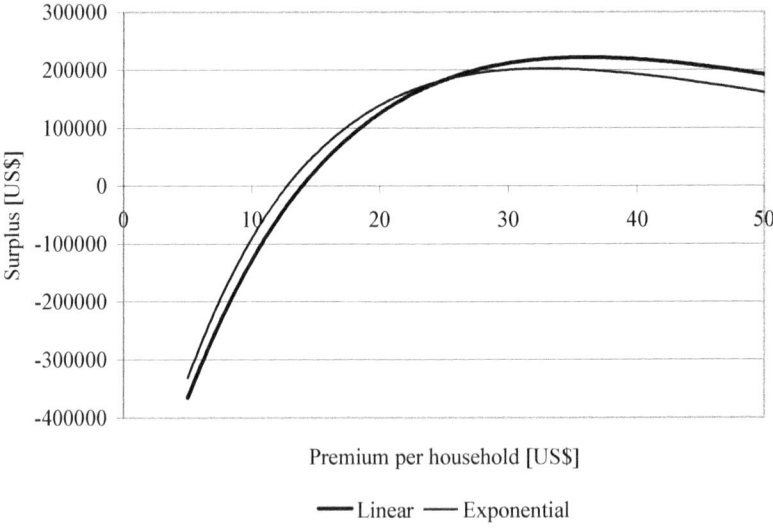

Figure 5.26   Break-Even analysis and exponential demand increase

5.3.2.3 Different Values for d_max and p_max

The following scenarios assume a linear increase in demand and different values for d_max and p_max. Scenario I is the basic model (linear demand increase, d_max = 5.6; p_max = 25 US$). Scenario II assumes a higher maximum premium (p_max = 40 US$), scenario III a lower maximum premium (p_max = 10 US$). Scenario IV assumes a stronger maximum demand increase (d_max = 8), scenario V a lower one (d_max=3). Scenario VI calculates the worst case, i.e. d_max = 8 and p_max = 40 US$. Finally scenario VII calculates the best case, i.e. d_max = 3 and p_max = 10 US$).

As Table 5.16 shows, an increase in p_max leads to an increase in demand, an increase in the premium and a decrease in the number of insured. An increase in d_max also leads to an increase in demand, an increase in the premium and a decrease in the number of insured. Consequently, the combined scenario VI with a high rate of d_max and p_max has a high increase in demand, a high premium and a low number of insured. Scenario VII has the lowest increase, the lowest premium and the maximum number of insured. The difference between the maximum premium (scenario VI) and the minimum premium (scenario VII) is 9.45 US$.

If we set a premium of 13.95 US$ (standard scenario) and if the worst case (scenario VI) occurs, CBI will have an annual loss of 120,970 US$. If the premium is 13.95 US$ and best case (scenario VII) occurs, the insurance will make an annual surplus of 498,455 US$. Instead of insuring 23,113 households, only 18,665 households would join with a premium of 13.95 US$.

Table 5.16   Scenarios of d_max and p_max

	d_max	p_max	p	d	NS
I	5.6	25	13.95	2.0	18,665
II	5.6	40	15.95	2.38	17,059
III	5.6	10	9.40	1.38	22,906
IV	8	25	15.55	2.32	17,368
V	3	25	11.50	1.54	20,747
VI	8	40	18.50	2.88	17,175
VII	3	10	9.05	1.08	23,113

These results demonstrate the importance of estimating d_max and p_max correctly. Without proper figures, setting the premium will remain a pure guess and the sustainability of the Community Based Insurance is at stake. Consequently, costing of health care services alone is insufficient for a sustainable and equitable health insurance. Behavioural studies must complete the effort to find the most appropriate premium.

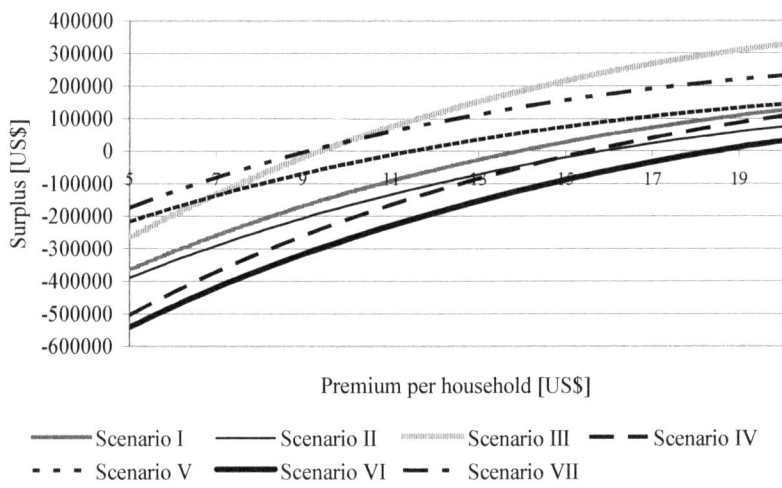

Figure 5.27   Break-Even analysis and different scenarios for p_max and d_max

5.3.2.4   Different Estimates of Willingness to Pay

The original model assumes a negative exponential Willingness to pay (WTP) curve as exhibited in Figure 5.28 [311]. A negative exponential curve assumes that a certain number of people will still join the insurance even if the premium is very high. In addition, three linear scenarios are demonstrated. Scenario "linear low" assumes that nobody will join the insurance if the annual premium per household is higher than 15 US$. Scenario "linear medium" is based on the assumption that nobody will join the insurance with a rate higher than 25 US$. Scenario "linear high" finally assumes that this point is only reached at a premium of 35 US$.

The negative exponential WTP-curve requires a premium of 13.95 CFA with 18,665 insured to break-even. Scenario "linear high" needs a premium of 13.99 US$ with 15,385 insured, scenario "linear medium" a premium of 13.93 US$ and 20,780 insured and scenario "linear low" a premium of 14.33 US$ with 1,399 insured. It is obvious that the WTP-curve has very little impact on the break-even premium, but very high impact on the number of insured. Therefore, if the WTP estimated by Dong, Kouyate & Sauerborn [311] is wrong, i.e., if the real WTP is lower, CBI will not necessarily go bankrupt. However, *if the number of insured is getting smaller, one might doubt whether implementing CBI is worthwhile at all.*

5.3 Setting a Premium for an Insurance Scheme

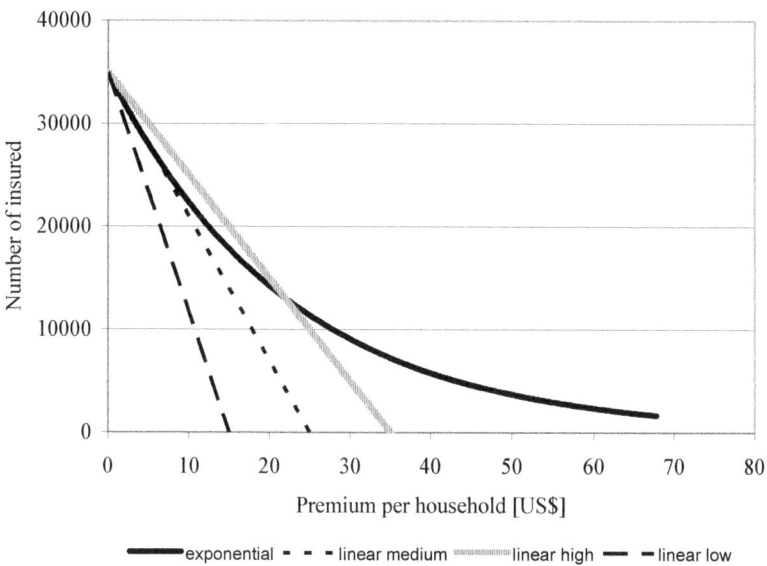

Figure 5.28   Willingness to pay

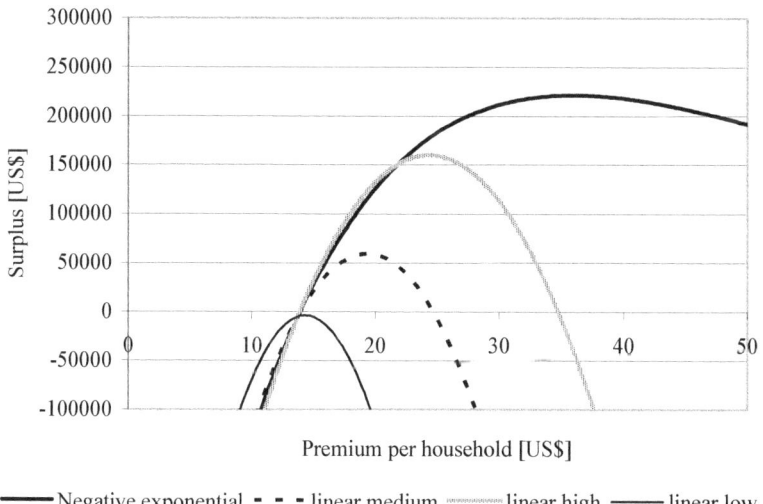

Figure 5.29   Break-Even analysis for different WTP

5.3.2.5 Effect of Pool Size

Finally, the premium depends on the *risk of bankruptcy* which is still considered to be acceptable. The above calculations represent the average cost per capita, i.e., with a probability of 50% the premium will not be sufficient to cover all cost. If the risk of bankruptcy shall be less than 50%, the premium must be increased. Consequently, we have to see the health care cost of the insured as a random variable and calculate the break-even point in respect to certain security levels. For that purpose we assume that the total variable cost of the insured are normally distributed. The individual increase or decrease in variable cost of the non-insured is (at least partly) compensated by increasing or decreasing fees as without an insurance scheme. Consequently, the break-even condition (7) can be specified as:

$$IH_f + II_f + NS \cdot p + f \cdot (Pop - NS) - \left\{ EH_f + EI_f + v\_n \cdot (Pop - NS) + \left(a\_v + \frac{s\_v \cdot u_{a\%}}{\sqrt{NS}} \right) \cdot d \cdot NS \right\} \geq 0$$

with

a_v expected value of the variable cost of an insured
s_v standard deviation of the variable cost of an insured
$u_{x\%}$ Security Level, $u_{50\%}=0$; $u_{95\%}=1.645$; $u_{97.5\%}=1.96$; $u_{99\%}=2.33$

The standard scenario calculated a premium of 13.95 US$ and 18,665 households insured with the likelihood of avoiding a bankruptcy of 50%. If this likelihood is decreased to 5%, the premium must be increased to 14.02 US$, 18,440 households will join the insurance. The corresponding figures for a probability of 1% are 14.05 US$ and 18,581 households. Therefore, for a population of 34,967 households a premium of about 14 US$ is an acceptable estimate.

However, the difference is the larger the smaller the risk pool is. In the start-up phase, CBI might begin with one village with a population of 50 households. Assuming that the fixed cost for this population are reduced proportionally, the premium must be 13.95 US$ for a risk of 50%, 16.27 US$ for 5%, 16.45 US$ for a risk of 2.5% and 17.14 US$ for a risk of 1%. Therefore, in order to reduce the risk of bankruptcy from 50% to 1% the premium must be increased by 23%. As Figure 5.30 demonstrates, the number of households insured determines the premium.

5.4 Sustainability

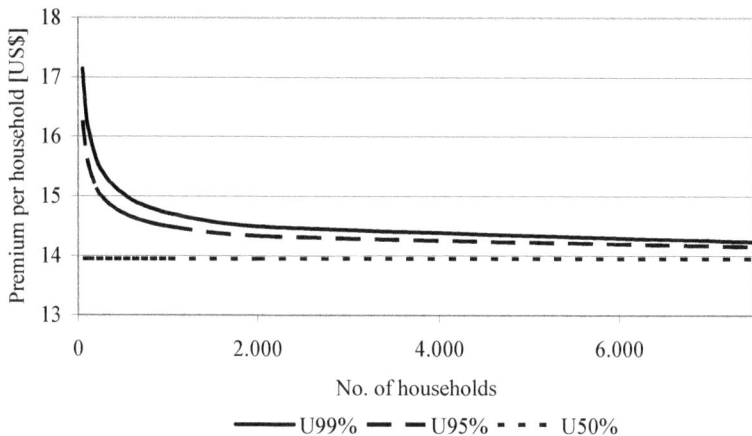

Figure 5.30   Minimum premium to avoid bankruptcy in respect to probability and number of households

The simulations demonstrate that CBI will have to charge an annual premium per household of about 14 US$ in order to break-even. However, this result is based on assumptions which will have to be re-assessed. First of all, the willingness to pay estimated in Nouna does not necessarily reflect the reality after having introduced CBI. Over-estimating WTP does not have a major impact on the likelihood of bankruptcy, but it has a tremendous effect on the number of insured. Secondly, the increase of demand after joining CBI cannot be estimated accurately. Many factors, such as tradition, distances, and behaviour of health care personnel influence the increase factor. This is beyond a mathematical model and will change over time.

Consequently, the calculations demonstrated here can only be *a first hint on how to set the premium*. In absence of external funding and back-up for bankruptcy it is wise to have a higher premium, i.e. 16 US$. If the management of the insurance realizes after two or three years that surpluses accumulate the premium can be reduced. However, this suggestion must be seen together with the call for equity, as presented in chapter 2.1 of this book.

5.4   Sustainability

In section 2.1 we demonstrated that sustainability is the answer of proper management to the call for inter-generational justice. In this section we will assess the sustainability of health care institutions based on the example in section 4.1. As Table 2.2 shows, we can distinguish between static and dynamic sustainability. Consequently, section 5.4.1 analyses the static sustainability of Lutheran hospitals in Tanzania, whereas section

5.4.2 discusses some basic concepts of dynamic sustainability. *The elaborations of sections 5.1.1 and 5.1.2 are based on the example of the Lutheran Church in Tanzania and are geared towards church-related health care services.* However, the arguments are valid for other non-profit and government services as well. We close (section 5.4.3) with a model examining the relation between time preference, interest rate and sustainability. We conclude that the *time preference is the key to understand sustainability*.

5.4.1 Assessing Static Sustainability

Table 5.17 exhibits the average cost per service unit in Lutheran hospitals in the year 1995. As described in section 4.1.1, *minimum costs* include personnel, drugs and other consumables which are absolutely necessary to keep the institution running for a short period. *Sustainable local costs* include all costs necessary to run the hospital for many years except those costs covered by donations. *Full costs* include the entire resource consumption, i.e. also for equipment and buildings paid by donations and for foreign staff. *Actual costs* are the monetary equivalent of all resources consumed in the year 1995, whereas *standard costs* are the equivalent for those resources which the hospitals would have required if they had followed their own standards of staffing, equipment and buildings. Standard full costs include a maintenance charge of 1% of initial costs of buildings and 5% of initial costs of equipment and a standard depreciation of annually 4% of the initial costs of buildings and of 10% of the initial costs of equipment.

Table 5.17 Average cost per equivalent inpatient day in Lutheran hospitals 1995 [US$] (comp. Table 4.2)

Category	Actual Cost	Standard Cost
Minimum costs	2.79	2.76
Sustainable local costs	2.96	3.52
Full costs	6.43	9.62

The management of the Lutheran hospitals was satisfied if they managed to close the annual books of accounts without a "deficit". However, the book-keeping of these institutions is a pure cash-flow accounting neglecting a major part of the total costs. In 1995, the actual expenditure was only 54% of the real costs, i.e., there was an underspending of 46%. The actual payment for equipment maintenance in 1995 was on average only 0.71% of the current budget. Based on standard equipment lists published by GtZ and WHO [236, 321] the standard equipment maintenance of the investigated hospitals should be on average 6.41% of the current budget. However, only 11% of the recommended amount was actually spent for equipment maintenance. At the same time, no hospital applied the concepts of depreciation or built up funds for reinvestments. In other words: the hospital structures were consumed without reflecting this in the accounts. In the long run the structure will vanish away and future patients will not find the same quality of services as patients of the present. This difference of 46% indicates that *the hospitals cannot achieve a static structural sustainability*.

5.4 Sustainability

The static functional sustainability must be based on an assessment whether the ELCT hospitals can fulfil their original function. According to the mission statement of the ELCT health and diaconic directorate, Lutheran hospitals in Tanzania were inaugurated to provide services for the "poor and needy" in the spirit of the Good Samaritan. This is the original function. However, some of these hospitals fail to serve a major share of the population at all.

Table 5.18   Occupancy and fees of ELCT hospitals 1995

	Occupancy [%]	Share of user-fees in total income [%]	Average user-fee per patient [Tshs]	Average user-fee per bedday [Tshs]
Marangu	26	82	4,945	1,693
Bumbuli	32	38	3,793	759
Machame	45	58	11,665	1,524
Itete	59	46	5,330	620
Iambi	61	57	5042	720
Selian	66	67	7,665	1,095
Ndolage	76	60	9,228	948
Lugala	81	43	3,494	538
Bulongwa	85	32	1,700	283
Karatu	90	66	9,366	1,626
Ilembula	90	57	4,282	714
Nyakahanga	101	23	3,794	332
Bunda	115	21	2,250	321
Haydom	119	53	8,183	827
Correlation with occupancy	1	-0,4784	-0,1428	-0,5035

Table 5.18 shows that almost half of the hospitals suffered from very poor occupancy. Many patients did not seek help from Lutheran hospitals. There is no evidence that the medical need had declined, but hospitals which were fully occupied in the 1980s had a strong drop in demand in the 1990s. According to the basic model presented in Figure 2.7, this can be due to poorer quality of ELCT hospital services, higher friction of distance or comparably higher fees. It is not very likely that the distances to the institutions had grown, and the general mobility had even increased so that distance cannot be the reason why hospitals which were originally fully occupied had occupancy rates of less than 70%.

A situation analysis of the early 1990s clarified that the competition of private and public providers had strongly increased. In particular government hospitals had improved their quality. In the 1970s and 1980s, these institutions were notoriously short of drugs and personnel. High quality services were only available in church-related health care institutions. The 1990s had seen major investments of the government into public health services, and the general economic situation allowed the import of drugs for government institutions. Consequently, government hospitals improved. At the same time, cost-sharing was introduced in Tanzanian government health care institutions which provided additional funds. But the user-fees were still much lower in governmental than in Lutheran hospitals so that the population had a higher tendency to seek help in government institutions than before and the demand for Lutheran hospital services declined.

Thus, we can conclude that ELCT hospitals do not serve as many people as they would like to. In addition, it is likely that they serve more the richer population which can afford to pay for these high-price services. Table 5.18 shows that there is a strong negative correlation between user-fees and occupancy. Hospitals with high fees have low occupancy. And hospitals with high fees have a tendency to exclude the poor.

The analysis of functional sustainability cannot be based entirely on costing-studies. We would have to discuss in detail why some Lutheran hospitals have so poor occupancy rates, i.e., why they fail to fulfil their original function. *Costing data of the health care institutions can provide a first and important insight, but it should be enriched by studies on willingness- and ability-to-pay.*

5.4.2 Assessing Dynamic Sustainability

In section 2.1 we defined dynamic sustainability as the *ability of a system to adjust to changes of its environment*. Health care systems are not in a static equilibrium. They are dynamic, i.e., a continuous series of changing system regimes with many fluctuations and bifurcations. Figure 5.31 illustrates this general statement with a brief history of the health care systems in Tanzania. The following analysis will focus on church-related health care institutions, but the underlying concepts of meta-stability and dynamic sustainability are applicable to any public health care system.

The traditional African system of health was holistic. Aspects of health and sickness were seen in a much wider context of the well-being of the individual in its social and spiritual environment. Searching for causes of diseases usually led to a violation of a traditional taboo or an insult of an ancestor or spirit, which had to be healed by acts of reconciliation, such as animal sacrifices [322]. Therefore, the traditional African health care system was highly interrelated with religion, and only few herbalist or traditional surgeons disclaimed the use of magic. A formal inter-regional system was not developed, but each tribe had its own traditions and cures.

The invasion of colonialism constituted a shock for most African tribes. In East Africa, the Arabs were the first to conquer the coast and later extended their influence via slave trade into inner Tanganyika. However, their influence was quite limited until Sultan Syyid Said Ibn settled in Zanzibar in 1840 and made it a centre of Arab influence, both on culture and slave trade in East Africa. The Arabs had a well established system of medicine called "unani". It builds on the ancient Greek galenic medicine and was developed in the 7th and 8th centuries A. D. Contrary to the African medical system, "unani" had developed a profession of medical practitioners with training institutions of their own and rather separate from religion. Arabs entering inner Africa brought with them their system of medicine and confronted African traditions with it. However, their influence was limited to few places. The population of Africa and the

5.4 Sustainability

traditional medical system had experienced a rather long period of continuity. A homeostatic system had developed and changes took place over a long time so that the necessary adjustment of regulation variables occurred almost imperceptibly.

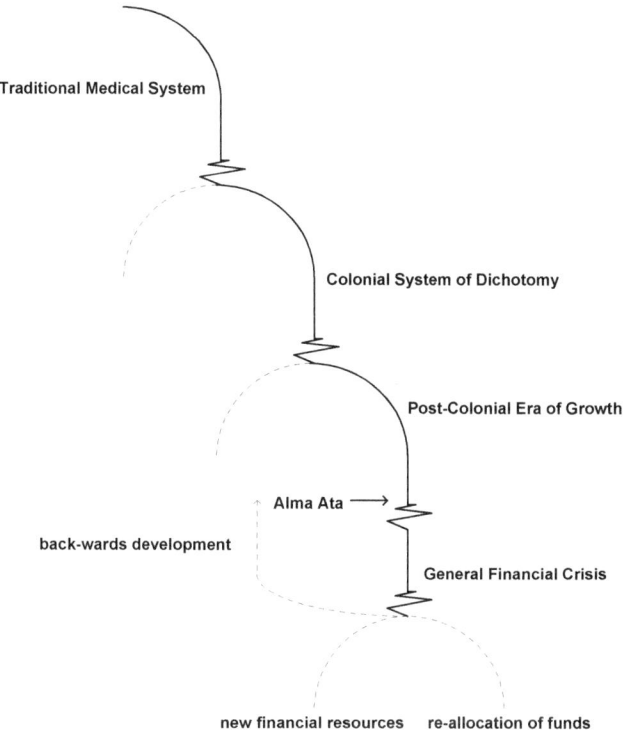

Figure 5.31   History of health care systems in Tanzania

Likewise, the influence of the Portuguese (1499-1698) in East Africa was restricted to a few miles of coastal areas and had hardly any impact on medical thought in Eastern Africa. This changed totally when German missionaries and colonial officers appeared. They started working in what today is called Tanzania about 1880. Used to western medicine and convinced of the superiority of western values, colonial officers started building hospitals in all major cities. Important research of tropical diseases took place and first attempts to control communicable diseases were initiated. The English Colonial Medical Service which became responsible for Tanganyika after the First World War developed the system of hospitals in central places further on and installed regional medical officers. The founding of different medical and nursing training centres falls into this period. Missionaries built church hospitals and professional medical doctors served in them.

However impressive some of the results of this time might appear, the impact on the daily life of the majority of the population in Tanganyika was negligible. The colonial era is characterized by a strong dichotomy between western medicine in towns and mission stations on the one hand, and on the other hand traditional medicine for the rural majority. As out-reach programmes were only few and mobility of the population was very limited, most of the hospitals had only a catchment area with a radius of a few kilometres around them. The vast majority of the country continued to rely on the services of traditional healers [323].

Toward the end of the colonial era and after independence the negligence of the majority of rural areas changed. The independence of the nation, the development of self governing churches and the years of nationalization brought strong fluctuations for the church health care system. Finally a point was reached where it became obvious that nothing would remain as it was before. At one point it was not clear whether the churches would continue at all to have hospitals in Tanzania. Some were nationalized and the government claimed full responsibility for all social services. On the other hand the new church leadership accepted the responsibility for the health care for the entire country and tried to build many new hospitals in areas which had been "forgotten" before. Theoretically it could have happened as well that a development back to a traditional health care system would have been initiated seeing that a poor and struggling nation and church cannot afford a western-type health care system.

At that time the medical missionaries of the China Inland Mission [324] had to leave China as they were expelled by the communist government. Many of them were life-long missionaries who were looking for new mission fields. Therefore, several came to East Africa and brought with them 100 years tradition of medical mission in China. This tradition was mainly a surgical tradition, as China had had a sophisticated system of internal medicine, whereas surgery had been a taboo. Therefore, medical mission in China was dominated by surgeons. After they had come to Africa they started restructuring mission hospitals. In Africa there was no equivalent system of internal medicine, so that only a very small part of medical problems in Africa were surgical. However, these missionaries built big operating theatres and founded major hospitals. The two biggest Lutheran hospitals in Tanzania, for instance, were both founded by former China inland missionaries.

The building of new hospitals yielded remarkable fruits in the first few years, as a wider share of the rural poor received access to western medicine. This was mainly financed by donations. The new system regime of widely spread church hospitals belonging to self-governing churches stabilized and a period of 25 years of constancy made many church leaders believe that the church hospital is a homeostatic system which can retain its energy level and structure without rapid changes or metamorphosis. The primary health care innovation (Alma Ata Declaration) came exactly in this period of stability and success of hospital-based health care. Therefore, it is no wonder that the implementation was very poor. There was no need to change anything. The innovations of primary health care were blocked long before they could reach the phase of diffusion.

5.4 Sustainability

Today the situation has changed completely: Peasants earn less for their crops and are unable to pay for health care services. Donations are diminishing and new diseases (e.g. AIDS) increase the demand for services. It becomes obvious that many church-related health care institutions have consumed their structure to such high an extent that they cannot fulfil their function anymore. The hospitals should adjust their function and structure to the new environment: they should be functionally sustainable. Hospitals will still have a function in a district health care system, but this function is not the same as it was a few years ago where church hospitals were almost entirely the only source of professional health care for the majority of rural people. Instead of being the centre of all curative care, the hospital must become a service centre for other health care activities. Its curative function must be restricted to referral cases. The changing function will also require a changing structure. Certain departments and professions (e.g. operating theatre, surgeons) will not have such a high status any more. Instead, health economists and social scientists will enter the health care hierarchy on top level.

However, it seems that the period of 25 years of constancy reduced the ability of church-related institutions to regulate and adjust to the new situation. This is only partly their fault. The steady stream of donations which was sent from the western world to low income countries has reduced their ability to adapt to the changing environment. Theoretically the majority of Christian hospitals in Tanzania would have required structural adjustments 25 years ago. But all failures and problems were cured with scores of developments workers and millions US$ of financial support from overseas. In this way these institutions lost their ability to adjust to minor changes of the environment. Now, where the changes have accumulated and call for a different function of the hospital, these institutions are unable to adjust: they are *dynamically unsustainable*. This might lead to their extinction.

In order to demonstrate this, we would like to consider a homeostatic system. The system can be very stable as long as the environment remains unchanged. Figure 5.32 exhibits the traditional control loop. The goals of the system (controlling variables) determine the regulation of the process (regulation variables). However, because of random disturbance by the environment (perturbance variables) and internal errors it can happen that the results (controlled variables) do not match the goals. Results and goals must be compared (control) and the regulation variables changed accordingly. It is the highest objective of any control loop to keep the steady flow of energy and the variables unchanged as long as possible. As long as the perturbance variables are not too influential, i.e., as long as the environment remains stable, there is no need to adjust the regulation variables. Societies, for instance, can remain in a homeostatic condition for generations without the necessity of changing their goals or means to achieve these goals. The church health care system was in such a stable condition for almost 25 years.

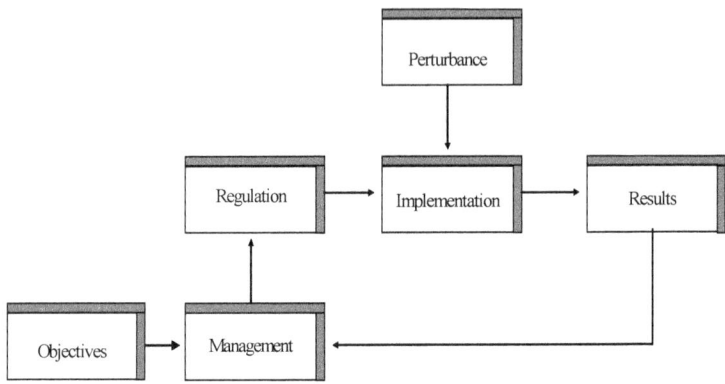

Figure 5.32   Control loop

However, this control-loop is completely changed by donations. The feed-back loop is the most important component of the entire control system. If this feed-back is interrupted or its message is disturbed by "noise", the system becomes without control. *The main problem of the control system of the Lutheran hospitals in Tanzania is that there are two sets of controlled variables. The first set constitutes the feed-back from the parish members and the hospital patients. The second is the feed-back from the donors.*

The big black arrow in Figure 5.33 which points from the controlled variables relevant to the donors to the evaluation process shall indicate that the ELCT control process must consider the donors much more than the local basis. As we have seen, up to 80% of the total hospital income is obtained from donors abroad. Thus, it is only logical if *the hospital leadership pays much more attention to the signals from abroad than to the signals of the own basis*, i.e. the patients. The hospitals of the Evangelical Lutheran Church in Tanzania are almost autonomous from their patients! In some hospitals patients indicated twenty years ago that something was wrong. The occupancy dropped and deficits accumulated. However, there was no need for the hospital leadership to change the hospital policy as the most important source of income and therefore the guarantee of financial sustainability remained unchanged. Donations came whether patients were cured or not. Hospitals like Nkoaranga, Marangu, Gonja or Bumbuli have completely lost contact with their basis. They can only survive as a stable organization because they are supported from abroad and all developments and changes are artificially blocked.

5.4 Sustainability

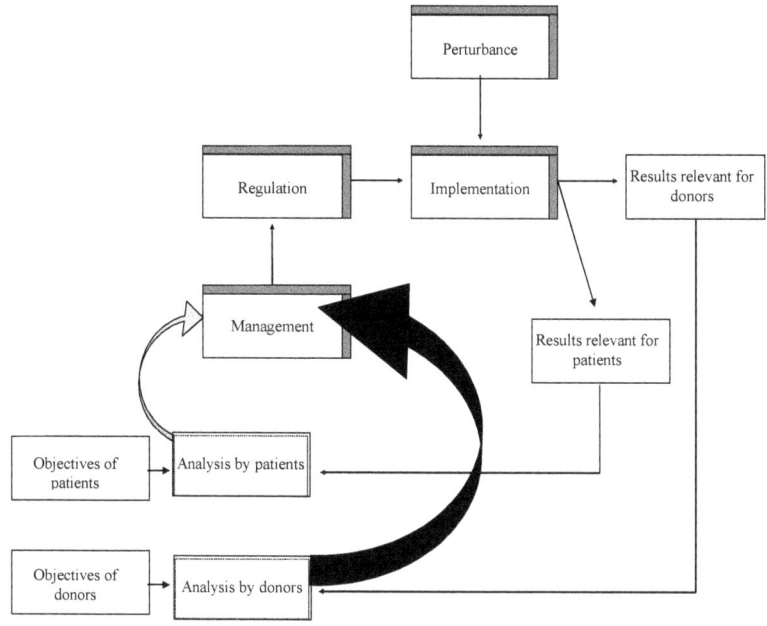

Figure 5.33 Control loop of ELCT hospitals

Quite a number of church and hospital leaders have replaced the original health-seeking mentality with a *transfer-seeking mentality*. The steady flow of donations made the system stable, but artificially stable. Generally, an artificial stability of a dynamic system by suppressing any perturbance caused by a changing environment is called *meta-stability* [325]. *The result of meta-stability is always inflexibility.* In the case of hospitals, the consequence of meta-stability is that the plans of the hospital leadership and the reality of the basis are becoming more and more irreconcilable. The inflexibility which is always the result of meta-stability has increased so much that it becomes doubtful whether a smooth mutation into a new system regime is still possible.

At the moment it seems possible to keep some hospitals artificially alive by external subsidies, but this will only worsen the inflexibility due to the meta-stable condition and finally the changing environment will cause these institutions to collapse. Instead of an ongoing evolution towards a new solution we are facing a process of involution. The Lutheran health care in Tanzania – as well as many other health care systems in developing countries – cannot adjust to the changes of the environment, it is dynamically unsustainable.

The reader will ask: "Why do you discuss these philosophical issues in a booklet on costing?" I fully agree that costing cannot provide all insights into the problems of dependency, meta-stability and distorted feedbacks. But *we have to know the costs, the income and the share of donations in the total income in order to assess the dependency and the risk of meta-stability. Without proper costing data, we will not be able to assess the magnitude of foreign influence on decision-making in health care institutions.*

The key to dynamic sustainability is the capability to react flexible on changes of the environment. This calls for professional management, continuous analysis and a leadership style that empowers employees and patients to act as sensors to the changes of the health care environment.

5.4.3 Sustainability and Time Preference

In section 2.1 we discussed the goal conflicts between the basic objectives of health care. Sustainability is in conflict with all other objectives as resources can either be spent today or tomorrow, for this generation or for future generations. From an economic perspective, the trade-off between today and the future can be expressed with the concept of the time preference. Consequently, we will first discuss the importance of the time preference for inter-temporal resource allocation. Afterwards we will present a model that allows some insights into the importance of the time preference rate for sustainable health care.

5.4.3.1 Model

Decision-makers have to decide whether a certain health status in the year t has the same or a different utility as the same health status in the year t+i (i>0). Usually, the utility (U) of a certain health status (H) is assessed as being the smaller, the further it lies in the future. This is due to the fact that this utility is uncertain and the individual is risk-avers [137, 144]. Therefore, the health status in t+i must be higher than the health status in t in order to have the same utility for the individual. Figure 5.34 presents this concept.

The inter-temporal indifferential curves U_0 and U_1 present combinations of present and future health status which are assessed as equal by the individual. The individual will only accept a reduction of the present health status if he receives a superproportional increase of health in future. This means that the future health status is discounted with a positive rate ρ. ρ is called the *time preference rate*, as it reflects the importance of the present against the future. The higher the time preference rate, the more important is the present, i.e., a future health status is highly discounted. Small time preference rates imply that future health has almost the same importance as a good health in the present.

The LP-model presented in section 5.2 optimized the resource allocation within one year. It did not consider an inter-temporal resource allocation, i.e., the model cannot be used to make statements about sustainability. In the following we present a model that maximizes an inter-temporal utility function. Depending on the time preference rate of

5.4 Sustainability

decision makers the programme calculates the number of dispensaries, health centres and hospitals in a health district as well as the funds allocated to preventive services. The planning period is 25 years, i.e., we are in the field of strategic planning. The results of the model can be utilized to explain the effects of a changing time preference rate on the allocation decision. The model is designed to provide insights into the processes of district health planning in developing countries ("Modelling for Insights, not Numbers"[276]).

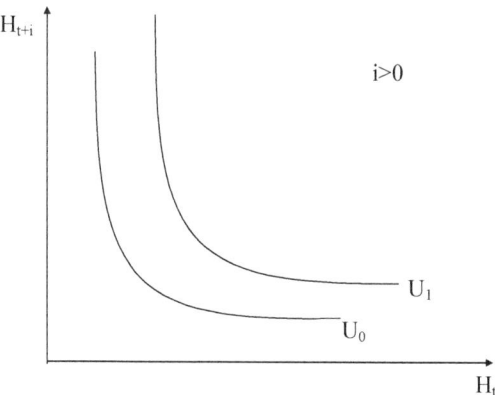

Figure 5.34   Inter-temporal allocation

The model must be limited to monetary aspects. It would be ideal to consider several diseases and the demand for health care services deriving from them in order to account for the highly complex epidemiology. However, such a detailed model could not be solved in acceptable time as a high number of integer variables is required.

The model defines the following variables (all variables are non-negative).

$K_{l,t}$	Demand for curative service units on level l in year t; l=1..3; t=1..25
$l =$	$\begin{cases} 1: dispensary \\ 2: health\,center \\ 3: hospital \end{cases}$
P_t	Prevention budget in year t; t=1..25
$In_{l,t}$	Number of institutions on level l in year t; integer variable; l=1..3; t=1..25
PW_t	Prevention effect in period t; t=1..25
$C_{l,t}$	Cost on level l in year t; l=1..3; t=1..25
$Beh_{l,t}$	Service units on level l in year t; l=1..3; t=1..25
$NIn_{l,t}$	New institutions on level l in year t; integer variable; l=1..3; t=1..25
$NB_{l,t}$	Demand unserved on level l in year t; l=1..3; t=1..25
$Be_{l,t}$	Number of beds on level l in year t; integer variable; l=2..3; t=1..25
$Nbe_{l,t}$	New number of beds on level l in year t; integer variable; l=2..3; t=1..25

Pe_t	$\begin{cases} 1 & \text{prevention begins in period } t \\ 0 & \text{else} \end{cases}$	
$Bu_{l,t}$	Budget for curative services on level l in year t; l=1..3; t=1..25	
BuP_t	Budget for prevention in year t, t=1..25	
X_t	Utility of health status in year t, t=1..25	
XS	Total utility of health status (unweighted)	
KCT	Total costs of curative health care services	
KPT	Total costs of prevention programmes	
$KPHT$	Total costs of primary services	
KHT	Total costs of hospital services	

The model defines the following constants:

$KMax_l$	Maximum demand for curative service units on level l; l=1..3
$KMin_l$	Minimum demand for curative service units on level l, if all means of prevention are used and effective; l=1..3
$PMax$	Maximum spending for prevention
$InMax_l$	Maximum number of institutions on level l; l=1..3
W_j	Efficacy of prevention in period t+j-1; j=1..4, with $\sum_{j=1}^{4} w_j = 1$
$MaxEZ_l$	Maximum capacity per unit of level l; l=1..3
CBF_l	Fixed cost of establishing the core buildings of one institution of level l; l=1..3
CBB_l	Fixed costs of establishing one bed on level l; l=2,3
$CBeF_l$	Annual fixed costs of running one institution on level l; l=1..3
$CBeV_l$	Variable costs per serve unit on level l; l=1..3
$MaxB_l$	Maximum number of beds per institution on level l; l=2,3
$CDMT$	Unique costs of establishing a district management team
M	100,000
A	Initial financial subsidy
Z	Annual subsidy per year
nV	Utility of preventing a disease
nb	Utility of curing a disease
nS	Utility of suffering from a disease
ε	Weight factor of the goal function
r	Interest rate
ρ	Time preference rate

The model of non-linear programming has the following *constraints*:

- *Effect of prevention:* It is a basic assumption of the model that funds allocated to prevention in period t will have impact on the incidence in the following periods. It is assumed that the maximum impact of prevention will need four periods to be es-

5.4 Sustainability

tablished. For instance, AIDS-control programmes have to teach people again and again how to prevent AIDS. The first year of education will have some impact on sexual behaviour, but it might take several years until behaviour changes significantly.

$$PW_1 = W_1 \cdot P_1$$
$$PW_2 = W_1 \cdot P_2 + W_2 \cdot P_1$$
$$PW_3 = W_1 \cdot P_3 + W_2 \cdot P_2 + W_3 \cdot P_1$$
$$PW_t = W_1 \cdot P_t + W_2 \cdot P_{t-1} + W_3 \cdot P_{t-2} + W_4 \cdot P_{t-3} \quad for \quad t = 4..25$$

- *Demand*: The demand of health care services depends on the impact of prevention. The model assumes the demand for curative services will decrease linearly with increasing prevention budgets, since a certain proportion of the illnesses can be avoided. However, not all diseases are preventable, so that a certain minimum demand for health care exists even if the prevention budget is unlimited.

$$P_t \leq PMax \; for \; t = 1...25$$
$$K_{l,t} \geq Kmin_l$$
$$K_{l,t} \leq KMax_l$$
$$K_{l,t} \geq KMax_l - \frac{(KMax_l - KMin_l)}{PMax} \cdot PW_t$$

- *Maximum capacity*: The demand for services on the different levels cannot be higher than the disease potential of the people in the catchment area of the institutions. Therefore, the health care institutions have a maximum capacity which corresponds to the maximum population of the catchment areas and their disease frequency.

$$Beh_{l,t} \leq MaxEZ_l \cdot \frac{K_{l,t}}{KMax_1} \cdot In_{l,t} \quad l = 1,2; \quad t = 1..25$$

$$Beh_{3,t} \leq MaxEZ_l \cdot Betten_{3,t}$$

- *Costs*: The building costs are divided into costs which vary with the number of beds (e.g. buildings wards) and those which are independent from the size of the institution (e.g. outpatient department, theatre, x-ray unit). Running costs are divided as well into fixed and variable costs.

$$C_{l,t} = CBF_l \cdot NIn_{l,t} + CBB_l \cdot Nbe_{l,t} + CBeF_l \cdot In_{l,t} + CBeV_l \cdot Beh_{l,t} \quad l=1..3; \quad t=1..25$$

$$NIn_{l,t} \geq In_{l,t} - In_{l,t-1} \quad t=2..25; l=1..3$$

$$Nbe_{l,t} \geq Be_{l,t} - Be_{l,t-1} \quad l=2..3; t=2..25$$

$$Be_{l,t} \leq MB_l \cdot In_{l,t} \quad l=2,3; \quad t=1..25$$

$$C_{l,t} \leq Bu_{l,t} \quad l=1..3, t=1..25$$

$$K_{l,t} - NB_{l,t} = Beh_{l,t} \quad l=1..3, t=1..25$$

- *Prevention*: Prevention programmes need administrative support. This support can be provided either by a hospital or by a special and independent district health management team. However, this team needs transport facilities, offices and training. If a hospital exists, there are hardly any additional costs.

$$Prev_t \leq M \cdot In_{3,t} + M \cdot \sum_{i=1}^{t} Prev\_Erstab_i \quad t=1..25$$

$$Prev_t + Cost\_DMT \cdot Prev\_Erstab_t = Budget\_Prev_t \quad t=1..25$$

$$\sum_{i=1}^{25} Prev\_Erstab_i \leq 1$$

- *Budget*: It is assumed that the health district receives external initial support in the beginning of the first year (t=1). In addition, they obtain a certain amount every year in order to provide health care services. Any funds can be used to buy bonds which earn an interest rate of r. At the same time, the health care district can obtain a loan and pay back the money in later years. In this case they will have to pay interest with a rate of r. The present value of all costs of all periods (t=1..25) must be less or equal to the present value of all health care resources in all periods (t=1..25).

$$\sum_{t=1}^{25} \frac{Z}{\left(1+\frac{r}{100}\right)^{t-1}} + A \geq \sum_{t=1}^{25} \left\{ \frac{\sum_{l=1}^{3} Bu_{l,t} + BuP_t}{\left(1+\frac{r}{100}\right)^{t-1}} \right\} \quad for \ t=1..25$$

The utility of year t is calculated as

$$X_t = nS \cdot \sum_{l=1}^{3}(NB_{l,t}) + nb \cdot \sum_{l=1}^{3}(Beh_{l,t}) + nV \cdot \sum_{l=1}^{3}(KMax_l - K_{l,t}) \quad for \ t=1..25$$

5.4 Sustainability

The present value of utilities of the health status of the population is maximised. Future utilities are discounted with a time preference rate ρ. Different utilities are assigned to diseases prevented, disease cured and disease untreated.

If the budget is higher than the financial requirements (e.g. if the time preference rate is extremely high so that all funds are entirely spent in the first year), there will be alternative solutions. Therefore, the objective function includes two terms which safeguard that the costs are minimised. The weight factor ε is a very small number so that costs will only be minimised if the utility is already at its maximum.

$$Z = \sum_{t=1}^{25} \frac{X_t}{\left(1 + \frac{\rho}{100}\right)^{t-1}} - \varepsilon \cdot \sum_{t=1}^{25} P_t - \varepsilon \cdot \sum_{l=1}^{3} \sum_{t=1}^{25} In_{l,t} \rightarrow Max!$$

The data is based on the calculations of section 4.1, 4.2 and 5.1.1. Table 5.19 presents the basic figures.

Table 5.19 Optimum allocation of health care resources in a district: constants

Constant	l=1	l=2	l=3	Other variables
$KMax_l$	150,000	37,350	46,538	
$KMin_l$	112,500	28,103	34,903	
$PMax$				100,000
$InMax_l$	16	4	1	
W_j				W_1=0.6; W_2=0.2; W_3=0.15; W_4=0.05
$MaxEZ_l$	9,361	310.25	310.25	
CBF_l	20,000	50,000	250,000	
CBB_l	0	1,000	4,186	
$CBeF_l$	6,000	10,000	100,000	
$CBeV_l$	0.2	0.36	0.96	
$MaxB_l$	0	30	150	
$CDMT$				50,000
M				100,000
A				1,000,000
Z				300,000
nV				100%
nb				50%
nS				1%
ε				0.0001

5.4.3.2 Results

The standard model assumes that interest and time preference rates are equal (r=5%, ρ=5%). Therefore, the decision maker is indifferent whether he should invest health care resources in period t or t+i (i>0) if the health effects of these investments are identical (H_t: health in period t; I_t: investment in period t). An investment in period t+i has the discounted utility $H_{t+i} \cdot (1 + \rho/100)^{-i}$, but the costs of this investment have a similar present value of $I_{t+i} \cdot (1 + r/100)^{-i}$. If the time preference rate equals the interest rate, the quotient of utility and present value is constant for all i, if the health effect of an investment is identical. Therefore, the decision maker is indifferent in which period to spend the health care budget, i.e., usually all periods will be treated in the same way.

As a consequence, health care services and the number of institutions are constant all over the 25 periods. There will be always 16 dispensaries and four health centres. However, no hospital is built. Instead, a health care management team is established and funded. The impact of the prevention programme is 60% in the first year, 80% in the second, 95% in the third. In the first year the number of patients declines accordingly to 85% of the initial value, in the second year to 80% and in the third year to 76.25%. Beginning of the fourth year, prevention programmes are fully effective so that merely 75% of the initial service units in the health care institutions are demanded. In the first year the four health centres are equipped with 102 beds. In the second year the effect of the prevention programmes allows to reduce the number to 96. In the third year the number of beds in health centres can again be reduced by 4 beds. In the fourth year and all further years it is 90.

The sum of the utilities is calculated as 3,204,221. As there is no hospital, all funds are invested into primary care (8,221,568 US$). 68.98% are spent for curative medicine. Therefore, the mathematical model of district health care underlines estimates of the World Bank that about 67% of health care budgets should be spent for curative health care services and the rest for prevention [143].

The results of this standard model shall be confronted with different scenarios of altered rates of interest and time preference rates. It is obvious that the results are constant if time preference and interest rates are equal (e.g. r=ρ=10%). The value of the objective function decreases if the rate increases. The situation changes if time preference and interest rates differ. One scenario (r=5%, ρ=0%) assumes that the interest rate is 5% and the time preference rate is zero. This means that there is no difference whether a utility is harvested today or in future. Another scenario (r=100%, ρ=0%) calculates with a time preference rate of zero and an extremely high interest rate of 100%. Again another scenario (r=0%, ρ=100%) shows the opposite. The time preference rate is high, whereas the interest rate is zero. The last scenario (r=5%, ρ=∞) reflects an extremely high time preference rate so that only utilities of the first period are maximised. Table 5.20 shows the results of these scenarios.

It is obvious that a steady development is prevented by the introduction of integer variables. For instance, in the second scenario (r=5%, ρ=0%) one would expect that the number of hospital beds will increase steadily. If the time preference rate is zero and the interest rate is greater than zero it is wise to invest the funds on the financial markets. The value of the funds invested increases with interests paid so that more can be spent for future health care. The utility will increase accordingly. Indeed the utility value of the second model (r=5%, ρ=0%) is greater than of the first model (r=5%,

5.4 Sustainability

$\rho=5\%$). Therefore, one would expect that health care facilities will be extended every year and new beds will be set up. If one calculates the model without integer variables the number of beds indeed increases from 0 to 133. Using integer variables the picture changes: Not before the 17th year the utility harvested by establishing a hospital is high enough to justify building a hospital. *Therefore, the functions which describe the optimal allocation of health care funds in a district to different levels of health care are neither steady nor monotonous. Health policy makers are challenged by this finding as it is very difficult to combine these jumps with the linear thinking of many decision makers.*

Table 5.20   Scenarios of interest and time preference rates

	$r=5\%, \rho=5\%$	$r=5\%, \rho=0\%$	$r=100\%, \rho=0\%$	$r=0\%, \rho=100\%$	$r=5\%, \rho=\infty$
Number of dispensaries	16 for t=1,...,25	16 for t=1,...,25	16 for t=1,...,25	16 for t=1..9, 0 for t≥10	16 for t=1, 0 for t≥2
Number of health centres	4 for t=1,...,25	3 for t=1, 4 for t≥2	4 for t=1,...,25	4 for t=1..9, 0 for t≥10	4 for t=1, 0 for t≥2
Beds in health centres	102 for t=1, 96 for t=2, 92 for t=3, 90 for t≥4	77 for t=1, 96 for t=2, 92 for t=3, 90 for t≥4	26 for t=1, 96 for t=2, 92 for t=3, 90 for t≥4	102 for t=1, 96 for t=2, 92 for t=3, 90 for t=4..9, 0 for t≥10	102 for t=1, 0 for t≥2
Number of hospitals	0 for t=1,...,25	0 for t=1..16, 1 for t≥17	0 for t=1, 1 for t≥2	1 for t=1..8, 0 for t≥9	1 for t=1, 0 for t≥2
Beds in hospitals	0 for t=1,...,25	0 for t=1..16, 133 for t≥17	0 for t=1, 122 for t=2, 150 for t≥3	150 for t=1..8, 0 for t≥9	150
Annual prevention budget	100,000 for t=1,...,25	100,000 for t=1,...,25	100,000 for t=1,...,25	100,000 for t=1..9, 0 for t≥10	100,000 for t=1, 0 for t≥2
Institutionalisation of DHMT	in t=1	in t=1	in t=1	in t=9	no DHMT
Sum of utilities	3,204,221	3,334,612	3,599,766	1,350,855	188,338
Share of primary care	100%	72.71%	64.30%	61.43%	46.67%
Share of curative care	68.98%	78.87%	77.69%	81.12%	94.76%

It is also obvious that a strong orientation towards the present (high time preference rate) will lead to a low total utility. The sum of annual utilities is 3,334,612 for the second scenario ($r=5\%, \rho=0\%$), whereas it is 188,338 for the last scenario ($r=5\%, \rho=\infty$). Thus, *a high time preference rate goes along with a low total utility* [326], *a decreasing time preference rate induces an increasing total utility.*

A high time preference rate will furthermore call for a high share of curative medicine in the total health care budget. If the time preference rate is high, future utilities have a low impact on decisions. This is due to the fact that curative care is effective on the spot, whereas prevention programmes will take several years until their full efficacy is reached. Most prevention programmes aim to change behaviour, so that they demand an ongoing education for many years. A high time preference rate implies that people prefer the results of curative medicine in the present to achievements of prevention programmes in the future. Therefore, a population with a high time preference rate will prefer curative medicine. *At the same time a population with a strong priority of the present will decide to run expensive hospital services today, even if this means that there will be not enough funds to provide health care services in dispensaries and health centres in the future. Therefore, a high time preference rate goes along with a low share of primary care in the total health care budget. One might be tempted to formulate a rule of thumb: "The higher the time preference rate, the lower the amount spent for prevention and primary curative care".*

However, this rule of thumb is not very helpful for decision makers as these functions are neither steady nor monotonous. For instance, reducing the time preference rate can even foster hospital services (scenario 1 to scenario 2)! If the time preference rate is lower, it might be worthwhile to save money in the first few periods which can be invested in later periods into health care services. Together with the interest earned there are sufficient funds in later periods – even to build a hospital! In this case reducing the time preference rate implies that the first period has a poorer provision of health services (e.g. 77 beds in health centres instead of 102 in t=1). The saved funds are invested with an interest rate of 5%, so that in period t=17 a hospital can be built. Finally, the share of curative medicine increases for all periods. With this result in mind, *one must be very careful to formulate a "golden rule" like "The higher the time preference rate the lower the budget of prevention". Health care planning calls for scientific and model-based analysis.*

6 Conclusions

Figure 6.1 summarizes the results of this booklet. It shows that the development of an equitable, sustainable and efficient health care system requires costing data. We cannot provide sufficient health care resources without knowing the resources and their monetary value that is required to run these services. We cannot make the best use of our resources unless we know the costs of the agents of production. We are unable to support the poor unless we know the costs of the subsidy required. And we will not be able to provide sustainable services accessible for future generations unless we have sufficient data for our strategic plans. *Costing of health care services is a prerequisite for affordability, sustainability and efficiency. Costing is the basic requirement for all efforts to improve the health status of human beings.*

This simple statement has a number of consequences for contemporary decision-making processes. Firstly, several developing countries develop academic training courses in health economics. There is a risk that these training programmes will focus on highly theoretical aspects of health economics, whereas Figure 6.1 shows that costing and a profound knowledge of general accounting are prerequisites for every health economist. Thus, *we have to overcome the traditional rift between economics and accounting training in order to equip future decision-makers with sufficient knowledge to make well-informed decisions.*

Secondly, *costing data can be used to assess vertical and horizontal programmes.* Is selective primary health care better than comprehensive primary health care [327-330]? If "better" implies higher accessibility, affordability, equity and efficiency, we have to define and calculate the cost of both regimes of primary health care and compare them with the outputs, outcomes and impacts. Are vertical disease control programmes better than horizontal basic packages [331]? Again, the answer requires a profound knowledge of cost. *As long as resources are scarce, costing is the prerequisite of the evaluation of different health care technologies.*

This is, third, in particular true for expensive interventions with long-term effects. It seems that decisions to invest in interventions against certain diseases are not always evidence-based. Antiretroviral Therapy (ART) in developing countries, for instance, might receive more funds than justifiable for a sustainable and equitable health care system. Already in the year 2002, Marseille, Hofmann and Kahn [332] had reservations against the cost-effectiveness of ART in comparison to other interventions, but the majority of researchers argued that ART has to be financed irrespective of existing health care budgets and other disease burdens. Thus, universal access to antiretroviral therapy has become a generally accepted objective for all countries. In the last few years, however, more authors dared to challenge this standard. MacKellar [333] discussed the prominence of HIV/AIDS on the donor agenda and showed that investments into field of HIV/AIDS lead to a negligence of nutrition and elements of a basic health care package. Shiffman [334] analysed donor funding priorities for communicable disease control in the developing world. He concludes that donor funding varies significantly across diseases, which could be due to the political influence of donor countries. For instance, he showed that acute respiratory infections represent a burden of disease approximately as high as AIDS in developing countries, but they receive only 2.5% of donor support, whereas AIDS is favoured with about 30% of all donor support. Recently England [335] asked the question "Are we spending too much on HIV?" He shows that many diseases cause a higher burden of disease but receive far less than HIV/AIDS. *A discussion about the rational allocation of health care resources has started* [336-338]*, and it will not be possible to give an answer to the question raised above without costing.*

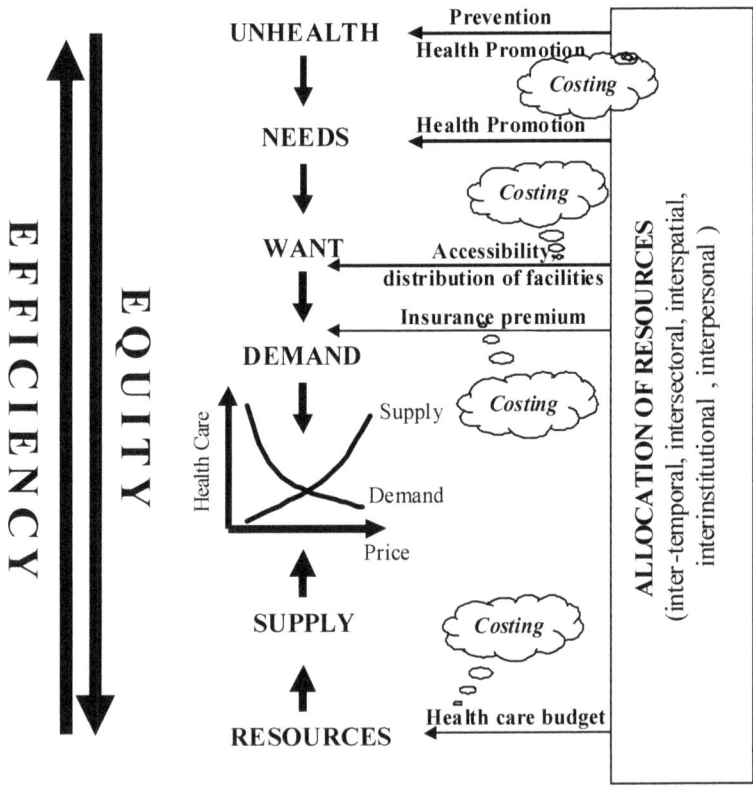

Figure 6.1 *Allocation of health care resources*

In addition, the long-term consequences of ART might be far reaching and completely undermine all efforts of sustainable health care systems. *Figure* 6.2 shows that some consequences of antiviral intervention can be neglected in a short-term analysis, but must be considered in a strategic approach with a vision of sustainability. The bold lines demonstrate the short-term system. It is obvious that no feedback loops exist between antiviral intervention and other elements of the system. Therefore, the total Cost-of-Illness can be calculated by just adding the independent cost components.

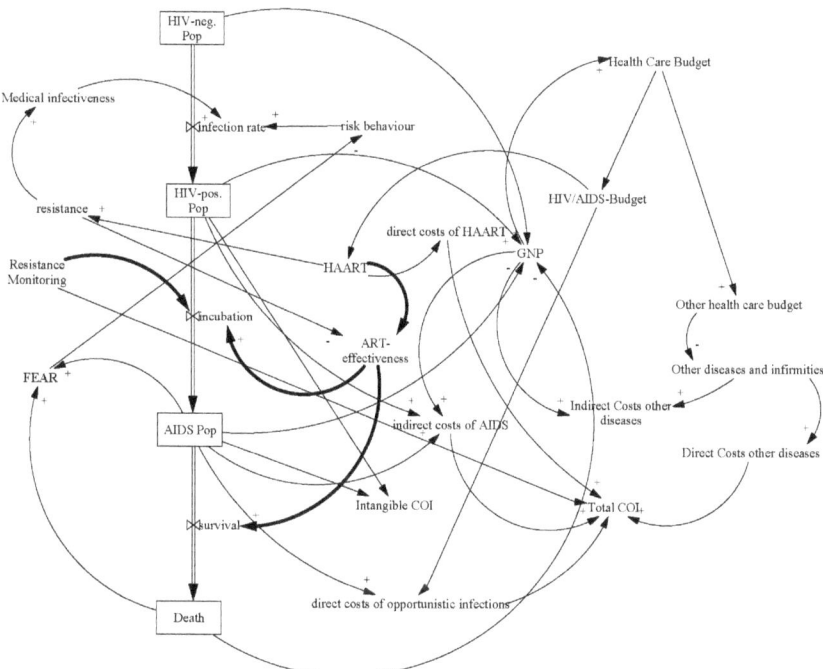

Figure 6.2   Causal Loop Diagram of Cost-of-AIDS

In a long-term perspective, however, a number of important feedback loops might exist with tremendous consequences on the COI and the cost-effectiveness of intervention programmes. Some of these loops were discussed in the Special Issue on HIV/AIDS of the Lancet [339], but their importance for the long-term socio-economic impact of antiviral intervention must be stressed.

Antiretroviral drugs might cause resistance. Already today we see that "emergence of drug resistance is the most common reason for treatment failure" [340], and "drug-resistant HIV-1 is transmissible and can be detected in up to 20% of newly infected individuals in countries with broad access to antiretrovirals. The prevalence of drug resistance in the untreated population remains low in regions with poor access to treatment". Drug resistance will definitely have an impact on costs as more expensive drugs will have to be developed and applied, and it might also increase the medical infectiveness resulting in an increase of AIDS-cases.

In addition, sexual behaviour might change if the "good message" of a treatment of HIV/AIDS spreads. Already today the incidence of HIV increases in some countries, such as Germany. This might be partly due to the long-term consequence of a reduced "horror". Finally, there is a strong interdependency between AIDS and economic strength (express in gross national product, GNP). On the one hand, patients treated with antiviral drugs are longer able to contribute to the economic wealth of a nation, on the other hand the drug regime requires high resources. Assuming a fixed health care budget, these costs have to be deducted from the health care resources of other diseases. Antiviral intervention might result in higher cost-of-illness of other diseases, but without appropriate budgets for these neglected diseases.

Thus, antiretroviral therapy seems to be economically favourable in the short-run, but we might expect the highest costs still to come. *Does this call for a cancellation of antiviral interventions? Definitely not! But it calls for a courageous long-term analysis of the cost-of-illness of AIDS and of the cost-effectiveness of certain interventions. Without knowing the cost, we will not be able to develop a sustainable and equitable intervention against this disease.*

Fourthly, *we need costing of health services in developing countries in order to provide evidence to different development strategies.* Should we invest more into education or hospitals? Should we focus our attention on humanitarian aid or capacity building? Are privatisation and public-private-partnership (PPP) the answer to our health care problems, or should development agencies and governments in developing countries strengthen their own institutions? Are non-governmental organisations more efficient than governmental providers? And should funds from international development cooperations be directly transferred to the respective governments, should they be given to a certain basket in a Sector Wide Approach (SWAp) or channelled directly to the health care providers? The answer can only be: *Choose the technology where sustainability, equity and efficiency are highest. It is obvious that the assessment of efficiency, equity and sustainability cannot be based on good intentions, wishes or guesses. It must be evidence based – it must be cost based. Thus, costing of health care services in developing countries is a prerequisite of affordability, sustainability and efficiency.*

Literature

1. WHO, *The World Health Report 2008: Primary Health Care - Now More Than Ever*, ed. W. Van Lerberghe and E. T. 2008, Geneva: World Health Organisation.
2. Gerhardus, A., J. Breckenkamp, and O. Razum, *Evidence-based Public Health. Prävention und Gesundheitsförderung im Kontext von Wissenschaft, Werten und Interessen*. Med Klin (Munich), 2008. **103**: p. 406-412.
3. Walt, G. and L. Gilson, *Reforming the health sector in developing countries: the central role of policy analysis*. Health Policy Plan, 1994. **9**(4): p. 353-70.
4. Walt, G., *WHO under stress: implications for health policy*. Health Policy, 1993. **24**(2): p. 125-44.
5. Leon, D.A., G. Walt, and L. Gilson, *Recent advances: International perspectives on health inequalities and policy*. Bmj, 2001. **322**(7286): p. 591-4.
6. Kuruvilla, S., N. Mays, and G. Walt, *Describing the impact of health services and policy research*. J Health Serv Res Policy, 2007. **12 Suppl 1**: p. S1-23-31.
7. Diderichsen, F., E. Varde, and M. Whitehead, *Resource allocation to health authorities: the quest for an equitable formula in Britain and Sweden*. Bmj, 1997. **315**(7112): p. 875-8.
8. Murray, C., et al., *Summary measures of population health: concepts, ethics, measurement and applications*. 2002, Geneva: World Health Organization.
9. Stefanini, A., *Sustainability of health care in developing countries - a selected annotated bibliography*. 1993: Padova, Italy.
10. Bankowski, Z., J.H. Bryant, and J. Gallagher, *Ethics, equity and health for all*. 1997, Geneva.
11. Olsen, I.T., *Sustainability of health care: a framework for analysis*. Health Policy Plan, 1998. **13**(3): p. 287-95.
12. Schwefel, D., *Gerechtigkeit und Gesundheit*, in *Globalisierung – Gerechtigkeit – Gesundheit. Einführung in International Public Health*, O. Razum, H. Zeeb, and U. Laaser, Editors. 2006, Huber: Bern. p. 65-78.
13. International Development Research Center, *Population and health in developing countries. Volume 1: Population, health, and survival at INDEPTH sites*. 2002, Ottawa: International Development Research Center.
14. Becher, H. and B. Kouyaté, *Health Research in Developing Countries*. 2005, Heideberg et al.: Springer.
15. Jack, W., *Principles of health economics for developing countries*. 1999, Washington D. C.
16. Flessa, S., *Gesundheitsökonomik. Eine Einführung in das wirtschaftliche Denken für Mediziner*. 2005, Heidelberg et al.: Springer.
17. Breyer, F., P. Zweifel, and M. Kifmann, *Gesundheitsökonomik*. Springer-Lehrbuch. 2005, Berlin et al.: Springer.
18. Henderson, J., *Health economics and policy*. 1999, Ohio, USA: South-Western College Publishing, Thomson Publishing Company.
19. Green, R.H., *Politics, power and poverty: health for all in 2000 in the Third World?* Soc Sci Med, 1991. **32**(7): p. 745-55.
20. James, C., et al., *Clarifying efficiency-equity tradeoffs through explicit criteria, with a focus on developing countries*. Health Care Anal, 2005. **13**(1). p. 33-51.
21. Menzel, P.T., *Equity, autonomy, and efficiency: what health care system should we have?* J Med Philos, 1992. **17**(1): p. 33-57.
22. Nichols, A.W., *Ethics of the distribution of health care*. J Fam Pract, 1981. **12**(3): p. 533-8.
23. Wikler, D., *Why prioritize when there isn't enough money?* Cost Eff Resour Alloc, 2003. **1**(1): p. 5.
24. Culyer, A.J. and A. Wagstaff, *Equity and equality in health and health care*. J Health Econ, 1993. **12**(4): p. 431-57.
25. Höffle, O., *Wirtschaftsbürger, Staatsbürger, Weltbürger. Politische Ethik im Zeitalter der Globalisierung*. 2004, Munich: UTB.

26. United Nations. *Millennium Development Goals.* 2007 [cited; Available from: http://www.un.org/millenniumgoals/.
27. Poole-Wilson, P.A., *Millennium development goals: an unbalanced approach to global health.* Nat Clin Pract Cardiovasc Med, 2007. **4**(6): p. 289.
28. Lawn, J.E., et al., *Countdown to 2015: will the Millennium Development Goal for child survival be met?* Arch Dis Child, 2007. **92**(6): p. 551-6.
29. Fleßa, S., *Why do Christians care? Values and objectives of church-related health services in developing countries.* Journal of Public Health, 2005. **13**: p. 236-247.
30. Kimmel, R.B., *Agreeing on a definition of quality care may be healthcare's biggest challenge.* Mod Healthc, 1989. **19**(12): p. 37.
31. Klint, R.B. and H.W. Long, *Toward a definition of quality.* Physician Exec, 1989. **15**(5): p. 7-11.
32. Suter, E., et al., *Continuing education of health professionals: proposal for a definition of quality.* J Med Educ, 1981. **56**(8): p. 687-707.
33. Kammermeier, R., *Konzeption und Einführungsstrategie eines Ansatzes zur unternehmensumfassenden Qualitätssteigerung: eine empirische Untersuchung.* 2000, Frankfurt a.M.
34. Corsten, H. and R. Gössinger, *Dienstleistungsökonomie. Beiträge zu einer theoretischen Fundierung* 2005, Berlin: Duncker & Humblot.
35. Fleßa, S., *Grundzüge der Krankenhausbetriebslehre.* 2007, München: Oldenbourg.
36. Akerele, O., I. Tabibzadeh, and J. McGilvray, *A new role for medical missionaries in Africa.* WHO Chron, 1976. **30**(5): p. 175-80.
37. Sines, D., *Impaired autonomy - the challenge of caring.* J Clin Nurs, 1995. **4**(2): p. 109-15.
38. Tauber, A.I., *Sick autonomy.* Perspect Biol Med, 2003. **46**(4): p. 484-95.
39. Baltussen, R.M., et al., *Perceived quality of care of primary health care services in Burkina Faso.* Health Policy Plan, 2002. **17**(1): p. 42-8.
40. Haddad, S., et al., *Patient perception of quality following a visit to a doctor in a primary care unit.* Fam Pract, 2000. **17**(1): p. 21-9.
41. Dowie, J., *Analysing health outcomes.* J Med Ethics, 2001. **27**(4): p. 245-50.
42. Donabedian, A., *Evaluating the quality of medical care.* Milbank Mem Fund Q, 1966. **44**(3): p. Suppl:166-206.
43. Donabedian, A., *The quality of medical care: a concept in search of a definition.* J Fam Pract, 1979. **9**(2): p. 277-84.
44. Donabedian, A., *Methods for deriving criteria for assessing the quality of medical care.* Med Care Rev, 1980. **37**(7): p. 653-98.
45. Freeman, R.E., *Strategic management. A stakeholder approach.* 1984, Marshfield: Pitman.
46. Meyer-Abich, K.M., *Soziale Verträglichkeit – ein Kriterium zur Beurteilung alternativer Energieversorgungssysteme.* Evangelische Theologie, 1979. **39**: p. 38-51.
47. Leder, M., *Innovationsmanagement - ein Überblick.* Zeitschrift für Betriebswirtschaft, 1989. **Ergänzungsheft 1**: p. 1-54.
48. Feldman, M.P., *The geography of innovation.* 1994, Dortbrecht, Boston, London: Kluwer Academic.
49. Claeson, M. and e. al., *Health, nutrition and population,* in *A sourcebook for poverty reduction strategies*, T.W. Bank, Editor. 2002, The World Bank: Washington DC. p. 201-230.
50. Weishaupt, M., *Krankendienst in Afrika. Aus Vergangenheit und Gegenwart der Leipziger Mission.* 1936, Leipzig: Leipziger Missionswerk.
51. Gilmurray, J., R. Riddell, and D. Sanders, *The struggle for health.* 1979, London: Macmillan Education.
52. Walsh, J.A., *Selective primary health care: strategies for control of disease in the developing world. IV. Measles.* Rev Infect Dis, 1983. **5**(2): p. 330-40.
53. Walsh, J.A., *Selectivity within primary health care.* Soc Sci Med, 1988. **26**(9): p. 899-902.
54. Walsh, J.A. and K.S. Warren, *Selective primary health care: an interim strategy for disease control in developing countries.* N Engl J Med, 1979. **301**(18): p. 967-74.
55. Walsh, J.A. and K.S. Warren, *Selective primary health care: an interim strategy for disease control in developing countries.* Soc Sci Med [Med Econ], 1980. **14**(2): p. 145-63.
56. Scott, R.W. and J.W. Meyer, *Institutional Environments and organisation. Structural complexity and individualism.* 1994, London: Sage Pub.
57. Heggenhougen, H.K. and L. Shore, *Cultural components of behavioural epidemiology: implications for primary health care.* Soc Sci Med, 1986. **22**(11): p. 1235-45.
58. King, M., *Medical care in developing countries.* 1986, Oxford: OUP East and Central Africa

59. Morley, D. and H. Lovel, *My name is today*. 1986, London: Blackwell.
60. McGilvray, J.C., *The quest for health. An interim report of a study process*. 1979, Tübingen: German Institute for Medical Missions.
61. McGilvrary, J.C., *The quest for health and wholeness*. 1981, Tübingen.
62. Wilson, M., *Exploration in health and salvation*. 1983, Birmingham: University of Birmingham.
63. Nthamburi, Z., *The ministry of healing*. 1990, Addis Abeba: Association of theological institutions in Eastern Africa, Staff Institute.
64. Ram, E., *Transforming health. Christian approaches to healing and wholeness*. 1995, Monrovia University of South Africa.
65. Makumira Consultation, *Health and healing*, in *The report of the Makumira Consultation on the healing ministry of the church*. 1967: Soni, Tansania.
66. Gimbi, A.L., *Clinical pastoral education and hospital chapalincy in East Africa*, in *Theological Seminary of St. Paul*. 1975, Theological Seminary of St. Paul: Minnesoty.
67. Christian Medical Board of Tanzania, *Proceedings from the Tanzania church consultation on PHC, June 10-15, 1985, Dar-es-Salaam*. 1985: Dar-es-Salaam.
68. McGilvray, J.C., *Der verlorene Gesundheit - das verheißene Heil*. 1982, Stuttgart: Radius.
69. Diesfeld, H.J., G. Talkenhorst, and O. Razum, *Gesundheitsversorgung in Entwicklungsländern. Medizinisches Handeln aus bevölkerungsbezogener Perspektive*. 2001, Berlin et al.: Springer.
70. World Health Organisation, *Organisational study on methods of promoting the development of basic health services*. 1973, Geneva: World Health Organisation.
71. World Health Organisation, *Alma-Ata 1978: primary health care. Report on the International Conference on Primary Health Care, 6-12. September 1978*. 1978, Geneva: World Health Organisation.
72. Ashorn, P., T. Kulmala, and M. Vaahtera, *Health for all in the 21st century?* Ann Med, 2000. **32**(2): p. 87-9.
73. Fendall, N.R., *Declaration of Alma-Ata*. Lancet, 1978. **2**(8103): p. 1308.
74. Passmore, R., *The declaration of Alma-Ata and the future of primary care*. Lancet, 1979. **2**(8150): p. 1005-8.
75. Romualdez, A., *Primary health care*. Maghreb Med, 1980. **20**(4): p. 3-4.
76. Werner, D. and D. Sanders, *Questioning the solution: The politics of primary health care and child survival*. 1997, Palo Alto: Healthwrights.
77. Parker, A.W., J.M. Walsh, and M. Coon, *A normative approach to the definition of primary health care*. Milbank Mem Fund Q Health Soc, 1976. **54**(4): p. 415-38.
78. Walsh, J., *New look at health in developing nations*. Science, 1987. **238**(4828): p. 746.
79. Warren, K.S., *Selective primary health care: strategies for control of disease in the developing world. I. Schistosomiasis*. Rev Infect Dis, 1982. **4**(3): p. 715-26.
80. Warren, K.S., *The evolution of selective primary health care*. Soc Sci Med, 1988. **26**(9): p. 891-8.
81. Zwi, A.B. and A. Mills, *Health policy in less developed countries: past trends and future directions*. J Int Dev, 1995. **7**(3): p. 299-328.
82. Basu, R.N., *Expanded programme on immunization and primary health care*. J Commun Dis, 1982. **14**(3): p. 183-8.
83. Keja, K., et al., *Expanded programme on immunization*. World Health Stat Q, 1988. **41**(2): p. 59-63.
84. Flessa, S., *Gesundheitsreformen in Entwicklungsländern. Eine kritische Analyse aus Sicht der kirchlichen Entwicklungshilfe*. 2002, Frankfurt a.M.: Lembeck.
85. Evans, D.B. and S.F. Hurley, *The application of economic evaluation techniques in the health sector: the state of the art*. Journal of International Development, 1995. **7**(3): p. 503-524.
86. Rice, N. and P.C. Smith, *Ethics and geographical equity in health care*. J Med Ethics, 2001. **27**(4): p. 256-61.
87. Murray, C.J.L. and A.D. Lopez, *The global burden of disease: a comprehensive assessment of mortality and disability from diseases, injuries, and risk factors in 1990 and projected to 2020*. 1996, Cambridge, Mass.: Harvard University Press.
88. Lopez, A.D., et al., *The global burden of disease and risk factors*. 2006, New York: Oxford University Press.
89. Jamison, D.T. and Disease Control Priorities Project., *Priorities in health*. 2006, Washington, D.C.: World Bank. xvii, 217.
90. Jamison, D.T., *Disease control priorities in developing countries*. 2nd ed. 2006, New York, Washington, DC: Oxford University Press, World Bank.

91. The World Bank, *World Development Report: Investing in Health*. 1993, Washington D.C.: The World Bank Group.
92. Russell, S., *Ability to pay for health care: concepts and evidence*. Health Policy Plan, 1996. **11**(3): p. 219-37.
93. Walraven, G., *Willingness to pay for district hospital services in rural Tanzania*. Health Policy Plan, 1996. **11**(4): p. 428-37.
94. The World Bank, *Health, nutrition, and population sector strategy paper*. 1997, Washington DC: The World Bank.
95. Fisher, I., *The theory of interest. As determined by impatience to spend income and opportunity to invest it*. 1930, New York: Porcupine Press
96. Mwabu, G., M. Ainsworth, and A. Nyamete, *Quality of medical care and choice of medical treatment in Kenya: an empirical analysis*. The Journal of Human Resources, 1993. **28**(4): p. 833-862.
97. Litvack, J.I. and C. Bodart, *User fees plus quality equals improved access to health care: results of a field experiment in Cameroon*. Soc Sci Med, 1993. **37**(3): p. 369-83.
98. Akin, J.S., D.K. Guilkey, and E.H. Denton, *Quality of services and demand for health care in Nigeria: a multinomial probit estimation*. Soc Sci Med, 1995. **40**(11): p. 1527-37.
99. Haddad, S. and P. Fournier, *Quality, cost and utilization of health services in developing countries. A longitudinal study in Zaire*. Soc Sci Med, 1995. **40**(6): p. 743-53.
100. Lachmann, W., *Entwicklungspolitik. Band 2: Binnenwirtschaftliche Probleme*. 1997, München, Wien: Oldenbourg.
101. Su, T.T., B. Kouyate, and S. Flessa, *Catastrophic household expenditure for health care in a low-income society: a study from Nouna District, Burkina Faso*. Bull World Health Organ, 2006. **84**(1): p. 21-7.
102. Carvalho, S. and H. White, *Combining the quantitative and qualitative approaches to poverty measurement and analysis*. World Bank Technical Paper, No. 366. 1997, Washington DC: The World Bank.
103. Su, T.T., et al., *Determinants of household health expenditure on western institutional health care*. Eur J Health Econ, 2006. **7**(3): p. 199-207.
104. Su, T.T., M. Sanon, and S. Flessa, *Assessment of indirect cost-of-illness in a subsistence farming society by using different valuation methods*. Health Policy, 2007.
105. Atim, C., *Social movements and health insurance: a critical evaluation of voluntary, non-profit insurance schemes with case studies from Ghana and Cameroon*. Soc Sci Med, 1999. **48**(7): p. 881-96.
106. Mariam, D.H., *Indigenous social insurance as an alternative financing mechanism for health care in Ethiopia (the case of eders)*. Soc Sci Med, 2003. **56**(8): p. 1719-26.
107. Obermann, K., et al., *Social health insurance in a developing country: the case of the Philippines*. Soc Sci Med, 2006. **62**(12): p. 3177-85.
108. Carrin, G., M.P. Waelkens, and B. Criel, *Community-based health insurance in developing countries: a study of its contribution to the performance of health financing systems*. Trop Med Int Health, 2005. **10**(8): p. 799-811.
109. Criel, B., P. Van der Stuyft, and W. Van Lerberghe, *The Bwamanda hospital insurance scheme: effective for whom? A study of its impact on hospital utilization patterns*. Soc Sci Med, 1999. **48**(7): p. 897-911.
110. Brundtland, G.H. and World Commission on Environment and Development (Genève), *Our common future*. 1987, Oxford et al.: Oxford University Press.
111. Grubb, M., *Earth Summit agreements a guide and assessment an analysis of the Rio '92 UN Conference on Environment and Development*. 1993, London: Earthscan Publications.
112. Flessa, S., *The costs of hospital services: a case study of Evangelical Lutheran Church hospitals in Tanzania*. Health Policy Plan, 1998. **13**(4): p. 397-407.
113. Flessa, S., *Sustainability and Meta-Stability of Health Care in Africa*. Zeitschrift für Gesundheitswissenschaften, 2001. **9**(4): p. 349-363.
114. Marckmann, G., *Zwischen Skylla und Charybdis: Reformoptionen im Gesundheitswesen aus ethischer Perspektive*. Gesundh ökon Qual manag, 2007. **12**: p. 96-100.
115. Mogyorosy, Z. and P. Smith, *The main methodological issues in costing health care services*. 2005: Centre for Health Economics, University of York.
116. Fleßa, S., *Gesundheitsökonomik: eine Einführung in das wirtschaftliche Denken für Mediziner*. Springer-Lehrbuch. 2007, Berlin et al.: Springer.

117. Santerre, R.E. and S.P. Neun, *Health economics: theories, insights, and industry studies*. 4 ed. 2007, Mason, Ohio: Thomson/South-Western.
118. Flessa, S., *Many worlds of health: a simulation of the determinants of the epidemiol-ogical transition in developing countries*. Zeitschrift für Bevölkerungswissenschaft, 1998. **23**(4): p. 459-494.
119. Eberly, L.E. and B.P. Carlin, *Identifiability and convergence issues for Markov chain Monte Carlo fitting of spatial models*. Stat Med, 2000. **19**(17-18): p. 2279-94.
120. Giudici, P., L. Knorr-Held, and G. Rasser, *Modelling categorical covariates in Bayesian disease mapping by partition structures*. Stat Med, 2000. **19**(17-18): p. 2579-93.
121. Karnon, J., *Alternative decision modelling techniques for the evaluation of health care technologies: Markov processes versus discrete event simulation*. Health Econ, 2003. **12**(10): p. 837-48.
122. Weidl, G., J.R. Iglesias-Rozas, and N. Roehrl, *Causal probabilistic modeling for malignancy grading in pathology with explanations of dependency to the related histological features*. Histol Histopathol, 2007. **22**(9): p. 947-62.
123. Amaghionyeodiwe, L.A., *Determinants of hte choice of health care provider in Nigeria*. Health Care Management Science, 2008. **11**: p. 215-227.
124. Mooney, G., *The demand for effectiveness, efficiency and equity of health care*. Theor Med, 1989. **10**(3): p. 195-205.
125. Doyal, L., *Needs, rights, and equity: more quality in healthcare rationing*. Qual Health Care, 1995. **4**(4): p. 273-83.
126. Sassi, F., L. Archard, and J. Le Grand, *Equity and the economic evaluation of healthcare*. Health Technol Assess, 2001. **5**(3): p. 1-138.
127. Culyer, A.J., *Equity - some theory and its policy implications*. J Med Ethics, 2001. **27**(4): p. 275-83.
128. Culyer, A.J., *Economics and ethics in health care*. J Med Ethics, 2001. **27**(4): p. 217-22.
129. Rawls, J., *A theory of justice*. 1997, Cambridge, Mass.: The Belknap Press of Harvard Univ. Press.
130. Bradshaw, G. and P.L. Bradshaw, *The equity debate within the British National Health Service*. J Nurs Manag, 1995. **3**(4): p. 161-8.
131. Lindholm, L., M. Rosen, and M. Emmelin, *An epidemiological approach towards measuring the trade-off between equity and efficiency in health policy*. Health Policy, 1996. **35**(3): p. 205-16.
132. Flessa, S., *Arme habt ihr allezeit! ein Plädoyer für eine armutsorientierte Diakonie*. 2003, Göttingen: Vandenhoeck und Ruprecht.
133. Viscusi, W.K. and M.J. Moore, *Rates of time preference and valuations of the duration of life*. 1989.
134. Lipscomb, J., M.C. Weinstein, and G.W. Torrance, *Time preference*. 1996.
135. Cairns, J.A., *Health, wealth and time preference*. Project Appraisal, 1992. **7**: p. 31-40.
136. Cairns, J., *Discounting and health benefits: another perspective*. Health Econ, 1992. **1**(1): p. 76-9.
137. Parsonage, M. and H. Neuburger, *Discounting and health benefits*. Health Econ, 1992. **1**(1): p. 71-6.
138. Sauerborn, R., P. Berman, and A. Nougtara, *Age bias, but no gender bias, in the intra-household resource allocation for health care in rural Burkina Faso*. Health Transit Rev, 1996. **6**(2): p. 131-45.
139. Wurthwein, R., et al., *Measuring the local burden of disease. A study of years of life lost in sub-Saharan Africa*. Int J Epidemiol, 2001. **30**(3): p. 501-8.
140. Shepard, D.S. and M.S. Thompson, *First principles of cost-effectiveness analysis in health*. Public Health Rep, 1979. **94**(6): p. 535-43.
141. Drummond, M., et al., *Standardizing methodologies for economic evaluation in health care. Practice, problems, and potential*. Int J Technol Assess Health Care, 1993. **9**(1): p. 26-36.
142. Weinstein, M.C. and W.B. Stason, *Foundations of cost-effectiveness analysis for health and medical practices*. N Engl J Med, 1977. **296**(13): p. 716-21.
143. The World Bank, *World Development Report 1993: Investing in Health*. 1993, Washington D. C.: The World Bank.
144. Krahn, M. and A. Gafni, *Discounting in the economic evaluation of health care interventions*. Med Care, 1993. **31**(5): p. 403-18.
145. Drummond, M.F., *Methods for the economic evaluation of health care programmes*. 3. ed. Oxford medical publications. 2005, Oxford et al.: Oxford Univ. Press.
146. Murray, C.J.L., *Health systems performance assessment: debates, methods and empiricism*. 2003, Geneva: World Health Organization.
147. Muennig, P., *Designing and conducting cost-effectiveness analysis in medicine and health care*. 2002, San Francisco: Jossey-Bass Inc.

148. Tan-Torres, E.T. and World Health Organization, *Making choices in health: WHO guide to cost-effectiveness analysis.* 2003, Geneva: World Health Organization.
149. Charnes, A., *Data envelopment analysis: theory, methodology, and application.* 1994, Boston: Kluwer Academic Publishers.
150. Murray, C.J.L., et al., *Development of WHO guidelines on generalised cost-effectiveness analysis.* Health Economics 2000. **9**: p. 235-251.
151. Rice, D.P., *Estimating the cost of illness.* Am J Public Health Nations Health, 1967. **57**(3): p. 424-40.
152. Rice, D.P. and B.S. Cooper, *The economic value of human life.* Am J Public Health Nations Health, 1967. **57**(11): p. 1954-66.
153. Rice, D.P., T.A. Hodgson, and A.N. Kopstein, *The economic costs of illness: a replication and update.* Health Care Financ Rev, 1985. **7**(1): p. 61-80.
154. Neubauer, S., et al., *Mortality, morbidity and costs attributable to smoking in Germany: update and a 10-year comparison.* Tob Control, 2006. **15**(6): p. 464-71.
155. Keith, R. and P. Shackleton, *Paying with their lives: the cost of illness for children in Africa.* 2006, London: Save the Children Fund.
156. Welte, R., H.H. König, and R. Leidl, *The costs of health damage and productivity losses attributabel to cigarette smoking in Germany.* European Journal of Public Health, 2000. **10**: p. 31-38.
157. Leidl, R., Deutsches Institut für Medizinische Dokumentation und Information, and Deutschland. Bundesministerium für Gesundheit, *Ansätze und Methoden der ökonomischen Evaluation: eine internationale Perspektive.* 1. Aufl ed. Health technology assessment 1999, Baden-Baden: Nomos-Verl.-Ges.
158. Henke, K.-D., K. Martin, and C. Behrens, *Direkte und indirekte Kosten von Krankheiten in der Bundesrepublik Deutschland 1980 und 1990.* Diskussionspapier/Wirtschaftswissenschaftliche Dokumentation, Technische Universität Berlin 1997, Berlin,.
159. Single, E., et al., *The economic costs of alcohol, tobacco and illicit drugs in Canada, 1992.* Addiction, 1998. **93**(7): p. 991-1006.
160. Xie, X., et al., *The economic costs of alcohol abuse in Ontario.* Pharmacol Res, 1998. **37**(3): p. 241-9.
161. Single, E., et al., *Morbidity and mortality attributable to alcohol, tobacco, and illicit drug use in Canada.* Am J Public Health, 1999. **89**(3): p. 385-90.
162. Xie, X., R.E. Mann, and R.G. Smart, *The direct and indirect relationships between alcohol prevention measures and alcoholic liver cirrhosis mortality.* J Stud Alcohol, 2000. **61**(4): p. 499-506.
163. Hodgson, T.A. and M. Meiners, *Guidelines for cost of illnesss studies in the Public Health Services*, T.f.o.c.o.i. studies, Editor. 1979, US Public Health Services.
164. Caro, J.J., et al., *Pertussis immunization of adolescents in the United States: an economic evaluation.* Pediatr Infect Dis J, 2005. **24**(5 Suppl): p. S75-82.
165. Dong, H., et al., *Inequality in willingness-to-pay for community-based health insurance.* Health Policy, 2005. **72**(2): p. 149-56.
166. van Roijen, L., et al., *Indirect costs of disease; an international comparison.* Health Policy, 1995. **33**(1): p. 15-29.
167. Carabin, H., et al., *The cost of measles in industrialised countries.* Vaccine, 2003. **21**(27-30): p. 4167-77.
168. Breidert, C., *Estimation of willingness-to-pay: theory, measurement, application.* 1. Aufl. ed. Gabler Edition Wissenschaft. 2006, Wiesbaden: Dt. Univ.-Verl.
169. Gertler, P. and d.G.J. van, *The willingness to pay for medical care: evidence from two developing countries.* 1990, BaltimoreMD: Johns Hopkins University Press. 133.
170. Koopmanschap, M.A., et al., *The friction cost method for measuring indirect costs of disease.* J Health Econ, 1995. **14**(2): p. 171-89.
171. Tarricone, R., *Cost-of-illness analysis. What room in health economics?* Health Policy, 2006. **77**(1): p. 51-63.
172. Arnett, R.H., 3rd, et al., *Revisions to the National Health Accounts and methodology.* Health Care Financ Rev, 1990. **11**(4): p. 42-54.
173. Berman, P.A., *National health accounts in developing countries: appropriate methods and recent applications.* Health Econ, 1997. **6**(1): p. 11-30.
174. Fetter, B., *Origins and elaboration of the national health accounts, 1926-2006.* Health Care Financ Rev, 2006. **28**(1): p. 53-67.
175. Huskamp, H.A., A.D. Sinaiko, and J.P. Newhouse, *Future directions for the national health expenditure accounts: conference overview.* Health Care Financ Rev, 2006. **28**(1): p. 1-8.

176. Halliday, R.G. and J. Darba, *Cost data assessment in multinational economic evaluations: some theory and review of published studies.* Appl Health Econ Health Policy, 2003. **2**(3): p. 149-55.
177. Dodge, R., *Foundations of cost and management accounting.* 1994, London: Chapman & Hall.
178. Drury, C., *Cost and management accounting: an introduction.* 5 ed. 2003, London: Thomson.
179. Drury, C., *Management and cost accounting.* 6th ed. 2004, London: Thomson Learning.
180. Horngren, C.T., *Management and cost accounting.* 3rd. ed. 2005, Harlow: Prentice Hall/Financial Times.
181. Horngren, C.T., S.M. Datar, and G. Foster, *Cost accounting: a managerial emphasis.* 11th ed. Charles T. Horngren series in accounting. 2003, Upper Saddle River, NJ: Prentice Hall.
182. Storey, R., *Introduction to cost and management accounting.* 1995, Basingstoke: Palgrave. xiii, 581.
183. Hankins, R.W. and J.J. Baker, *Management accounting for health care organizations: tools and techniques for decision support.* 2004, Sudbury, Mass. London: Jones and Bartlett. xvi, 467.
184. Jacobs, P. and J. Bachynsky, *Costing methods in the Canadian literature on the economic evaluation of health care. A survey and assessment.* Int J Technol Assess Health Care, 1996. **12**(4): p. 721-34.
185. Koopmanschap, M.A., K.C. Touw, and F.F. Rutten, *Analysis of costs and cost-effectiveness in multinational trials.* Health Policy, 2001. **58**(2): p. 175-86.
186. Pines, J.M., S.S. Fager, and D.P. Milzman, *A review of costing methodologies in critical care studies.* J Crit Care, 2002. **17**(3): p. 181-6.
187. Smith, M.W. and P.G. Barnett, *Direct measurement of health care costs.* Med Care Res Rev, 2003. **60**(3 Suppl): p. 74S-91S.
188. King, M., *Activity based costing in hospitals: a case study investigation.* 1994, London: Chartered Institute of Management Accountants.
189. Larsen, J. and U.S. Skjoldborg, *Comparing systems for costing hospital treatments. The case of stable angina pectoris.* Health Policy, 2004. **67**(3): p. 293-307.
190. Llewellyn, S. and D. Northcott, *The average hospital.* Accounting, Organisations and Society, 2005. **30**: p. 555-583.
191. Oostenbrink, J.B., et al., *Unit costs of inpatient hospital days.* Pharmacoeconomics, 2003. **21**(4): p. 263-71.
192. Oostenbrink, J.B., M.A. Koopmanschap, and F.F. Rutten, *Standardisation of costs: the Dutch Manual for Costing in economic evaluations.* Pharmacoeconomics, 2002. **20**(7): p. 443-54.
193. Oostenbrink, J.B. and F.F. Rutten, *Cost assessment and price setting of inpatient care in The Netherlands. The DBC case-mix system.* Health Care Manag Sci, 2006. **9**(3): p. 287-94.
194. Reed, S.D., et al., *Comparison of hospital costing methods in an economic evaluation of a multinational clinical trial.* Int J Technol Assess Health Care, 2003. **19**(2): p. 396-406.
195. Shuman, L.J. and H. Wolfe, *The origins of hospital microcosting.* J Soc Health Syst, 1992. **3**(4): p. 61-74.
196. Smet, M., *Cost characteristics of hospitals.* Soc Sci Med, 2002. **55**(6): p. 895-906.
197. Adam, T., D.B. Evans, and C.J. Murray, *Econometric estimation of country-specific hospital costs.* Cost Eff Resour Alloc, 2003. **1**(1): p. 3.
198. Lane, J., *The state of the Tanzanian economy 1984*, in *E. R. B. Paper*. 1984: Dar-es-Salaam.
199. Ferranti, D.d., C. Lovelace, and O. Pannenborg, *Preface*, in *Health expenditures, services, and outcomes in Africa. Basic data and cross-national comparisons, 1990-1996*, D.H.e.a. Peters, Editor. 1999, Human Development Network, Health, Nutrition, and Population Series: Washington DC. p. v-vi
200. Phillips, M.A., *Why do costings?* Health Policy Plan, 1987. **2**(3): p. 255-7.
201. Mills, A., *The economics of hospitals in developing countries. Part I: Expenditure patterns.* Health Policy and Planning, 1990. **5**(2): p. 107-117.
202. Mills, A., *The economics of hospitals in developing countries. Part II: Costs and sources of incomes.* Health Policy and Planning, 1990. **5**(3): p. 203-218.
203. Barnum, H. and J. Kutzin, *Public hospitals in developing countries.* 1993, Washington DC: The World Bank
204. Creese, A. and D. Parker, *Cost analysis in primary health care: a training manual for programme managers.* 1994, Geneva: W. H. O.
205. Hanson, K. and L. Gilson, *Cost, resource use and financing methodology for basic health services: a pratical manual.* Bamako Initiative Technical Report Series. Vol. No.16. 1993, New York: UNICEF.
206. Shepard, D., D. Hodgkin, and Y. Antony, *An analysis of hospital costs: a manual for managers.* 1998, Geneva: World Health Organisation.

207. Kumaranayake, L., *The real and the nominal? Making inflationary adjustments to cost and other economic data.* Health Policy Plan, 2000. **15**(2): p. 230-4.
208. Witter, S., *Health economics for developing countries: a practical guide.* 2000, London: Macmillan.
209. Walker, D., *Cost and cost-effectiveness guidelines: which ones to use?* Health Policy Plan, 2001. **16**(1): p. 113-21.
210. Walker, D. and L. Kumaranayake, *Allowing for differential timing in cost analyses: discounting and annualization.* Health Policy Plan, 2002. **17**(1): p. 112-8.
211. Conteh, L. and D. Walker, *Cost and unit cost calculations using step-down accounting.* Health Policy Plan, 2004. **19**(2): p. 127-35.
212. Vaca, V.H., K. S. D., and M.S. Kreider, *Financing church-related community-based primary health care.* 1987, Geneva: Christian Medical Commission.
213. Asante, K., *Sustainability of church hospitals in developing countries. A search for criteria for success.* 1998, Geneva: Christian Medical Commission.
214. Cao, P., S. Toyabe, and K. Akazawa, *Development of a practical costing method for hospitals.* Tohoku J Exp Med, 2006. **208**(3): p. 213-24.
215. Murru, M., et al., *Costing health services in Lacor hospital.* Health Policy and Development, 2003. **1**: p. 61-68
216. Olukoga, A., *Unit costs of inpatient days in district hospitals in South Africa.* Singapore Med J, 2007. **48**(2): p. 143-7.
217. Green, A., et al., *Using costing as a district planning and management tool in Balochistan, Pakistan.* Health Policy and Planning, 2001. **16**(2): p. 180-186.
218. Hutton, G. and R. Baltussen, *Cost valuation in resource-poor settings* Health Policy and Planning, 2005. **20**(4): p. 252-259.
219. Manzi, F., et al., *Out-of-pocket payments for under-five health care in rural southern Tanzania.* Health Policy Plan, 2005. **20 Suppl 1**: p. i85-i93.
220. Guinness, L., R. Levine, and M. Weaver, *10 best resources in ... cost analysis for HIV/AIDS programmes in low and middle income countries.* Health Policy Plan., 2004. **19**: p. 242 - 245.
221. Hansen, K., et al., *The costs of HIV/AIDS care at government hospitals in Zimbabwe.* Health Policy Plan., 2000. **15**: p. 432 - 440.
222. Wandwalo, E., B. Robberstad, and O. Morkve, *Cost and cost-effectiveness of community based and health facility based directly observed treatment of tuberculosis in Dar es Salaam, Tanzania.* Cost Eff Resour Alloc, 2005. **3**: p. 6.
223. Johns, B., R. Baltussen, and R. Hutubessy, *Programme costs in the economic evaluation of health interventions.* Cost Eff Resour Alloc., 2003. **1**: p. 1.
224. Adam, T., M. Aikins, and D.B. Evans, *CostIt Software. Version 4.3. Short User''s Notes.* 2002, Geneva: World Health Organisation.
225. Adam, T. and D.B. Evans, *Determinants of variation in the cost of inpatient stays versus outpatient visits in hospitals: a multi-country analysis.* Soc Sci Med, 2006. **63**(7): p. 1700-10.
226. Johns, B., T. Adam, and D.B. Evans, *Enhancing the comparability of costing methods: cross-country variability in the prices of non-traded inputs to health programmes.* Cost Eff Resour Alloc, 2006. **4**: p. 8.
227. Wöhe, G. and U. Döring, *Einführung in die Allgemeine Betriebswirtschaftslehre.* 22., neubearb. Aufl. ed. Vahlens Handbücher der Wirtschafts- und Sozialwissenschaften. 2005, München: Vahlen.
228. Lucey, T., *Costing.* 2002, London: Thompson Learning.
229. Krueger, D. and T. Davidson, *Alternate approaches to cost accounting.* Topics in Health Care Financing, 1987. **13**(4): p. 1-9.
230. Baptist, A.J., *A general approach to costing procedures in ancillary departments.* Topics in Health Care Financing, 1987. **13**(4): p. 32-47.
231. Lerner, W.M. and W.L. Wellman, *Pricing hospital units of service using microcosting techniques.* Hosp Health Serv Adm, 1985. **30**(1): p. 7-28.
232. Green, A., *An introduction to health planning in developing countries.* 1999, Oxford: Oxford Medical Press.
233. Raftery, J., *Costing in economic evaluation.* Bmj, 2000. **320**(7249): p. 1597.
234. Halbwachs, H., *Health care equipment management.* Health Estate J, 1994. **48**(10): p. 14, 17-9, 22.
235. Halbwachs, H., *The technical and financial impact of systematic maintenance and repair services within health systems of developing countries.* Health Estate, 1999. **53**(4): p. 6-8, 10-1.

236. Halbwachs, H., *Maintenance and the life expectancy of healthcare equipment in developing economies.* Health Estate, 2000. **54**(2): p. 26-31.
237. Donabedian, A., *Explorations in Quality Assessment and Monitoring, Volume I: The Definition of Quality and Approaches to its Assessment.* 1980, Ann Arbor, Michigan.
238. Heidemann, E.G., *The contemporary use of standards in health care.* 1993, Geneva: World Health Organisation.
239. Flessa, S. and N.T. Dung, *Costing of services of Vietnamese hospitals: identifying costs in one central, two provincial and two district hospitals using a standard methodology.* Int J Health Plann Manage, 2004. **19**(1): p. 63-77.
240. Flessa, S. and B. Kouyate, *Implementing a comprehensive cost information system in rural health facilities: the case of Nouna health district, Burkina Faso.* Trop Med Int Health, 2006. **11**(9): p. 1452-65.
241. Eriksson, P., V. Diwan, and I. Karlberg, *Health sector reforms: what about hospitals?*, in *NHV report.* 2002, The Nordic School of Public Health: Goteborg.
242. Furber, A.S., *Referral to hospital in Nepal: 4 years' experience in one rural district.* Trop Doct, 2002. **32**(2): p. 75-8.
243. Knowles, J., *Integrated health programmes.* Trop Doct, 1995. **25**(2): p. 50-3.
244. Nichter, M.A., *The primary health center as a social system: PHC, social status, and the issue of teamwork in South Asia.* Soc Sci Med, 1986. **23**(4): p. 347-55.
245. Stefanini, A., *District hospitals and strengthening referral systems in developing countries.* World Hosp Health Serv, 1994. **30**(2): p. 14-9.
246. Taylor, C.E., *Surveillance for equity in primary health care: policy implications from international experience.* Int J Epidemiol, 1992. **21**(6): p. 1043-9.
247. Newbrander, W., J. Kutzin, and H. Barnum, *Hospital economics and financing in developing countries.* Series; no. WHO/SHS/NHP1992/2. 1992, Geneva: WHO. 39.
248. Gish, O., *Planning the health sector: the Tanzanian experience.* 1975, London: Croom Helm.
249. World Health Organisation, *How to investigate drug use in health facilities. Selected drug use indicators.* 1993, Geneva: World Health Organisation.
250. Pho, P.T., *Regarding the model of socialist oriented market economy in Vietnam.* Journal of Economics and Development, National Economics University, Hanoi – Vietnam, 2002. **7**: p. 3-6.
251. National Economics University, *Monthly Statistics.* Journal of Economics and Development, National Economics University, 2002. **7**: p. 36-37.
252. Minh, L., *Public health – private remedy.* Vietnam Economics Times, 2002. **101**: p. 20-24.
253. Ministry of Health of Vietnam, *Health statistics of Vietnam from 1994 to 2001*, D.o.P. Health Statistics and Informatics, Editor. 2001d Ministry of Health of Vietnam.
254. Vietnam, M.o.H.o., *Health Statistics Year Book 2001.* 2002, Ministry of Health, Vietnam.
255. Hung, P.M., et al., *Efficient, equity oriented strategies for health.* 2000, Victoria: University of Melbourne Press.
256. The World Bank, *African Development Indicators.* 2004, Washington D.C.: The World Bank.
257. Kynast-Wolf, G., et al., *Mortality patterns, 1993-2001, in sub-Saharan Africa: Results from a Demographic Surveillance System in Nouna, Burkina Faso* 2001, SFB 544 Study Paper 01/2003: Heidelberg.
258. Mugisha, F., et al., *Costing health care interventions at primary health facilities in Nouna, Burkina Faso.* Afr J Health Sci, 2002. **9**(1-2): p. 69-79.
259. Mugisha, F., et al., *Examining out-of-pocket expenditure on health care in Nouna, Burkina Faso: implications for health policy.* Trop Med Int Health, 2002. **7**(2): p. 187-96.
260. Kouyate, B., et al., *Process and effects of a community intervention on malaria in rural Burkina Faso: randomized controlled trial.* Malar J, 2008. **7**: p. 50.
261. Ministere de la Sante Burkina Faso, *Annuiare statistique/sante 2005.* 2006, Ouagadougou: Ministere de la Sante.
262. World Health Organisation, *World Health Report: Health Systems: Improving performance.* 2000, Geneva: World Health Organisation.
263. Sauerborn, R., *Low quality of care in low income countries: is the private sector the answer?* Int J Qual Health Care, 2001. **13**(4): p. 281-2.
264. Benzler, J. and R. Sauerborn, *Rapid risk household screening by neonatal arm circumference: results from a cohort study in rural Burkina Faso.* Trop Med Int Health, 1998. **3**(12): p. 962-74.
265. Secretariat General du Ministère de la Saluté du Burkina Faso, *Annuaire statistique de la santé.* 2002, Ouagadougou: Ministère de la Saluté.

266. Fleßa, S., *Gesundheitsreformen in Entwicklungsländern: eine kritische Analyse aus Sicht der kirchlichen Entwicklungshilfe*. 2002, Frankfurt am Main: Lembeck.
267. The World Bank, *Better health for Africa*. 1994, Washington, DC: The World Bank.
268. Sauerborn, R., et al., *Population-based, actuarial data for estimating the needs for curative health care under community-based insurance in Burkina Faso*. 2003, Discussion paper, University of Heidelberg.
269. Mugisha, F., et al., *The two faces of enhancing utilization of health-care services: determinants of patient initiation and retention in rural Burkina Faso*. Bull World Health Organ, 2004. **82**(8): p. 572-9.
270. World Health Organisation, *World Health Report 2007*. 2007, Geneva: World Health Organisation.
271. Unicef and W.H. Organisation, *Immunization Summary 2006. A Statistical Reference. Data through 2004*. 2006, Geneva: Unicef, World Health Organisation.
272. Pokhrel, S., et al., *Gender role and child health care utilization in Nepal*. Health Policy, 2005. **74**(1): p. 100-9.
273. Streefland, P. and J. Chabot, *Implementing primary health care*. 1990, Amsterdam: KIT Publishers
274. World Health Organisation, *District Hospitals: Guildelines for Development*. WHO Regional Publications, Western Pacific Series No. 4. 1996, Geneva: World Health Organisation.
275. Flessa, S., *Reconciling the Irreconcilable*, in *Recommendations for the Evangelical Lutheran Church in Tanzania*. 1997, ELCT Health Directorate: Arusha, Tanzania.
276. Huntington, H.G., J.P. Weyant, and J.L. Scweeney, *Modelling for insights, not numbers: the experience of the energy modelling forum, OMEGA*. The International Journal of Management Science, 1982. **10**: p. 449.
277. Cocking, C., S. Flessa, and G. Reinelt, *Locating health facilities in Nouna district, Burkina Faso*. Operations Research Proceedings 2005, ed. H.-D. Haasis, H. Kopfer, and J. Schönberger. 2006, Berlin, Heidelberg, New York: Springer. 431-436.
278. Walt, G., *Health Policy: An introduction to process and power*. Vol. 5. 2001, New York: St. Martins Press.
279. Boldy, D., *A review of the application of mathematical programming to tactical and strategic health and social services problems*. Operational Research Quarterly, 1976. **3**: p. 439-448.
280. Heidenberger, K., *Strategic Investment in Preventive Health Care: Quantitative Modelling for Programme Selection and Resource Allocation*. Operations Research Spektrum 1996. **18**: p. 1-14
281. Heidenberger, K. and S. Flessa, *A system dynamics model for AIDS policy suppor tin Tanzania*. European Journal of Operational Research, 1993. **70**: p. 167-176.
282. Harfner, A., *Spezialisierungs- und Konzentrationsprozesse im deutschen Krankenhauswesen bei einem fallbezogenen Finanzierungssystem. Eine quantitative Analyse mit Hilfe computergestützter Szenarienrechnungen*. Vol. Arbeitsbericht 99-2. 1999, Nürnberg: Forschungsgruppe Medizinökonomie, Universität Erlangen-Nürnberg.
283. ReVelle, C., F. Feldman, and W.R. Lynn, *An optimization model of tuberculosis epidemiology*. Management Science, 1969. **16**: p. 190-211.
284. Parker, B.R., *A program selection/resource allocation model for control of malaria and related parasitic diseases*. Computers & Operations Research, 1983. **10**(4): p. 375-389.
285. Parker, B.R., *In quest of useful health care decision models for developing countries*. European Journal of Operational Research, 1990. **49**: p. 279-288.
286. Feldstein, M.S., M.A. Piot, and T.K. Sundaresan, *Resource allocation model for public health planning: a case study of tuberculosis control*. Bulletin of the World Health Organisation, 1973. **48 Suppl.**: p. 1-110.
287. Berman, P.A., *Selective primary health care: is efficient sufficient?* Soc Sci Med, 1982. **16**(10): p. 1054-9.
288. Segall, M., *Planning and politics of resource allocation for primary health care: promotion of meaningful national policy*. Soc Sci Med, 1983. **17**(24): p. 1947-60.
289. Tarimo, E. and E.G. Webster, *Primary health care concepts and challenges in a changing world: Alma-Ata revisited*. WHO ARA Paper No. 7. 1996, Geneva: World Health Organisation.
290. Dong, H., et al., *The differences in characteristics between health-care users and non-users: implication for introducing community-based health insurance in Burkina Faso*. Eur J Health Econ, 2006.
291. Bachmann, M.O., *Would national health insurance improve equity and efficiency of health care in South Africa? Lessons from Asia and Latin America*. S Afr Med J, 1994. **84**(3): p. 153-7.

292. El-Mahalli, A.A. and B.F. Abdel-Aziz, *Health sector reform and equity: a study at a family health center affiliated to health insurance organization in Alexandria.* J Egypt Public Health Assoc, 2005. **80**(5-6): p. 547-61.
293. Hidayat, B., et al., *The effects of mandatory health insurance on equity in access to outpatient care in Indonesia.* Health Policy Plan, 2004. **19**(5): p. 322-35.
294. Kang, H.C., et al., *Changes in distributive equity of health insurance contribution burden.* J Prev Med Pub Health, 2005. **38**(1): p. 107-16.
295. Liu, G.G., et al., *Equity in health care access to: assessing the urban health insurance reform in China.* Soc Sci Med, 2002. **55**(10): p. 1779-95.
296. Yip, W. and P. Berman, *Targeted health insurance in a low income country and its impact on access and equity in access: Egypt's school health insurance.* Health Econ, 2001. **10**(3): p. 207-20.
297. Barnighausen, T., et al., *Willingness to pay for social health insurance among informal sector workers in Wuhan, China: a contingent valuation study.* BMC Health Serv Res, 2007. **7**(1): p. 114.
298. Kirigia, J.M., et al., *An overview of health financing patterns and the way forward in the WHO African Region.* East Afr Med J, 2006. **83**(9 Suppl): p. S1-28.
299. Devadasan, N., et al., *Indian community health insurance schemes provide partial protection against catastrophic health expenditure.* BMC Health Serv Res, 2007. **7**: p. 43.
300. Devadasan, N., et al., *The landscape of community health insurance in India: an overview based on 10 case studies.* Health Policy, 2006. **78**(2-3): p. 224-34.
301. Noterman, J.P., et al., *A prepayment scheme for hospital care in the Masisi district in Zaire: a critical evaluation.* Soc Sci Med, 1995. **40**(7): p. 919-30.
302. Baltussen, R., et al., *Management of mutual health organizations in Ghana.* Trop Med Int Health, 2006. **11**(5): p. 654-9.
303. Ekman, B., *Community-based health insurance in low-income countries: a systematic review of the evidence.* Health Policy Plan, 2004. **19**(5): p. 249-70.
304. Mubyazi, G.M., et al., *Community views on health sector reform and their participation in health priority setting: case of Lushoto and Muheza districts, Tanzania.* J Public Health (Oxf), 2007. **29**(2): p. 147-56.
305. Kamuzora, P. and L. Gilson, *Factors influencing implementation of the Community Health Fund in Tanzania.* Health Policy Plan, 2007. **22**(2): p. 95-102.
306. Gilson, L., *Management and health care reform in sub-Saharan Africa.* Soc Sci Med, 1995. **40**(5): p. 695-710.
307. Bura, M., *Community health funds and managed health care. A practical guide for provider-based health funds for communities in developing countries*, in *Evangelical Lutheran Church in Tanzania, Health and Diaconia Directorate.* 1999: Arusha, Tanzania.
308. Chee, G., K. Schmith, and A. Kapinga, *Assessment of the community health fund in Hanang District*, in *Partners for Health Reformplus Project.* 2002: Bethesda, MD.
309. De Allegri, M., et al., *Understanding consumers' preferences and decision to enrol in community-based health insurance in rural West Africa.* Health Policy, 2006. **76**(1): p. 58-71.
310. De Allegri, M., M. Sanon, and R. Sauerborn, *"To enrol or not to enrol?": A qualitative investigation of demand for health insurance in rural West Africa.* Soc Sci Med, 2006. **62**(6): p. 1520-7.
311. Dong, H., et al., *Willingness-to-pay for community-based insurance in Burkina Faso.* Health Econ, 2003. **12**(10): p. 849-62.
312. Dong, H., et al., *A comparison of the reliability of the take-it-or-leave-it and the bidding game approaches to estimating willingness-to-pay in a rural population in West Africa.* Soc Sci Med, 2003. **56**(10): p. 2181-9.
313. Dong, H., et al., *Differential willingness of household heads to pay community-based health insurance premia for themselves and other household members.* Health Policy Plan, 2004. **19**(2): p. 120-6.
314. Dong, H., et al., *Gender's effect on willingness-to-pay for community-based insurance in Burkina Faso.* Health Policy, 2003. **64**(2): p. 153-62.
315. Dong, H., et al., *The feasibility of community-based health insurance in Burkina Faso.* Health Policy, 2004. **69**(1): p. 45-53.
316. Sommerfeld, J., et al., *Informal risk-sharing arrangements (IRSAs) in rural Burkina Faso: lessons for the development of community-based insurance (CBI).* Int J Health Plann Manage, 2002. **17**(2). p. 147-63.

317. Criel, B. and M.P. Waelkens, *Declining subscriptions to the Maliando Mutual Health Organisation in Guinea-Conakry (West Africa): what is going wrong?* Soc Sci Med, 2003. **57**(7): p. 1205-19.
318. Criel, B., et al., *Editorial: Community health insurance (CHI) in sub-Saharan Africa: researching the context.* Trop Med Int Health, 2004. **9**(10): p. 1041-3.
319. Waelkens, M.P. and B. Criel, *Les mutuelles de santé en Afrique sub-Saharienne - Etat des Lieux et Reflexions su un Agenda de Recherche.*, in *Health, Nutrition and population Discussion Paper.* 2004, The World Bank: Washington D.C.
320. Sauerborn, R., A. Nougtara, and E. Latimer, *The elasticity of demand for health care in Burkina Faso: differences across age and income groups.* Health Policy and Planning, 1994. **9**: p. 185-192.
321. Halbwachs, H. and A. Issakov, *Essential equipment for district health facilities in developing countries.* 1994, Eschborn: Deutsche Gesellschaft für technische Zusammenarbeit.
322. Mbiti, J.S., *Introduction to African religion.* 1992, Nairobi.
323. Schweikart, J., *Räumliche und soziale Faktoren bei der Annahme von Impfungen in der Nord-West Provinz Kameruns.* Heidelberger geographische Arbeiten, Heft 92. 1992, Heidelberg: Geographisches Institut, Universität Heidelberg.
324. Grundmann, C.H., *Gesandt zu heilen.* 1992, Gütersloh: Gütersloher Verlagshaus.
325. Ritter, W., *Wirtschaftsgeographie.* 2001, München: Oldenbourg.
326. Neumann, M., *Theoretische Volkswirtschaftslehre III. Wachstum, Wettbewerb und Verteilung.* 1982, München: Vahlen.
327. Farmer, J.E., et al., *Comprehensive primary care for children with special health care needs in rural areas.* Pediatrics, 2005. **116**(3): p. 649-56.
328. Magnussen, L., J. Ehiri, and P. Jolly, *Comprehensive versus selective primary health care: lessons for global health policy.* Health Aff (Millwood), 2004. **23**(3): p. 167-76.
329. Obimbo, E.M., *Primary health care, selective or comprehensive, which way to go?* East Afr Med J, 2003. **80**(1): p. 7-10.
330. Sharma, A. and A.K. Gupta, *Selective versus comprehensive PHC (primary health care).* J Acad Hosp Adm, 1993. **5**(1): p. 9-11.
331. Jinabhai, C.C., P.D. Ramdas, and V. Govender, *Cost analysis of the basic package, resource utilisation and financing of health services at Halley Stott Health Centre and Umbumbulu Clinic in KwaZulu-Natal.* S Afr Med J, 1997. **87**(10): p. 1359-64.
332. Marseille, E., P. Hofmann, and J. Kahn, *HIV prevention before HAART in sub-Saharan Africa.* Lancet 2002. **359**: p. 1851-1856.
333. MacKellar, L., *Priorities in global assistance for health, AIDS, and population.* Population and Development Review, 2005. **31**: p. 293-312.
334. Shiffman, J., *Donor funding priorities for communicable disease control in the developing world.* Health Policy and Planning, 2006. **21**: p. 411-420.
335. England, R., *Are we spending too much on HIV?* Bmj, 2007. **334**(7589): p. 344.
336. Boerma, J.T. and S.K. Stansfield, *Health statistics now: are we making the right investments?* Lancet, 2007. **369**(9563): p. 779-86.
337. Fleßa, S., *Basic health care package without antiretroviral therapy?* Journal of Public Health, 2008. **16**: p. 145-150.
338. Gordon, J.G., *A critique of the financial requirements to fight HIV/AIDS.* The Lancet, 2008. **372**: p. 333-36.
339. Editorial, L., *Betting on HIV prevention.* Lancet 2006. **368**: p. 424.
340. Simon, V., D.D. Ho, and Q. Abdool Karim, *HIV/AIDS epidemiology, pathogenesis, prevention, and treatment.* Lancet, 2006. **368**(9534): p. 489-504.

Medizin in Entwicklungsländern

Herausgegeben von Prof. Hans Jochen Diesfeld

Band 1 Wolfgang Bichmann: Die Problematik der Gesundheitsplanung in Entwicklungsländern. Ein Beitrag zur Geschichte, der Situation und den Perspektiven der Planung des nationalen Gesundheitswesens in den > Least Developed Countries < Afrikas. 1979.

Band 2 Jens Herrmann: Ambition and Reality - Planning for Health and Basic Health Services in the Yemen Arab Republic. 1979.

Band 3 J.M. Pönninghaus: The Cost Benefit of Measles Immunisation. A Study from Southern Zambia. 1979.

Band 4 Hilde Wander (Hrsg.): Bedingungen und Möglichkeiten der Integrierung bevölkerungspolitischer Programme in die nationale und die internationale Entwicklungspolitik. 1980.

Band 5 M. Heidegger/H.J. Diesfeld/A. Selheim: Demographische und soziale Wirkungen von Familienplanung. 1980.

Band 6 H.J. Diesfeld (Hrsg.): Importierte Krankheiten und ärztliche Untersuchungen vor und nach Tropenaufenthalt. Kongreßbericht über die X. Tagung der Deutschen Tropenmedizinischen Gesellschaft vom 22.-24. März 1979 in Heidelberg. 1980.

Band 7 Alexander Boroffka: Benedict Nta Tanka's Commentary and Dramatized Ideas on "Disease and Witchcraft in our Society". A Schreber Case from Cameroon Annotated Autobiographical Notes by an African on his Mental Illness. 1980.

Band 8 Hartmut Brandt: Work Capacity Restraints in Tropical Agricultural Development. 1980.

Band 9 nicht erschienen

Band 10 Tilman Nitzschke / Donata von Lüttwitz: Annehmbarkeit präventiver und promotiver Maßnahmen eines Health Centre für die Bevölkerung. Dargestellt am Beispiel der ländlichen Gesundheitsversorgung der Vereinigten Republik Kamerun. 1981.

Band 11 H.J. Diesfeld (Ed.): Health Research in Developing Countries. Proceedings of the Joint Meeting of the Belgische Vereniging voor Tropische Geneeskunde, Societé Belge de Medecine Tropicale, the Nederlandse Vereniging voor Tropische Geneeskunde and the Deutsche Tropenmedizinische Gesellschaft. 1982.

Band 12 Axel Kroeger/Francoise Barbira-Freedman: Cultural Change and Health: The Case of Southamerican Rainforest Indians. With special reference to the Shuar/Achuar of Ecuador. 1982.

Band 13 Dorothea Sich: Mutterschaft und Geburt im Kulturwandel. Ein Beitrag zur transkulturellen Gesundheitsforschung aus Korea. 1982.

Band 14 Uwe K. Brinkmann: Onchozerkose in Westafrika. 1982.

Band 15 Peter Oberender/Hans Jochen Diesfeld/Wolfgang Gitter (Hrsg.): Health and Development in Africa. International, Interdisciplinary Symposium, 2-4 June 1982, University of Bayreuth. 1983.

Band 16 Josef Boch (Hrsg.): Tropenmedizin, Parasitologie, Trypanosomiasis, Malaria, Bilharziose, Onchozerkose, Importierte Virusinfektionen, Lepra, Intermediate Technology, Zecken und durch sie übertragene Krankheiten, Immundiagnostik. 1983.

Band 17 Abdin Hamid Shaddad: Anforderungen an Gesundheitseinrichtungen der Basisversorgung im Sudan. Ein Beitrag zur Gesundheitsversorgung und zu baulichen Maßnahmen für die Gesundheitseinrichtungen unter besonderer Berücksichtigung der vorhandenen Ressourcen, der sozialen Verhältnisse und der klimatischen Bedingungen. 1984.

Band 18 Gerhard Heller: Krankheitskonzepte und Krankheitssymptome. Eine empirische Untersuchung bei den Tamang von Cautara/Nepal zur Frage der kulturspezifischen Prägung von Krankheitserleben. 1985.

Band 19 Hans-Jochen Diesfeld / Sigrid Wolter (Hrsg.): Medizin in Entwicklungsländern. Handbuch zur praxisorientierten Vorbereitung für medizinische Entwicklungshelfer. 5. neubearbeitete Auflage. 1989.

Band 20 Verena Kücholl: Soziokulturelle Wege des Heilens. Eine ethnomedizinische Analyse und Interpretation des Samkhya und der Heiltradition der Navajo. 1985.

Band 21 Frank-Peter Schelp (Ed.): Health Problems in Asia and in the Federal Republic of Germany. How to solve them? Proceedings of a seminar on "Techniques and Problems of Intervention Trials in Developing and Developed Countries". 1985.

Band 22 Rolf Heinmüller, Winfried Kern: Primäre Gesundheitsversorgung im südwestlichen Sudan. Eine Feldforschung bei den südsudanesischen Azande zur Evaluierung der Einflüsse des 'Primary Health Care'-Programms auf gesundheitliche Lage und allgemeine Lebensbedingungen. Detailed English Summary. 1987.

Band 23 Andreas Hahold/Axel Kroeger: Krankheitsbewältigung im Andenhochland Perus. Ergebnisse einer Bevölkerungsbefragung. 1986.

Band 24 Georg Kamm / Peter Witton / Hatibu Lweno: Anaesthesia Notebook for Medical Auxilaries. With special Reference to Anaesthesia Practice in Developing Countries. 1989.

Band 25 Alice S. Kuhn: Heiler und ihre Patienten auf dem Dach der Welt. Ladakh aus ethnomedizinischer Sicht. 1988.

Band 26 Wolfgang Bichmann: Community Involvement in Nepal's Health System. A case study of district health services management and the Community Health Leader scheme in Kaski district. 1989.

Band 27 M. Luisa Vázquez / Renate Lipowsky / Axel Kroeger: Malaria und kutane Leishmaniase in Kolumbien. Vorkommen, Volkskonzepte und traditionelle Behandlungsformen. 1989.

Band 28 Heinrich Berg / Axel Kroeger / Carmen Perez-Samaniego / Fernando Malo: Kranke Menschen – krankes Gesundheitswesen? Eine epidemiologische Untersuchung in Nord-Mexiko. 1989.

Band 29 Emmie Ho-Tsui / Margit Urhahn: Medizin und Gesundheitsforschung in Entwicklungsländern. Bibliographie des Instituts für Tropenhygiene 1984-1988. 1991.

Band 30 Thomas Lux: Gespräche mit afrikanischen Krankenpflegern und Heilern. Bilder von Krankheit im Mikrokosmos von Malanville(Benin), 1991.

Band 31 Christopher Knauth: Arzneimittelgebrauch armer Bevölkerungsschichten in städtischen Elendsvierteln Perus. Möglichkeiten und Grenzen der Gesundheitserziehung zum rationalen Arzneimittelgebrauch. 1991.

Band 32 Erhard Hinz: Geomedizinische und biogeographische Aspekte der Krankheitsverbreitung und Gesundheitsversorgung in Industrie- und Entwicklungsländern. 1991.

Band 33 Klaus Hoffmann: Psychiatrie in Afrika. Eine Einführung für Entwicklungshelfer. 1992.

Band 34 Dorothea Sich / Hans Jochen Diesfeld / Angelika Deigner / Monika Habermann (Hrsg.): Medizin und Kultur. Eine Propädeutik für Studierende der Medizin und der Ethnologie mit 4 Seminaren in Kulturvergleichender Medizinischer Anthropologie (KMA). 1993. 2., unveränd. Aufl. 1995.

Band 35 Annette Wiemann-Michaels: Die verhexte Speise. Eine ethnopsychosomatische Studie über das Depressive Syndrom in Nepal. 1994.

Band 36 Christine Loytved: Hebammen in Ozeanien zwischen traditioneller und westlicher Medizin. Weiterbildung traditioneller Hebammen in Westsamoa und Tonga. 1994.

Band 37 Andrea Materlik: Medizinisch-anthropologische Aspekte von Lepra im Amazonas und ihre Bedeutung für die Gesundheitserziehung. 1994.

Band 38 Oliver Razum: Improving Service Quality through Action Research, as applied in the Expanded Programme on Immunization (EPI). 1994.

Band 39 Ulrich Schramm: Einflußfaktoren auf die Akzeptanz von baulichen Anlagen der ländlichen Gesundheitseinheiten in Ägypten. Fallstudie am Beispiel der staatlichen Einheit in Zebeda unter Verwendung der Post-Occupancy Evaluation. 1995.

Band 40 Rainer Sauerborn / Adrien Nougtara / Hans Jochen Diesfeld (Eds.): Recherche sur les systèmes de santé: Le cas de la zone médicale de Solenzo, Burkina Faso. Auteurs: Rainer Sauerborn, Adrien Nougtara, Hans Jochen Diesfeld, Gaston Sorgho, Joseph Bidiga, Lougousse Tiébélessé, Eric Latimer, Roberto Sallier de La Tour, Uwe Brinkmann, Don Shepard. 1995.

Band 41 Rainer Sauerborn / Adrien Nougtara / Hans Jochen Diesfeld (Eds.): Les Côuts Economiques de la Maladie pour les Ménages au Milieu Rural du Burkina Faso. Avec des contributions de Rainer Sauerborn, Adrien Nougtara, Maurice Hien, Issouf Ibrango, Matthias Borchert, Justus Benzler, Eberhard Koob, Hans Jochen Diesfeld. 1996.

Band 42 Erhard Hinz: Helminthiasen des Menschen in Thailand. 1996.

Band 43 Matthias Perleth: Historical Aspects of American Trypanosomiasis (Chagas' Disease). 1997.

Band 44 Christiane Fischer: Über die Effektivität der Dorfgesundheitsarbeiterinnen innerhalb der Nichtregierungsorganisation ACCORD in Tamil Nadu/Südindien. Aktionsforschung im Rahmen der Gesundheitssystemforschung. 1998.

Band 45 Maureen Dar Iang: Assessment of antenatal and obstetric care services in a rural district of Nepal. 1999.

Band 46 Julia Katzan: sòi mendan – Die Sache mit dem Wasser... Eine medizinethnologische Untersuchung zum Zusammenhang von Wasser und Krankheit aus indigener Sicht. 2001.

Band 47 Catharina Will: Malaria-Selbstmedikation mit Chloroquin in einem hyperendemischen Gebiet (Mali). 2001.

Band 48 Ansgar Gerhardus: Entscheidungsprozesse im Gesundheitssektor. Der Beitrag der Theorie der politischen Ökonomie. 2001.

Band 49 Sylvie Schuster: Der Schwangerschaftsabbruch im Grasland Kameruns. Medizin, Kultur und Praxis. 2004.

Band 50 Sascha Klotzbücher: Das ländliche Gesundheitswesen der VR China. Strukturen – Akteure – Dynamik. 2006.

Challenges in Public Health

Editor: Prof. Dr. Oliver Razum

Band 51 Ulrich Ronellenfitsch: Cardiovascular Mortality among Ethnic German Immigrants from the Former Soviet Union. 2007.

Band 52 Manuela De Allegri: To Enrol or not to Enrol in Community Health Insurance. Case Study from Burkina Faso. 2007.

Band 53 Catherine Kyobutungi: Ethnic German Immigrants from the Former Soviet Union: Mortality from External Causes and Cancers. 2008.

Band 54 Maren Bredehorst: Information Systems for the Rehabilitation of Landmine Survivors. 2007.

Band 55 Sven Voigtländer / Gabriele Berg-Beckhoff / Oliver Razum: Gesundheitliche Ungleichheit. Der Beitrag kontextueller Merkmale. 2008.

Band 56 Oliver Razum / Jürgen Breckenkamp / Pitt Reitmaier (Hrsg.): Kindergesundheit in Entwicklungsländern. 2008.

Band 57 Steffen Fleßa: Costing of Health Care Services in Developing Countries. A Prerequisite for Affordability, Sustainability and Efficiency. 2009.

www.peterlang.de

Ingrid Zechmeister

Mental Health Care Financing in the Process of Change

Challenges and Approaches for Austria

Frankfurt am Main, Berlin, Bern, Bruxelles, New York, Oxford, Wien, 2005.
183 pp., 19 tab. 13 graf.
Forschungsergebnisse der Wirtschaftsuniversität Wien.
Edited by Wirtschaftsuniversität Wien. Vol. 8
ISBN 978-3-631-54338-2 · pb. € 41.10*

While mental health care has undergone substantial reforms, little attention has been paid to financing issues. This book addresses this shortcoming and brings more transparency into the complex relationship between mental health care reform, service provision and financing. Additionally, it provides rich information about the characteristics of mental health care financing in Western Europe. The author analyses the recent mental health care reform discourse against the backdrop of broader political economic developments and demonstrates the role of financing arrangements herein. The book vividly shows how financing is related to specific effects for service users and their relatives in the process of change. In the final part practitioners, planers and policy makers find useful guidelines for developing alternative financing approaches including support to improve understanding of financing issues amongst those involved in mental health care.

Contents: Perspectives of Mental Illness · Mental Health Care Structures in Austria · Mental Health Care Financing · Paradigm Shift in Mental Health Care: An Exploration of Mental Health Care Reform Objectives and Reform Processes · Mental Health Care Financing in the Light of Reform Objectives and Discourse · Concluding Remarks: What Financing for Mental Health Care?

Frankfurt am Main · Berlin · Bern · Bruxelles · New York · Oxford · Wien
Distribution: Verlag Peter Lang AG
Moosstr. 1, CH-2542 Pieterlen
Telefax 00 41 (0) 32 / 376 17 27

*The €-price includes German tax rate
Prices are subject to change without notice
Homepage http://www.peterlang.de

www.ingramcontent.com/pod-product-compliance
Ingram Content Group UK Ltd.
Pitfield, Milton Keynes, MK11 3LW, UK
UKHW020857160426
5217IPUK00035B/1357